Southeast Asia After the Cold War

Southeast Asia After the Cold War

A Contemporary History

Ang Cheng Guan

NUS PRESS
SINGAPORE

Published by:

NUS Press
National University of Singapore
AS3-01-02, 3 Arts Link
Singapore 117569

Fax: (65) 6774-0652
E-mail: nusbooks@nus.edu.sg
Website: http://nuspress.nus.edu.sg

ISBN 978-981-3250-78-9 (paper)

National Library Board, Singapore Cataloguing in Publication Data

Name(s): Ang, Cheng Guan.
Title: Southeast Asia After the Cold War: a contemporary history/Ang Cheng Guan.
Description: Singapore: NUS Press, [2019]|Includes bibliographical references and index.
Identifier(s): OCN 1089720450|ISBN 978-981-3250-78-9 (paperback)
Subject(s): LCSH: Southeast Asia--Foreign relations--20th century.|Southeast Asia--Foreign relations--21st century.|Southeast Asia--History--20th century.|Southeast Asia--History--21st century.
Classification: DDC 327.59--dc23

Cover: "Image: Freepik-com". This cover has been designed using resources from Freepik.com

Printed by: Markono Print Media Pte Ltd

Contents

Acknowledgements

This book (and its prequel) can be considered as the bookends of my academic interest in the international history and politics of contemporary/post-World War II Southeast Asia. I wish to take this opportunity to remember a number of people who helped, guided and influenced me on my learning journey. The first four of them have since passed on: Professor Ralph Smith, my graduate teacher and supervisor at SOAS; Professor Michael Leifer, who taught me about the international politics of Southeast Asia at LSE; Professor Nicholas Tarling, a friend and mentor; and Mr S.R. Nathan, the founding director of the Institute of Defence and Strategic Studies (now the S. Rajaratnam School of International Studies). I am grateful to Professor Robert Taylor, who taught me government and politics of Southeast Asia, also at SOAS. Professor Taylor continues to be a friend and mentor years after I graduated from SOAS.

The S. Rajaratnam School of International Studies provided a conducive environment for me to research and write this book. I wish to thank my colleagues, particularly Mushahid Ali and Chong Yee Ming, as well as the anonymous reviewers of the manuscript. At NUS Press, I would like to thank Peter Schoppert, Sunandini Arora Lal and Lena Qua for their editorial guidance. Last but not least, I thank Weilun Chia.

Introduction

> *"An understanding of history has its limits. History cannot fully explain the past and it cannot foresee the future. But it can reliably tell us where we are and how we have reached this provisional destination in time. Without such historical understanding or an interest in acquiring it, we can have no idea of where we are going or how to get there."* [1]

Purpose of This Book

This book traces the development of the international relations of Southeast Asia from the end of the Cold War to 2017–18. It takes stock of how the international relations of the region have evolved since 1990, the changes, continuities and likely trajectories. Looking back almost 30 years since the Cold War ended, this book attempts to answer the following questions: What was the international politics of the region like at the end of the Cold War or at the beginning of the post-Cold War era? What were the goals and aspirations of the different Southeast Asian states and the region as a whole? Have they been realized or achieved? If not, why not?

The focus is primarily on foreign relations. The domestic politics of the Southeast Asian states will be discussed where they have a bearing on the conduct of foreign policy of the countries and/or the region as a whole. The Association of Southeast Asian Nations features prominently in this narrative, inevitably so. On 30 April 1999, with the admission of Cambodia into ASEAN, the association became synonymous with the region we call Southeast Asia, and vice versa. Before that, ASEAN was only a subregional organization. That said, ASEAN is the sum of

[1] Frank Ninkovich, "Trumpism, History and the Future of U.S. Foreign Relations", H-Diplo | ISSF Policy Series, 18 Apr. 2017, https://issforum.org/roundtables/policy/1-5ad-ninkovich, accessed 18 Sept. 2017.

its ten parts, and in the course of this narrative the individual parts will be discussed separately from the collective when appropriate.

This book continues from an earlier study that focused on the international politics of Southeast Asia during the Cold War period. It also draws inspiration from the British historian Edward Hallett Carr's *The Twenty Years' Crisis, 1919–1939*, which traces and analyzes the international relations of Europe from the end of World War I to the eve of World War II. Carr's book reached the page proof stage when war broke out on 3 September 1939. According to Carr, the book was written "when war was already casting its shadow on the world, but when all hope of averting it was not yet lost".[2] Carr subtitled his book "An Introduction to the Study of International Relations". He was writing at the beginning of the discipline of international relations as it carved its way out of international law and political studies. First published in 1939, the book remains a classic in the literature of international relations theory. This book, *Southeast Asia After the Cold War: A Contemporary History*, which covers the years from the end of the Cold War in 1990 to 2017–18—the cusp of a new (and still unknown/evolving) era—is far less ambitious. It does not attempt to present any groundbreaking theory of history writing. Neither does it offer solutions to problems faced by the Southeast Asian states. Unlike Carr, I am neither a political scientist nor a public intellectual advocate.

This book, however, aims to present an example, hopefully a good one, of the writing of the contemporary international history of Southeast Asia. International history has been very much in vogue since the end of the Cold War. It has been described as a new field (although it is by now not so new). But it certainly has an old and long pedigree.[3] There is thus no need to delve into its methodology here. "Contemporary history", on the other hand, remains a controversial subfield of history, which according to Jonathan Haslam is "the most

[2] Edward Hallett Carr, *The Twenty Years' Crisis, 1919–1939: An Introduction to the Study of International Relations* (New York: HarperCollins, 2001), p. ix.

[3] Zara Steiner, "On Writing International History: Chaps, Maps and Much More", *International Affairs* 73, 3 (1997): 531–46. See also Patrick Finney (ed.), *International History* (Houndmills: Palgrave Macmillan, 2005); Marc Trachtenberg, *The Craft of International History: A Guide to Method* (Princeton: Princeton University Press, 2006).

contentious and problematic history of all".[4] Haslam made that remark in the context of writing the history of the Cold War years, but it is even more relevant to the post-Cold War period, which remains open-ended.

Indeed, some may argue that it is too soon to treat the post-Cold War period as "history". However, as the late Ralph Smith, who wrote the highly regarded multivolume *International History of the Vietnam War* in the 1980s, argued in a different book project, "It is never too early for scholars to begin the attempt to see events in historical perspective; and the discipline of history need not in itself depend on the availability of archives". Furthermore, "one way or another, the history of the war has already begun to be written".[5]

Existing Literature

Indeed, there is no shortage of scholarly writings on Southeast Asian international relations after the Cold War, which has been dominated by political scientists and international relations specialists. The literature can be divided into two broad categories: works that focus on the topical issues of the time and those that develop a broader canvas of the international relations of the region. Most of the writings are of the first kind. There are only a handful of books in the second category, most of which are standard texts in almost all courses on the international relations of Southeast Asia. One of them is *International Relations in Southeast Asia* by Donald E. Weatherbee. Weatherbee has often been described as the dean of American scholars on the international relations of Southeast Asia. First published in 2005, his book is now in its third edition. The first edition was multi-authored, and the second (2009) and most recent (2015) editions were singly authored by Weatherbee.[6]

---

[4] Jonathan Haslam, "The Cold War as History", *Annual Review of Political Science* 6 (2003): 77–98.

[5] Ralph B. Smith, *An International History of the Vietnam War*, Vol. 1: *Revolution Versus Containment, 1955–61* (London: Macmillan, 1983); Vol. 2: *The Struggle for Southeast Asia, 1961–65* (London: Macmillan, 1985); Vol. 3: *The Making of a Limited War, 1965–66* (London: Macmillan, 1991). The first two volumes were published within ten years after the end of the Vietnam War in 1975.

[6] Donald E. Weatherbee, *International Relations in Southeast Asia: The Struggle for Autonomy* (Lanham: Rowman & Littlefield, 2015).

The book adopts a thematic approach with an eye on current interest. Thus, in the second edition there was, in the words of the author, "less emphasis on the war on terror" and "more structured discussion of human security as an issue in international relations in Southeast Asia". The second edition also highlighted the new ASEAN Charter and gave "more extended consideration" to the China-ASEAN-United States triangle, both issues much talked about when the book was written.

A second book is *Southeast Asia in the New International Era*, initially by Clark D. Neher. It was originally published in 1991 and went through four editions by 2001. The fifth (2010) and sixth (2013) editions were jointly authored by Neher and Robert Dayley.[7] The present edition, the seventh (2017), is by Dayley. This book adopts a country-by-country approach, and foreign relations is only one of four themes discussed; the others are "Institutions and Social Groups", "State-Society Relations and Democracy", and "Economy and Development".

Both Weatherbee and Neher, although political scientists, wore their "theory" hat rather lightly. In contrast, Amitav Acharya's *The Quest for Identity* (2000) and its sequel, *The Making of Southeast Asia* (2012), are written very much with a theoretical framework in mind.[8] The end of the Cold War ushered in a renewed debate amongst competing theoretical traditions within the international relations academic community. Acharya is acknowledged as the leading international relations scholar who approaches the study of Southeast Asia through the lens of constructivism, specifically the creation of a Southeast Asian regional identity. Finally is Evelyn Goh's *The Struggle for Order* (2013).[9] Although the book is not specifically on Southeast Asia, Goh pays considerable attention to developments in the region from an "international society" perspective (often described as the English School of International Relations). Like Acharya, Goh is primarily interested in engaging in the ongoing theoretical debates within the international relations academia,

---

[7] Robert Dayley and Clark D. Neher, *Southeast Asia in the New International Era* (Boulder: Westview, 2013).

[8] Amitav Acharya, *The Quest for Identity: International Relations of Southeast Asia* (Singapore: Oxford University Press, 2000); *The Making of Southeast Asia: International Relations of a Region* (Ithaca: Cornell University Press, 2012).

[9] Evelyn Goh, *The Struggle for Order: Hegemony, Hierarchy, and Transition in Post-Cold War East Asia* (Oxford: Oxford University Press, 2013).

in her case with East Asia as her focus. Both Acharya and Goh are, however, more historically grounded than many of their peers.

All the above books have been widely praised and certainly have their merits. However, it is my view that a study that focuses on topical themes or takes a country-by-country approach misses the complexities and interconnectedness of issues and events. Privileging one theoretical lens over another leaves out the inconvenient facts that may not fit into one's construct or worldview. Furthermore, as the historian Pieter Geyl reminds us, many factors determine historical change, and to isolate one of them would be unhistorical.[10]

There are two books relevant to my study written by the late Nicholas Tarling, the eminent historian of Southeast Asia, which must be mentioned: The first is *Regionalism in Southeast Asia* (2006). This is the final volume of his trilogy that also includes *Imperialism in Southeast Asia* (2001) and *Nationalism in Southeast Asia* (2004).[11] The book ends in the 1990s. The other is *Southeast Asia and the Great Powers* (2010). This book is an epilogue to his trilogy. Tarling felt that he had devoted too much space to the role of outside powers in Southeast Asia in the first two books and insufficient attention in the final book. *Southeast Asia and the Great Powers* is thus his attempt to redress the balance and "examine what had interested great powers in the region in the past and what had involved them there".[12] Each chapter focuses on one external power. While both books are extremely informative, erudite and thought provoking, the approach tends to simplify the complex interplay between the external powers and the Southeast Asian elites. They were also written more for specialists.

Given that a historian of Southeast Asia venturing into what is apparently the domain of political scientists and international relations experts is a rarity, it is perhaps useful to first acquaint the reader with the concept and method of "contemporary history".

---

[10] Marnie Hughes-Warrington, *Fifty Key Thinkers on History* (London: Routledge, 2000), p. 118.

[11] Nicholas Tarling, *Imperialism in Southeast Asia* (London: Routledge, 2001); *Nationalism in Southeast Asia* (London: Routledge, 2004); *Regionalism in Southeast Asia: To Foster the Political Will* (London: Routledge, 2006).

[12] Nicholas Tarling, *Southeast Asia and the Great Powers* (London: Routledge, 2010), p. 2.

Contemporary History

Contemporary history is often described as an imprecise concept and as such difficult to understand. There are disagreements about its meaning and its chronological limits. What is contemporary at a given time can change, as Bruce Mazlish rightly noted.[13] Some have criticized the term "contemporary history" as an oxymoron.[14] More significantly, the writing (and teaching) of contemporary history is not so well regarded or, as H. Stuart Hughes put it in *History as Art and as Science* (1964), "not quite respectable" in the eyes of many historians, especially in the 1950s and 1960s. Thus, the title of Hughes' chapter on the subject is in the form of a question: "Is Contemporary History Real History?" The prevalent view then was that at least a century should pass before a subject was deemed ready for historical analysis.[15] Arthur Schlesinger Jr. described contemporary history as having held "a precarious status in the annals of historiography".[16] As late as 1997, Arthur Marwick, who had joined the editorial team of the *Journal of Contemporary History*,[17] still noted a certain prejudice towards this subfield of history.[18] Today, however, writing contemporary history is not such an oddity as it used to be. Martin Johnes, at the end of 2011, noted that "if there is any prejudice or hesitancy towards studying the recent past it is rooted in

[13] Bruce Mazlish, "Revisiting Barraclough's Contemporary History", *Historically Speaking* 8, 6 (July/Aug. 2007): 45.

[14] For a genealogy of the writing of contemporary history, see Gordon Wright, "Contemporary History in the Contemporary Age", in *The Future of History: Essays in the Vanderbilt University Centennial Symposium*, ed. Charles F. Delzell (Nashville: Vanderbilt University Press, 1977); John Lewis Gaddis, *On Contemporary History: An Inaugural Lecture Delivered Before the University of Oxford on 19 May 1993* (Oxford: Clarendon Press, 1995); Terry Smith, *What Is Contemporary Art?* (Chicago: University of Chicago Press, 2009), p. 253.

[15] H. Stuart Hughes, *History as Art and as Science: Twin Vistas on the Past* (Chicago: University of Chicago Press, 1964), chapter 5: "Is Contemporary History Real History?"

[16] Arthur Schlesinger Jr., "On the Writing of Contemporary History", *The Atlantic*, 22 Dec. 2017, http://www.theatlantic.com/magazine/archive/1967/03/on-the-writing-of-contemporary-history/305731/, accessed 18 Mar. 2019.

[17] Richard J. Evans, "The Journal of Contemporary History and Its Editors", *Journal of Contemporary History* 50, 4 (2015): 710–37.

[18] Arthur Marwick, "A New Look, a New Departure: A Personal Comment on Our Changed Appearance", *Journal of Contemporary History* 32, 1 (Jan. 1997): 5–8.

its difficulties rather than any sense that contemporary history is not as important or valid for study",[19] a view that is increasingly shared by historians.[20]

A simple but useful definition of "contemporary history" is the "history of a period lying within the adult life of the historian".[21] While the definition may be straightforward, scholars concur that the writing of contemporary history is problematic although the difficulties may not be altogether unique to historians writing on the contemporary period. Three interrelated issues or challenges are often cited: (a) sources, (b) subjectivity, and (c) perspective.[22]

Concerning sources—the raw material without which no history can be written—scholars are divided over whether the contemporary historian has too many or too few at their disposal. Either case is problematic. Those who believe that there are too many argue that the enormous bulk of contemporary records makes selection and deciding what is or what is not important extremely difficult. In the process, the historian is thus much more susceptible to external influences. As Johnes puts it, contemporary historians "write about people who

---

[19] Martin Johnes, "On Writing Contemporary History", *North American Journal of Welsh Studies* 6, 1 (Winter 2011); "Category: Contemporary History", 12 Sept. 2017, https://martinjohnes.wordpress.com/category/contemporary-history/, accessed 28 Mar. 2019.

[20] Michael D. Kandiah, "Contemporary History", Making History, http://www.history.ac.uk/makinghistory/resources/articles/contemporary_history.html, accessed 28 Mar. 2016; Bradley W. Hart, "The Journal of Contemporary History: Fifty Years of Change and Continuity", *Journal of Contemporary History* 50, 4 (2015): 738–49.

[21] K.R. Greenfield, "An Adventure in the Writing of Contemporary History", talk before the Trinity College Historical Society, Durham, NC, 19 April 1950, revised for a talk at New York University, 19 Mar. 1953, cited in Martin Blumenson, "Can Official History Be Honest History?" *Military Affairs* 26, 4 (Winter 1962–63): 158fn15. For more on contemporary history as a subfield of history, see the anniversary issue editorials of *Journal of Contemporary History* 1, 1 (1966); 11, 4 (Oct. 1976); 21, 2 (Apr. 1986); 32, 1 (Jan. 1997); 39, 4 (2004); Evans, "Journal of Contemporary History and Its Editors", and Hart, "Journal of Contemporary History", both in *Journal of Contemporary History* 50, 4 (2015): 710–37 and 738–49 respectively.

[22] See, for example, Wright, "Contemporary History in the Contemporary Age", chapter 10.

can answer back".[23] In short, it is difficult to be objective and not be affected by ongoing developments. This is compounded by the fact that the contemporary historian, unlike those who write about the past, "does not know what follows the events he describes", which makes it difficult to fully assess the historical event or trend and put developments in perspective.[24]

Anthony D'Amato offers a different perspective. In his view, while the disadvantage of writing about recent events is that "some relevant information is unavailable because it has not been made public", there is one advantage, which is "there is less danger of rationalisation":

> [I]f ten years from now a scholar looking at the state archive materials on the Taiwan Strait incident of 1966 finds numerous memos on the international law aspects of the problem, the scholar may be led to believe that concerns about international law played a large role. Yet the paper trail may unduly magnify itself in historical contemplation; unrecorded conversations in soundproof rooms may have played a larger role in policy decisions.[25]

On the other hand, there are those (particularly of the Rankean school) who simply argue that contemporary history cannot be written because of inadequate (archival) documentary evidence. For all these reasons, historians should eschew writing about contemporary developments, which ought to be best left to political scientists or journalists. Indeed, one often-heard criticism of contemporary history is that it can only be journalistic.[26]

Others have countered the above views by arguing that the enormous amount of contemporary records at the disposal of the historian is in fact an advantage. Llewellyn Woodward, writing in the inaugural issue of *Journal of Contemporary History*, cited the great British historian Lewis Namier, who said most secrets are in print if you know where

---

[23] Johnes, "On Writing Contemporary History": 21.

[24] W.H. Burton and D. Thompson (eds), *Studies in the Nature and Teaching of History* (New York: Humanities Press, 1967), pp. 116–8, see chapter titled "The Nature and Teaching of Contemporary History".

[25] Anthony D'Amato quoted in W. David Clinton, *The Realist Tradition and Contemporary International Relations* (Baton Rouge: Louisiana State University Press, 2007), p. 82. D'Amato was a professor of law. He passed away in April 2018.

[26] Blumenson, "Can Official History Be Honest History?": 158.

to look for them.[27] Namier might have exaggerated, but there is a grain of truth. *The WikiLeaks Files* (2015) comes to mind.[28] Herbert Butterfield, in fact, took great pride in not having access to confidential documents and in not having to be subjected to the constraints of the Official Secrets Act or having to submit his writings to be approved by a Foreign Office official.[29] Hugh Trevor-Roper, Regius Professor of Modern History, recalled that his many well-regarded historical accounts were based largely on contemporary evidence, which in his view was "more accurate, in some respects, than later reconstructions" precisely because of its "contemporaneity".[30] This was a point also noted by the noted Indo-Fijian historian Brij V. Lal, who pointed out that there were "distinct advantages" in writing about recent times, "in terms of evidence and more varied opportunities to cross-check it". He highlighted the significance of oral evidence as a source, "which if properly used ... could enrich and deepen a study in ways that archival documents cannot".[31]

Wang Gungwu makes an interesting observation on this issue. According to him, this "immense challenge ... having to chase up every relevant document to ensure relative objectivity" (which he ascribed to the training of a professional historian in the 19th-century mould) is "largely self-inflicted". Although "a necessary skill and responsibility", it "does not necessarily capture the essence" of the chosen historical subject, be it event, personality or trend.[32] Eric Hobsbawm acknowledges that "as the historian of the twentieth century draws closer to the present he or she becomes increasingly dependent on two types of sources: the daily or periodical press and the periodic reports, economic

[27] Llewellyn Woodward, "The Study of Contemporary History", *Journal of Contemporary History* 1, 1 (1966): 6.

[28] See *The WikiLeaks Files: The World According to US Empire*, introd. Julian Assange (London: Verso, 2015).

[29] David Thomson, "The Writing of Contemporary History", *Journal of Contemporary History* 2, 1 (Jan. 1967): 26.

[30] Brian Brivati, Julia Buxton and Anthony Seldon (eds), *The Contemporary History Handbook* (Manchester: Manchester University Press, 1996), pp. xi–xii.

[31] Interview with Brij V. Lal in Carolien Stolte and Alicia Schrikker (eds), *World History: A Genealogy, Private Conversations with World Historians, 1996–2016* (Leiden: Leiden University Press, 2017), p. 45.

[32] Wang Gungwu (ed.), *Nation-Building: Five Southeast Asian Histories* (Singapore: Institute of Southeast Asian Studies, 2005), p. 11.

and other surveys, statistical compilations and other publications by national governments and international institutions".[33]

It was George Orwell who said, "Who controls the past controls the future; who controls the present controls the past." Historians therefore cannot abdicate their professional responsibility, as Donald C. Watt warns, by yielding the writing of contemporary history to the "prejudiced and untrained".[34] There is a demand for "higher synthesis, for more coherent and comprehensive presentation of the long-term trends of our times", an observation that David Thomson made in 1967 and is still true today. Like Watt, Thomson also warns that if this demand is not satisfied by competent professional historians, "it will be fobbed off with slipshod generalities or propagandist doctrines, masquerading as historical truths".[35]

In writing this book, I am thus mindful of the challenges and pitfalls of writing contemporary history and takes guidance from the dictums of a number of well-respected historians who share a similar interest in this subfield of history. It is worth starting with a reminder by Fernand Braudel (though he is not a contemporary historian). Braudel warns that those who study the immediate past continually risk being "caught by anything which moves quickly or glitters", and thus it is "absolutely vital to know whether what one is witnessing is the rise of a new movement, the tail end of an old one, an echo from the distant past, or a monotonously recurring phenomenon".[36] Second is the need always to "retain professional objectivity and be mindful of professional responsibility".[37] In this regard, the contemporary historian in particular must be self-aware of their politics.[38] Third, the contemporary historian should possess what Peter Catterall describes as a "hinterland", which is knowledge that goes well beyond the immediate past. This knowledge can minimize, if not remove, the risk highlighted

---

[33] Eric Hobsbawm, *The Age of Extremes* (New York: Vintage Books, 1996), p. xi.

[34] See Donald C. Watt, "Contemporary History: Problems and Perspectives", *Journal of the Society of Archivists* 3, 10 (1969): 511–25.

[35] Thomson, "Writing of Contemporary History": 30.

[36] Quoted in Gaddis, *On Contemporary History*, p. 22; Peter Catterall, "What (If Anything) Is Distinctive About Contemporary History?" *Journal of Contemporary History* 32, 4 (1997): 450.

[37] Watt, "Contemporary History": 512–3.

[38] Johnes, "On Writing Contemporary History": 25.

by Braudel as well as differentiate the historian from the journalist and columnist.[39] In the words of Catterall, "... our understanding of the contemporary needs to be shaped, not just by headlines, or by the study of social, political or economic structures, but by how these have changed over time and been moulded by the past".[40]

In sum, contemporary history may not be the only type of history for understanding the world we live in, but, in the words of Marwick, "the crucial importance of contemporary history, rigorously studied and persuasively presented" is obvious.[41] With the advent of the Internet and with it the proliferation of social media and the explosion of information —both fake and real news—in today's world, there is indeed a great and urgent need for a responsible, balanced and careful recording of contemporary events. I will end this section by describing to readers how I have applied the craft of writing contemporary history (described above) to the writing of this book. This book was conceived in the 1990s, not long after the Cold War ended. I had envisaged a two-book project, beginning with the reconstruction of the Cold War in Southeast Asia[42] and after that bringing the story from the end of the Cold War to the present (I took as a rough guide Carr's time frame in *The Twenty Years' Crisis, 1919–1939*). With this plan in mind, I began to follow assiduously developments in the region every day for almost 30 years since the Cold War ended. It can thus be said that it took that long to write this book. I made two other important early decisions. I chose to take both a "lumper" and "splitter" approach to understanding the region. "Lumpers" refer to those who write about the region, in this case Southeast Asia/ASEAN, from a "corporate strategic perspective", whereas "splitters" refer to those (such as the late Michael Leifer) who find "the differing strategic visions of the ASEAN states more interesting and important".[43] I also adopt an international history approach in

---

[39] "G. Barraclough, 76, Historian", http://www.nytimes.com/1985/01/10/world/g-barraclough-76-historian.html, accessed 30 Mar. 2016.

[40] Kandiah, "Contemporary History"; Catterall, "What (If Anything) Is Distinctive About Contemporary History?": 450.

[41] Marwick, "A New Look, a New Departure": 8.

[42] See Ang Cheng Guan, *Southeast Asia's Cold War: An Interpretive History* (Honolulu: University of Hawai'i Press, 2018).

[43] Yuen Foong Khong, "The Elusiveness of Regional Order: Leifer, the English School and Southeast Asia", *Pacific Review* 18, 1 (2005): 23.

the writing of this narrative. One of the most challenging problems in writing international history is to strike the right balance between the analysis of situations in terms of everything happening at one time (within the chosen perspective) and the pursuit of a narrative of the sequence of events in one place or institution over a period of time. (International history gives precedence to the former.)

In constructing this narrative of post-Cold War Southeast Asia, like all historians, I have relied on a a combination of sources: (a) news reports, (b) offical publications, (c) investigative reports, (d) memoirs, (e) oral history, (f) archives, and (g) secrets. As Hobsbawm (1996) notes, as the historian draws closer to the present, he or she inevitably becomes increasingly dependent on (a) and (b), whereas (f) and (g) are hardest to come by, with the others in between. Having a perch at the Institute of Defence and Strategic Studies (subsequently renamed the S. Rajaratnam School of International Studies) gave me numerous opportunities to listen to and interact with scholars, political analysts and officialdom (both active and retired) in the course of the last 20-odd years. John Tosh reminds us that "each type of source possesses certain strengths and weaknesses; considered together, and compared one against the other, there is at least a chance that they will reveal the true facts—or something very close to them".[44]

Finally, I have taken heed of the caution and advice of Braudel and Catterall. To apply them requires a developed sense of history and a dynamic grasp of geopolitical reality, to be able to see both the woods and the trees. These qualities can only be attained through years of studying the region.

We can now turn back to the subject at hand: the international politics of Southeast Asia coming to three decades after the end of the Cold War era. The thematic coherence of this narrative is held together by two ideas: order and regionalism.[45] Whereas the central historical

---

[44] John Tosh, *The Pursuit of History: Aims, Methods and New Directions in the Study of Modern History* (London: Pearson Longman, 2006), p. 66.

[45] The terms have been described by international relations scholars as "slippery" and "complex" respectively, and they have been much discussed and debated in international relations literature. See, for example, Khong, "Elusiveness of Regional Order": 23–41; See Seng Tan, "Spectres of Leifer: Insights on Regional Order and Security for Southeast Asia Today", *Contemporary Southeast Asia* 34, 3 (Dec. 2012): 309–37; Amitav Acharya, *Constructing Global Order: Agency and Change in World Politics* (Cambridge: Cambridge University Press, 2018), chapter 1.

trajectories of the years between the ends of World War II and the Cold War were decolonization and the Cold War, the priority after 1990 was to focus on regional integration and the search for a new political framework to replace the Cold War structures.[46] Order is a condition whereby states "have established by dialogue and consent common rules and institutions for the conduct of their relations, and recognise the common interest in maintaining these arrangements".[47] Regionalism is the "formation of interstate associations or groupings on the basis of regions" that brings "adjoining states, societies, and economies into intensified interaction. Through this interaction, members of a particular cluster of states may be said to have a distinctive orientation to each other and to constitute a region."[48] This remains a work in progress to this day.

The book adopts a narrative form because, in my view, it is the most effective, authentic method and has the most explanatory power to address the questions raised at the beginning of this Introduction. This is because "narratives offer rich possibilities for self-understanding and the exploration of new worlds".[49] And, as John Ellis notes, "narrative is not only a structuring of events towards a conclusion, but also a structuring of judgement".[50] The narrative form of most histories, in fact, constitutes a distinct form of explanation.

---

[46] A concise and useful article on regionalism is Edward D. Mansfield and Etel Solingen, "Regionalism", *Annual Review of Political Science* 13 (2010): 145–63, http://web.waseda.jp/gsaps/eaui/educational_program/PDF_2/KU_KIM%20DongHun_Reading2_Regionalism.pdf, accessed 14 Aug. 2018.

[47] Hedley Bull and Adam Watson (eds), *Expansion of International Society* (Oxford: Oxford University Press, 1984), p. 1. For a useful discussion of order, see also John J. Mearsheimer, "The Rise and Fall of the Liberal International Order", paper presented at Notre Dame International Security Center, 11 Sept. 2018, https://ndisc.nd.edu/assets/288231/rise_and_fall_of_the_liberal_international_order.september_11_2018.pdf, accessed 8 Jan. 2019.

[48] Jorn Dosch, "Southeast Asia: ASEAN and the Challenge of Regionalism in the Asia-Pacific", in *The New Global Politics of the Asia-Pacific: Conflict and Co-operation in the Asian Century*, Michael K. Connors, Remy Davison and Jorn Dosch (London: Routledge, 2018), pp. 161–2.

[49] Quoted in Hughes-Warrington, *Fifty Key Thinkers on History*, p. 118.

[50] John Ellis, *Documentary: Witness and Self-revelation* (London: Routledge, 2011), p. 70.

The Chapters

Chapter 1 lays out the terrain. It attempts to capture the mood of the early years after the Cold War era, when the geopolitics of the region was malleable, pliable and fluid, and it was "a period of potential geopolitical complication".[51] It describes how the region was different from the 1980s in some ways and a continuation in others. There was much doubt about the future of ASEAN and its raison d'être with the closure of the Cambodian issue. The chapter introduces the debates about American decline, the China threat, the early years of the South China Sea dispute, human security (or non-traditional security, the term Southeast Asian governments prefer), amongst others, which resurface in subsequent chapters as the narrative unfolds. Human security includes environmental issues, piracy, drug and human trafficking, communicable diseases, natural disasters, and terrorism.[52]

Two connected themes run through this book, beginning from the first chapter. The first is the pursuit of regionalism. It began with the transformation of ASEAN from a subregional organization to a full regional organization. This came with some costs. Besides diluting internal unity, the issue of Myanmar would hang over ASEAN's neck like an albatross for many years. In the first 20-plus years after the end of the Cold War, the preoccupation was economic and security integration. The second theme is the pursuit of a new kind of order different from the Cold War period—some call it "security architecture" —an order that places at the centre the region, namely Southeast Asia or, after 1999, ASEAN-10. Chapter 1 recounts the formation of the ASEAN Regional Forum (ARF), which Termsak Chalermpalanupap describes as "the first instance of using the ASEAN model in a multilateral setting involving non ASEAN partners".[53]

[51] Bilahari Kausikan, "Dealing with an Ambiguous World Lecture IV: The Myth of Universality: The Geopolitics of Human Rights", IPS-Nathan Lectures, 29 Apr. 2016, http://lkyspp2.nus.edu.sg/ips/event/201516-ips-nathan-lectures-lecture-iv-a-false-universality-human-rights-and-democracy, accessed 22 Sept. 2017.

[52] Rodolfo C. Severino, "Asean in Need of Stronger Cohesion", *Straits Times*, 9 Dec. 2006.

[53] Termsak Chalermpalanupap, "The ASEAN Regional Forum: Genesis, Development, and Challenges", *ASEAN Matters for All of Us*, Issue 3 (6 Aug.) (Singapore: Institute of Southeast Asian Studies, 2018).

The idea that security lies in trade ties was received wisdom. Chapter 2 describes the formation of APEC (Asia-Pacific Economic Cooperation) and the fulfilment of the ASEAN dream of becoming a full-fledged regional organization. The chapter also highlights the first major crisis of the post-Cold War period that affected the region and its implications for the Southeast Asian states and ASEAN: the Asian Financial Crisis that began in 1997. "Is ASEAN dead?" was a commonly asked question during those years. The period of the financial crisis would also be remembered as the juncture where disappointment with the United States and the West coincided with the reality of the significance of China, both positive and negative, leading to the beginning of a recalibration of Southeast Asia's relations with China (and East Asia). The Asian Financial Crisis also led to the emergence of a new state in the region—Timor-Leste. Whether Timor-Leste will become the 11th member of ASEAN remains an open question. As Marty Natalegawa reminds us, "… the attainment of ASEAN-10 did not foresee the separation of the former Indonesian province of *Timor Timur* (East Timor) and its emergence as a sovereign state in 2002".[54]

Chapter 3 deals with two main issues: ASEAN's efforts to recover its status in the aftermath of the Asian Financial Crisis, and the emergence of the terrorist threat in Southeast Asia. This chapter describes how ASEAN tried to reinvent itself by resuscitating the ASEAN Free Trade Area (AFTA) and proposing the establishment of an ASEAN Economic Community as well as the East Asia Summit (EAS). The focus was principally on economics.

This brings us to Chapter 4, which covers the years 2007 to 2010. This chapter takes stock of where the region was at the halfway point of this narrative. It describes the domestic politics of the ASEAN countries, which had geopolitical implications. It reviews the ASEAN Regional Forum, which has been the platform for the discussion of security in the region. The chapter also introduces the ASEAN Defence Ministers Meeting (ADMM) and the ASEAN Defence Ministers Meeting Plus (ADMM-Plus) (which include ASEAN's eight dialogue partners). It was during this period that ASEAN began to move slightly away from its preoccupation with economics (although this was never

[54] Marty Natalegawa, *Does ASEAN Matter? A View from Within* (Singapore: Institute of Southeast Asian Studies, 2018), p. 61.

far from the minds of Southeast Asian leaders) to stress regional identity and awareness and to promote ASEAN citizenship. Thus the proposal to introduce the ASEAN Community as well as an ASEAN Charter "to improve its decision-making processes and structures".[55] After much soul-searching, twists and turns, the organization in 2003 resolved to establish an ASEAN Community comprising three pillars: political-security, economic and socio-cultural, initially by 2020 and subsequently brought forward to 2015. At the 40th anniversary of ASEAN in 2007, the ten members also signed the ASEAN Charter, which committed ASEAN to becoming a "rules-based legal organisation". The ASEAN Charter came into force in 2008. Both remain a work in progress; as one diplomat opined, "You can't turn a frog into a prince overnight."[56]

Chapter 5 deals principally with the South China Sea dispute, described in chapters 1 and 2. It provides an overview of the dispute and picks up the narrative from the Second Mischief Reef incident (1998) followed by the task of drafting a Code of Conduct for the South China Sea, which remains a work in progress till today. The South China Sea dispute would become an increasingly important issue as the years went by, and the United States, initially positioning itself as a bystander, became drawn into the conflict. As Bilahari Kausikan noted:

> [T]he South China Sea issue is not the only issue in US-China relations; it is perhaps not even the most important issue in their relationship. But the SCS is today the issue where the parameters of US-China relations and their interests are most clearly defined. Like it or not, the region will draw conclusions about American resolve and Chinese intentions from the SCS issue, which will also shape perceptions of Asean.[57]

The region had so far managed to keep the simmering South China Sea dispute—one of the most sensitive post-Cold War issues affecting Southeast Asia and a potential flashpoint, because it involved multiple disputes amongst ASEAN member states and with China over the issue

[55] "ASEAN Charter: The Model Decision", *Straits Times*, 9 Sept. 2005.
[56] Ibid.
[57] "Pavlovian Conditioning and 'Correct Thinking' on the South China Sea", *Straits Times*, 1 Apr. 2016.

of sovereignty—from escalating. Between 1996 and 2010, Southeast Asia indeed had more immediate concerns (beginning with the Asian Financial Crisis). Chapter 7, titled "The South China Sea Dispute Moves Centre Stage", brings the narrative up to date. In between these two chapters is chapter 6, which describes the Southeast Asian states' and, by association, ASEAN's relations with the United States and China, a tension that began in chapter 1. The South China Sea dispute inevitably appears in chapters 6 and 8 as well.

Finally, chapter 8, which ends this narrative in 2017, also marks the 50th anniversary of the formation of ASEAN, an opportune time for reflection and also for looking forward. It is worth noting that if one started the count from 1999, which is when the ASEAN we know of today began, the new ASEAN (or ASEAN-10) is in fact less than 20 years old. Having said that, the organization (since 1967) has survived against all odds. The goal of the Southeast Asian states has always been to ensure that ASEAN remains in the "driver's seat" (ASEAN's favourite terminology) or "at the core of the regional architecture". In its pursuit of a post-Cold War regional order centred on ASEAN, the organization—particularly after 1997—realized that it would first and foremost need to get its own house in order, "to keep its unity intact" and also rejuvenate itself to keep up with the times.[58] It had so far succeeded in remaining in the driver's seat in all the regional mechanisms set up after the Cold War (ASEAN Plus Three, ARF, EAS, ADMM-Plus), and with all the new upgrades to the organization, it hoped to continue to play a key role in regional security. However, the organization is now facing another crossroad, perhaps more dangerous than ever before, as it confronts a twin challenge: keeping the group united and maintaining a balance between the growing rivalry of the United States and China. Apart from that, there is also the potential of a resurgence of terrorism in Southeast Asia. Underlying all the above is, of course, national stability, without which there can be no regionalism. Without the unity of a region, there can be no order of the type that the Southeast Asian states all desire.

---

[58] "CSCAP Retreat: Reviewing of Regional Security Order and Architecture", *Think Tank* 40 (Apr. 2017), S. Rajaratnam School of International Studies, p. 13.

CHAPTER 1

1990–96: Gazing at Signboards That Are All Blank

"The 1990s will be a decade of exciting changes in the world."[1]

"... with the demise of the Cold War, the regional security order is likely to evolve."[2]

The Cusp of a New Era

No one predicted the Cold War would end in 1989. In the words of Bartholomew Sparrow, "if someone on the twentieth of January, 1989, had predicted that in just one year all of Eastern Europe would be liberated and the Warsaw Pact would be obsolete, Robert Gates later remarked, that 'person would have been confined to a loony bin'".[3] With the fall of the Berlin Wall on 9 November 1989, the period

[1] "Speech by Prime Minister Lee Kuan Yew at the Foreign Correspondents' Club, Hong Kong, on 26 October 1990", http://www.nas.gov.sg/archivesonline/speeches/record-details/73fe558e-115d-11e3-83d5-0050568939ad, accessed 5 May 2016.

[2] Tommy Koh, "ASEAN Charts a New Regional Order", *Wall Street Journal Asia*, 21 Aug. 1992.

[3] Bartholomew Sparrow, *Brent Scowcroft and the Call of National Security: The Strategist* (New York: Public Affairs, 2015), pp. 266, 295. Robert Gates was deputy director of the CIA (1987–89), national security advisor (1989–91) and director of the CIA (1991–93). George H.W. Bush was inaugurated as the 41st president of the United States on 20 January 1989. For a discussion on dating the end of the Cold War, see, John Mueller, "What Was the Cold War About? Evidence from Its Ending", *Political Science Quarterly* 119, 4 (2004–05).

known as the Cold War ended. If one were looking for a more "official" date, it would be when Presidents Bush and Gorbachev declared its end in Malta on 3 December 1989. No one expected the disintegration of the Soviet Union in 1991 either. As Peter Duignan and L.H. Gann noted, it was not Gorbachev's intention to dismantle the Soviet Union. He only "wished to mend communism, not end it, to render the state more efficient, more humane, and more acceptable to the citizenry".[4] The disintegration of the Soviet Union was the last nail in the coffin of the Cold War.

While on the one hand the confrontation between the United States and the Soviet Union (after 1991, Russia) ended, on the other, Washington's relations with Beijing started to fray. Relations had been developing positively since the 1972 Nixon visit, and particularly after the Vietnamese invasion of Kampuchea in 1978. In February 1989, when President George H.W. Bush met with General Secretary Zhao Ziyang in Beijing, the two leaders agreed that notwithstanding their differences, Sino-US relations had "reached a level of significant mutual understanding" and the leaders were on "the same general wave length".[5] A few months later, the Tiananmen Square Incident (April–June 1989) caused a turn for the worse in Sino-US relations as Washington (and some of its allies) imposed a number of economic and diplomatic sanctions against China.

In Southeast Asia the Cold War ended without much of an announcement.[6] The "wall" that divided the Communists and the anti-Communists in Southeast Asia had been breaking down brick by brick, albeit at different paces in each country, for almost a decade before 9 November 1989. Indeed, by 1989 all the Communist Parties in the ASEAN countries as well as the Burmese Communist Party had

---

[4] Peter Duignan and L.H. Gann, *The Cold War: End and Aftermath* (Stanford: Hoover Institution on War, Revolution, and Peace, 1996), p. 8.

[5] Memorandum of Conversation between George H.W. Bush and Zhao Ziyang, 26 Feb. 1989, http://digitalarchive.wilsoncenter.org/document/133956, accessed 9 May 2016.

[6] See, for example, Kimie Hara, "Rethinking the 'Cold War' in the Asia-Pacific", *Pacific Review* 12, 4 (1999): 515–36; Sergey Radchenko, "Unwanted Visionaries: The Soviet Failure at the End of the Cold War", Oxford Scholarship Online (Apr. 2014), http://www.oxfordscholarship.com/view/10.1093/acprof:oso/9780199938773.001.0001/acprof-9780199938773, accessed 18 Apr. 2016.

been either destroyed or neutralized. Only the Communist Party of the Philippines remains today, but it does not pose any existential threat to the government. Its heyday was during the martial law period in the 1980s under President Marcos. The Cold War in Southeast Asia had a rhythm of its own.[7] If one had to choose a date or event that identified the end of the old and the beginning of the new, and an appropriate starting point for this book, it would be the signing of the Framework for a Comprehensive Political Settlement of the Cambodia Conflict in Paris on 23 October 1991.

The "official" end of the Cambodia conflict in 1991 was the first concrete indication that the Cold War was finally over in Southeast Asia. There would not have been a resolution had it not been for two rapprochements that took place in the late 1980s: US-Soviet on the one hand, and Sino-Soviet on the other. With the decade-long Cambodian issue resolved, the Southeast Asian states could henceforth move ahead to complete the ASEAN project, which had started in 1967. In 1999 ASEAN, which until then was a subregional association, finally achieved its organizational goal, set out in Article 18 of the Founding Charter of ASEAN, of uniting all the Southeast Asian states within one entity.

Malaysia, Thailand and the Philippines had established diplomatic relations with China soon after the Sino-US rapprochement in the 1970s. ASEAN states had also cooperated with China against the Vietnamese occupation of Kampuchea/Cambodia through the 1980s (out of expediency). But it was the Sino-Soviet rapprochement and the settlement of the Cambodian issue that paved the way for the normalization of Southeast Asian relations with China, particularly for Vietnam, Indonesia and Singapore. Sino-Soviet rapprochement made it possible for Beijing to abandon its support for Communist Parties in the Southeast Asian states, which the Chinese were reluctant to do when they were still in competition with the Soviet Union for leadership of the Communist movement. Beijing's refusal to cut off links with the fraternal Communist Parties was the major obstacle to China's advancing its relations with the ASEAN countries. Indonesia finally resumed formal relations with China (suspended since 1967) in August 1990.

[7] See Ang, *Southeast Asia's Cold War*, chapter 6.

Soon after, in October 1990, Singapore established formal diplomatic relations of its own volition—the last Southeast Asian state to do so.

The tension in US-China relations would eventually come to affect the Southeast Asian states. In a speech delivered just two months before the fall of the Berlin Wall, Singapore Prime Minister Lee Kuan Yew warned that while the confrontation between the Communist and non-Communist blocs since World War II was over, "the competition between big powers for influence and power" would continue in a "multi-polar world". Lee noted, "It has always been thus, whether it was the Three Kingdoms in China or the Warring States in Japan. The Big wants to assure its supremacy by growing bigger, and the Small tries to prevent this by alliances between themselves to block the Big, and to make him smaller ..."[8] The international environment in the early 1990s was indeed extremely malleable, pliable and fluid.[9] There was the anticipation that "a new international environment was emerging",[10] although no one knew what it would turn out to be like. As Bush noted, "the new world facing us—and I wish I were your age—it's a wonderful world of discovery, a world to unlocking the promise of freedom. It's no more structured than a dream, no more regimented than an innovator's burst of inspiration."[11] Even Lee Kuan Yew, who had cautioned against being unduly sanguine over the passing of an era described above, saw a silver lining. In his October 1989 speech delivered at the 11th Commonwealth Heads of Government Meeting one

[8] Lecture by the prime minister of Singapore at the Thai National Defence College, Bangkok, 19 Sept. 1989, http://www.nas.gov.sg/archivesonline/data/pdfdoc/lky19890919.pdf, accessed 3 May 2016. See also Jane Perlez, "One Envoy's Take on China's Hardball Diplomacy", *New York Times*, 31 Mar. 2016, http://nyti.ms/1RPxGOH, accessed 10 May 2016; Edward Wong, "Queen Elizabeth II Says Chinese Officials Were 'Very Rude' on State Visit", *New York Times*, 11 May 2016, http://www.nytimes.com/2016/05/12/world/asia/china-britain-queen-xi-jinping.html?smid=fb-nytimes&smtyp=cur, accessed 12 May 2016.

[9] Paul Keating, *Engagement: Australia Faces the Asia-Pacific* (Sydney: Macmillan, 2000), p. 24; David Shambaugh, "Prospects for Asian Security After the Cold War", in *After the Cold War: Security and Democracy in Africa and Asia*, ed. William Hale and Eberhard Kienle (London: I.B. Tauris, 1997), chapter 5.

[10] Keating, *Engagement*, p. 24.

[11] "Remarks at Maxwell Air Force Base War College in Montgomery, Alabama", 13 Apr. 1991, https://www.presidency.ucsb.edu/documents/remarks-maxwell-air-force-base-war-college-montgomery-alabama, accessed 5 May 2016.

month before the fall of the Berlin Wall, he noted that "as the balance between the major powers changes, other states in the world have little choice but to adjust. But not all these developments are adverse." Lee observed that there was "a strong desire in the East and West, in the North and South, to concentrate energies and resources on economic development, and to restrain expenditure on arms". This, in his view, "could usher in an era of worldwide international cooperation through multilateral institutions". Lee in fact advocated for the strengthening of multilateral institutions, starting with the UN and its agencies.[12] The establishment of APEC, first broached by Australian Prime Minister Bob Hawke in January 1989, initially as an informal ministerial-level dialogue group of 12 countries in November 1989, was a reflection of the "increasingly [*sic*] interdependence of regional economies" at the cusp of the end of the Cold War. APEC as an institution was formalized in 1993.[13] Looking back at the decade of the 1990s, Andres Martinez noted how "the sense that we were no longer stuck in a divided, zero-sum world proved enormously beneficial for cross-border collaboration".[14] As President Bill Clinton said at the inaugural APEC Summit, hosted by the United States, "we agreed that the Asian-Pacific region should be united, not divided".[15]

---

[12] "Toast by the Prime Minister at a Dinner for Commonwealth Heads of Government on Wednesday, 25 Oct. 1989 at the Shangri-La Hotel [Kuala Lumpur]", http://www.nas.gov.sg/archivesonline/speeches/record-details/73c5fe19-115d-11e3-83d5-0050568939ad, accessed 6 May 2016.

[13] First Ministerial Meeting, Canberra, 6–7 Nov. 1989, http://www.apec.org/~/media/Files/MinisterialStatements/Annual/1989/89_amm_jms.pdf, accessed 9 May 2016. (The ministers were from Australia, Brunei, Canada, Indonesia, Japan, Republic of Korea, Malaysia, New Zealand, the Philippines, Singapore, Thailand and the United States); APEC Leaders Economic Vision Statement, Blake Island, Seattle, 20 Nov. 1993. In addition to the original 12 countries, the 1993 meeting included China (President Jiang Zemin) as well as representatives from Taiwan and Hong Kong, http://www.apec.org/~/media/Files/LeadersDeclarations/1993/1993_LeadersDeclaration.pdf, accessed 9 May 2016.

[14] Andres Martinez, "The 1990s: Exuberant Interlude Between Cold War and Sept. 11", *Sunday Times*, 8 May 2016.

[15] "President Clinton Convenes APEC Summit on Blake Island on 20 November 1993", *Seattle Times*, 17 and 21 Nov. 1993, http://www.historylink.org/index.cfm?DisplayPage=output.cfm&file_id=5333, accessed 9 May 2016.

The Unipolar Moment

In the latter years of the Cold War there was an ongoing debate about American decline, aptly illustrated by the discussions of Paul Kennedy's best-selling book *The Rise and Fall of the Great Powers* (1987).[16] Both the unexpected end of the Cold War and the ability of the United Nations (UN)—and in particular the UN Security Council—to collectively respond to Iraq's invasion and annexation of Kuwait in August 1990 (led by the United States) gave hope of a promising post-Cold War era as well as a rejuvenated America. The Gulf War was the first major conflict of the post-Cold War era (and to this day the only conflict that had a swift and unified international response led by the United States).

It led the Americans to declare a "new world order", one with a special role for the United States. As George H.W. Bush remarked:

> [T]he new world order really is a tool for addressing a new world of possibilities. This order gains its mission and shape not just from shared interests but from shared ideals. And the ideals that have spawned new freedoms throughout the world have received their boldest and clearest expression in our great country, the United States. Never before has the world looked more to the American example. Never before have so many millions drawn hope from the American idea ...[17]

In short, Washington saw its post-Cold War mission as changing the world in its image because the assumption was that the world wanted to be like the United States.

This was the beginning of America's brief post-Cold War triumphant and unipolar moment,[18] which would give Southeast Asia its share of pain (we will come back to this later). Charles Krauthammer,

---

[16] Paul Kennedy, *The Rise and Fall of the Great Powers* (New York: Vintage Books, 1987).

[17] "Address Before a Joint Session of the Congress on the Cessation of the Persian Gulf Conflict", 6 Mar. 1991, https://www.presidency.ucsb.edu/documents/address-before-joint-session-the-congress-the-cessation-the-persian-gulf-conflict, accessed 6 May 2016.

[18] See Charles Krauthammer, "The Unipolar Moment", *Foreign Affairs: America and the World* (1990–91): 23–33; "The Unipolar Moment Revisited", *National Interest* (Winter 2002/03): 5–17.

who coined the term "unipolar moment", did not expect this status to last forever: "no doubt, multi-polarity will come in time." However, he expected "decades" or even "another generation" before the unprecedented gap in power between the leading nation and all the others could be closed.[19] Lee Kuan Yew, as well as other Southeast Asian leaders, shared Krauthammer's view. In his appraisal of the strategic problems that confronted the post-Cold War world, Lee viewed the 1990s in the context of a new geopolitical configuration that would pose new challenges for Asian countries. He foresaw the shift in global balance to Asia-Pacific with the inevitable rise of China economically (followed by that of India). Thus, it was necessary for the United States to maintain a presence in the region as a countervailing power.[20]

It is perhaps useful to pause here and revisit US policy specifically towards East Asia (including Southeast Asia) as described in the reports submitted by the US Department of Defense to Congress titled "A Strategic Framework for the Asia Pacific Rim: Looking Toward the 21st Century", more commonly shortened to "East Asia Strategic Initiative" (EASI). There were three such reports in the early-post Cold War years: EASI-I (April 1990), EASI-II (mid-1992) and EASI-III (February 1995). The first of the three stated that US interest in Asia-Pacific remained the same as it was before the end of the Cold War. As such, US military presence in the region should remain (more or less) unchanged. The report paid particular attention to the situation in Northeast Asia, which, despite the end of the Cold War, was still unstable and volatile. EASI-I was crafted during the very early days of the so-called New World Order. It was during the period that saw the Soviet withdrawal from Afghanistan and the collapse of Communism in Eastern Europe and when the decade-long Cambodian issue was not yet fully resolved. However, taking into account the overall improved

---

[19] Krauthammer, "Unipolar Moment"; " Unipolar Moment Revisited". See also Hal Brands, *Making the Unipolar Moment: U.S. Foreign Policy and the Rise of the Post-Cold War Order* (Ithaca: Cornell University Press, 2016). Brands argued that the "unipolar moment" was a relatively brief period from 1989 to 1992 when the United States enjoyed "an extraordinarily favourable configuration of power and influence in the international area, and whose values, preferences, and overall global leadership seemed as privileged as ever before" (p. 274).

[20] See Ang Cheng Guan, *Lee Kuan Yew's Strategic Thought* (London: Routledge, 2013), p. 71.

international climate and the US budget deficit, EASI-I stated that there should be some reductions, particularly of US ground forces, in the region to be carried out in three phases. The first would be 1990–93, when about 14,000–15,000 of the 135,000 US military personnel in the Pacific would be withdrawn. Adjustments in the second and third phases, 1993–95 and 1995–2000, would be "dependent on the prevailing international climate". According to EASI-I, the US would play the role of a regional balancer and "honest broker" in three ways: by maintaining a strong forward deployment military force in the region, by coordinating policies with other Asian countries through bilateral and multilateral channels, and by being a neutral arbiter to help resolve problems between the Asian nations themselves. In February 1991 the US Department of Defense reported to Congress that the Asian countries supported EASI-I and that it was being implemented according to schedule. While that might have been true to a degree, there was certainly concern from some quarters within the region that Washington was retrenching from East and Southeast Asia to focus on newly liberated Eastern Europe, in what Paul Kennedy called "imperial overstretch". Following the collapse of the Soviet Union at the end of 1991 and the closure of US bases in the Philippines, the Department of Defense produced EASI-II in mid-1992. Regional disquiet over US withdrawal in EASI-I might have led to some recalibration in EASI-II. In EASI-II, Asia, which had been of secondary importance in US strategic calculations, now assumed primary significance. The study stated that maintaining a credible security presence was an important element of the US effort "to build a sense of Asia-Pacific community vital to the post-Cold War international system now taking place". It did not specify any particular threat to US interests in Asia but noted the following sources of instability: North Korea, a post-Deng China, Taiwan, Cambodia, the Spratly Islands, Burma and nuclear proliferation in Northeast Asia. With the loss of the Philippines bases, the study stated that the US would have to change its force structure from one of a large permanent presence in the region to one of having a forward presence through access agreements with countries such as Australia and Singapore. It also highlighted the strategic importance of US forces in Japan.

Like Paul Kennedy, who believed that "the importance of economics seemed to have been much undervalued by military and diplomatic historians",[21] Lee Kuan Yew also highlighted the need for a new balance of power, one founded on economic strength rather than military power.[22] In Lee's analysis, a US military presence in both Europe and the Pacific was still essential, but he warned that "unless the US economy becomes more dynamic and less debt-ridden, this presence will be much reduced by the end of the decade". Even if the US deficits were reduced and productivity and exports increased, the US could not afford—and would not be willing—to bear the whole cost of the global security burden. Thus, other nations—particularly Germany and Japan—must take a more active role in international security.[23] One critical question was thus whether the United States could continue its role as a key security and economic player in Asia-Pacific beyond the year 2000. Lee hoped Washington could and would:

> No alternative balance can be as comfortable as the present one with the US as a major player. But if the US economy cannot afford a US role, then a new balance it will have to be ... However, the geopolitical balance without the US as a principal force will be very different from that which it now is or can be if the US remains a central player.

According to Lee, his generation of Asians,

> who have experienced the last war, its horrors and miseries, and who remember the US role in the phoenix-like rise from the ashes of that war to prosperity of Japan, the NIE's and ASEAN, will feel a sense of regret that the world will become so vastly different because the US becomes a less central player in the new balance.[24]

---

[21] "Imperial Cycles: Bucks, Bullets and Bust", *New York Times*, 10 Jan. 1988, http://www.nytimes.com/1988/01/10/books/imperial-cycles-bucks-bullets-and-bust.html?pagewanted=all, accessed 16 May 2016.

[22] Ang, *Lee Kuan Yew's Strategic Thought*, p. 71.

[23] "Speech by Mr Lee Kuan Yew, Senior Minister of Singapore, at Asahi Shimbun Symposium in Tokyo on 9 May 1991", http://www.nas.gov.sg/archivesonline/speeches/record-details/74075a2d-115d-11e3-83d5-0050568939ad, accessed 8 Apr. 2019.

[24] "Speech by Mr Lee Kuan Yew, Senior Minister of Singapore, at the Harvard-Fairbank Center Conference in New York: 'East Asia in the New Era: The Prospects of Cooperation' on 11 May 1992", http://www.nas.gov.sg/archivesonline/data/pdfdoc/lky19920511.pdf, accessed 8 Apr. 2019; "Speech by Mr Lee Kuan Yew, Senior Minister of Singapore, at the 1992 Pacific Rim Forum in San Diego on 13 May 1992", http://www.nas.gov.sg/archivesonline/speeches/record-details/74088d56-115d-11e3-83d5-0050568939ad, accessed 8 Apr. 2019; Ang, *Lee Kuan Yew's Strategic Thought*.

He believed that "thinking Americans who understand power and their relations, the equation between power and American economic well-being" would want to remain in the region.[25]

More than any other Southeast Asian country, Singapore felt the need for an American presence in Asia. When the Philippine Congress in 1991 voted to shut down the American bases there, Singapore offered to upgrade its naval base to service the US fleet and serve as a transit point for US naval operations in the region, an offer that had the tacit support of the other Southeast Asian countries with the possible exception of Malaysia. Prime Minister Mahathir, who was against an over-reliance on the United States, was reported to have said that he did not want to see "an enhanced American military presence in the region".[26] Jason Swergold noted that prior to the retirement of Mahathir, "an outspoken critic of many US policies, the amount of cooperation that could be expected out of Kuala Lumpur was often unclear".[27] Lee explained:

> Nature does not like a vacuum. And if there is a vacuum, we can be sure that somebody will fill it. I don't see Japan particularly wanting to fill that space unless it feels that its trade routes and access to Gulf oil are threatened. If the Americans are not around, they (the Japanese) cannot be sure who will protect their oil tankers. So they have to do something themselves. That will trigger the Koreans, who fear the Japanese, then the Chinese. Will India then come down to our seas with two aircraft carriers? It could be a disastrously unstable state of affairs. So why not stick with what has worked so far? The US presence has maintained peace on the high seas of the Pacific since 1945. The American presence, in my view, is essential for the continuation of international law and order in East Asia.[28]

Under the Clinton presidency (1993–2001), the administration's policy of engagement and "assertive multilateralism" was aimed at ensuring that the US would not fight a war in the region, and even if it needed

---

[25] Ang, *Lee Kuan Yew's Strategic Thought.*

[26] Sheldon W. Simon, *The Economic Crisis and ASEAN States' Security* (Strategic Studies Institute, US Army War College, 23 Oct. 1998), p. 19.

[27] Jason Swergold, "U.S. Military Transformation and the Rise of China: Restructuring Regional Alliances", http://hdl.handle.net/2345/496, accessed 17 Nov. 2016.

[28] "Why American Economic and Security Presence Vital for Asia", *Straits Times*, 17 Dec. 1991.

to, it would not have to bear most of the burden as it did during the Vietnam War. On more than one occasion, American officials said that the region could—and must—assume a growing share of the security burden, a point made as early as 1969 by President Nixon and commonly known as the Nixon or Guam Doctrine. Thus, whether the United States maintained the 100,000 troop level in Asia (spelled out in EASI-III in February 1995) was perhaps not the crucial question. What was critical was whether Washington had the national will to retain its presence (whatever the size and nature) and to exercise its power decisively when the situation demanded. The question of what constituted American critical interests was one that only the Americans could answer.

The China Threat

For historical reasons, the Southeast Asian states, often described as China's backyard, have always been wary of China. In a seminar paper titled "The China Threat", Michael Yahuda noted that it was widely believed in Southeast Asia, "with varying degrees of intensity, that China constitutes some sort of a threat (actual or potential) to the region ... Whether or not China constitutes such a threat to Southeast Asia therefore belongs essentially to the subjective realm of perceptions and misperceptions".[29] Yahuda's observation was made in 1986, a few years before the phrase became popular in both academic and policy circles. China's Zhao Ziyang told President Bush in 1989:

> [T]en years have elapsed since reform was launched in China. The steps taken have not been small. However, we are only half way through ... it is indeed a tough pursuit to transform the Chinese economy from a highly centralised system to a planned commodity system. It is a long process that cannot be done in a short period of time, particularly for a large country like China.[30]

Militarily, China still lacked the capacity to project power beyond its borders. But its increased real defence spending since 1989 did not

---

[29] Michael Yahuda, *The China Threat* (Kuala Lumpur: Institute of Strategic and International Studies, 1986), p. 1.

[30] Memorandum of Conversation between George H.W. Bush and Zhao Ziyang.

go unnoticed.[31] No one, however, could predict how fast and soon China would develop economically to challenge the United States and/or Japan and the implications of a rising or powerful China. Indeed, its economic transition was fraught with obstacles, which accounted for Deng Xiaoping's "historic tour of South China, popularly known as *Nanxun*" in February 1992. Michel Oksenberg noted that although physically declining, Deng remained mentally sharp and was "determined to keep China on the path that he and his associates had set in the 1980s".[32] The Chinese tried to allay such concerns in the region by constantly emphasizing that they needed a peaceful and stable international environment in which to achieve their economic goals. As Deng told Bush when they met in February 1989, "With regards to the problems confronting China, let me say to you that the overwhelming need is to maintain stability. Without stability, everything will be gone, even accomplishments will be ruined. We hope our friends abroad can understand this point."[33]

Even though "the early 1990s was a time of great political and economic uncertainty in China ... with a messy, half-reformed economy",[34] much to the chagrin of the Chinese leadership a small but influential "cottage industry predicated on forecasts about growing regional insecurity and in particular, on China as a great power threat" emerged during the same period.[35] To the Chinese, Washington and Tokyo conjured up China's military threat in order to achieve their ulterior motives, which were Washington's intention to sell F-16 fighters to

---

[31] Margaret Thatcher, *Statecraft: Strategies for a Changing World* (London: HarperCollins, 2002), p. 180.

[32] John Wong and Zheng Yongnian (eds), *The Nanxun Legacy and China's Development in the Post-Deng Era* (Singapore: Singapore University Press, 2001), pp. 3, 21; see also chapters 1, 2.

[33] Memorandum of Conversation between George H.W. Bush and Chairman Deng Xiaoping.

[34] Zheng Yongnian and John Wong (eds), *Goh Keng Swee on China: Selected Essays* (Singapore: World Scientific, 2013), p. 2; see in particular chapter 8, "What's Gone Wrong in China?" Goh Keng Swee was an economic adviser to China's top leadership from 1985 to 1990.

[35] Gary Klintworth, "Greater China and Regional Security", *Australian Journal of International Affairs* 48, 2 (Nov. 1994); Denny Roy, "The 'China Threat' Issue", *Asian Survey* 36, 8 (Aug. 1996).

Taiwan and Tokyo's plan to allow its Self-Defense Forces to participate in UN peacekeeping operations.[36] The beginning of the China threat theory thus could be traced to the end of 1992. It was brought about by a "confluence of factors": (a) Deng Xiaoping's *Nanxun*, which, in the words of Yong Deng, "resuscitated China's market reforms, leading to the economic rise of a unified China that lent credence to the fear of China's strength in lieu of the commonplace prognosis of imminent 'China collapse'" in the aftermath of the Tiananmen Square Incident; (b) China's territorial claims over the Spratly Islands, which were (and still are) strongly disputed by a number of Southeast Asian countries; and (c) Washington's and Japan's agendas as mentioned above.

Just as Kennedy's *The Rise and Fall of the Great Powers* generated a debate on whether the United States was in decline, which lasted for a number of years and was periodically rehashed (such as during the global economic crisis in 2007–08 and again in 2016–17), a parallel and lively debate ensued between those who viewed the rise of China as a threat and those who were more sanguine about it. The debate continues to this day.

The Chinese did not help their own cause. Of the many issues, the South China Sea dispute was the most worrisome to Southeast Asian states. Although the South China Sea had long been identified as a potential trouble spot, it did not became *the* security issue of the day throughout the 1970s and 1980s. This was so despite a number of unfriendly and even hostile developments that took place in the South China Sea. Although China had all along claimed that it had indisputable sovereignty over the Nansha Islands and adjacent waters, from the mid-1970s through the 1980s the disputes over the South China Sea had been very much a China-Vietnam affair.[37] This began to change from 1992. In July 1992 Vietnam (and Laos) became observers in ASEAN, which was the first step towards eventual membership in the association.

In February 1992 Beijing passed the Territorial Waters Law, which essentially claimed Chinese suzerainty over the whole of the South China

[36] For a discussion on the origins of the "China Threat" theory or theories, see Yong Deng, *China's Struggle for Status: The Realignment of International Relations* (Cambridge: Cambridge University Press, 2008), pp. 104–19.

[37] See Ang Cheng Guan, "The South China Sea Dispute Revisited", *Australian Journal of International Affairs* 54, 2 (July 2000).

Sea. In May of the same year, Vietnam and China were involved in a high-profile argument over the contract signed between China Offshore Oil Corporation and Crestone Energy Corporation to conduct joint oil exploration in an area that Vietnam claimed to be within its territorial waters. Beijing was unable to debunk the China threat theory because Chinese actions in the South China Sea lent further credibility to the arguments put forward by the China threat camp. The opaqueness of the decision-making process in Beijing, matched by the contradiction between words and deeds, compounded the matter. When Premier Li Peng visited Singapore in August 1990 and Malaysia in December 1990, he said that China was willing to discuss joint efforts to develop the Spratlys and shelve the question of sovereignty. Chinese President Yang Shangkun conveyed a similar message during his visit to Thailand and Indonesia at the beginning of 1992. However, soon after, Beijing passed the controversial Territorial Waters Law on 25 February 1992. Almost immediately after attending the Third Indonesian-sponsored Workshop on "Managing Potential Conflicts in the South China Sea" (29 June–3 July 1992) in Jogjakarta, the Chinese occupied Da Lac Reef, which was claimed by Vietnam.[38] At the same time, Beijing expressed lukewarm support for the five-point ASEAN Declaration on the South China Sea (issued at the 25th ASEAN Ministerial Meeting in July 1992), which called for self-restraint, joint cooperation and putting aside the issue of sovereignty. An ASEAN official disclosed that China did not budge from its official stand about asserting Chinese sovereignty in the Spratlys during its meeting with the ASEAN ministers in Manila.[39] Wong Kan Seng, then Singapore's foreign minister, said that the declaration "raised the political consciousness of all countries about the South China Sea and its potential problems".[40] We will return to the South China Sea issue in chapter 2.

---

[38] *Voice of Vietnam*, 7 July 1992, *SWB*/*FE*/1428/A2/1.

[39] "Settle Spratlys Dispute Amicably: ASEAN Ministers", *Straits Times*, 22 July 1992; "Spratlys Declaration 'Gives Asean New Role in Dispute'", *Straits Times*, 31 July 1992. For the declaration, see https://cil.nus.edu.sg/rp/pdf/1992%20ASEAN%20Declaration%20on%20the%20South%20China%20Sea-pdf.pdf, accessed 18 Aug. 2016.

[40] "Spratlys Declaration 'Gives Asean New Role in Dispute'".

ASEAN at 25 and the Formation of the ASEAN Regional Forum

The five Southeast Asian states that made up ASEAN at the end of the Cold War emerged from the Cold War on the side of the victors. However, the largest and most important member of ASEAN—often considered the first amongst equals in the association—Indonesia under the leadership of Suharto (since 1966) was "showing some signs of vulnerability".[41] It was a gradual decline marked by a sudden plunge in 1997 into the unknown, which would have grave implications for the group. However, we should not run too far ahead of our narrative. Until 1996 Suharto, R.E. Elson noted, "was thought by the influential magazine *Asiaweek* to be the most powerful man in Asia".[42]

Despite being victorious, ASEAN did not leave "politics and international affairs to chance". There is general agreement that the resolution of the decade-long Cambodian issue was "the greatest diplomatic success" of ASEAN, which had gone through a long teething period—some would refer to it as stagnation—from its formation in August 1967. Indeed, the end of the Cold War, and with it the end of the Cambodia conflict, was the pinnacle of ASEAN's triumph. The oft-asked question in the early 1990s was, "what would be its post-Cold War *raison d'être*".[43]

In 1992 ASEAN celebrated the 25th anniversary of its formation. The year began with the Fourth ASEAN Summit, which took place on 27–28 January 1992 in Singapore. It was only the fourth in the 25 years of ASEAN, and the first since the Cold War ended in Southeast Asia with the signing of the Paris Agreement on 23 October 1991. In the words of Tommy Koh, "the summit will show that ASEAN does not need Cambodia to justify its existence ..." Convened "at a turning point in history", the summit was also important as an occasion for the ASEAN leaders to assess the implications of the end of the Cold War for East and Southeast Asia.[44]

---

[41] R.E. Elson, *Suharto: A Political Biography* (Cambridge: Cambridge University Press, 2001), p. 265.
[42] Ibid., p. 297.
[43] Ang Cheng Guan, *Singapore, ASEAN and the Cambodian Conflict 1978–1991* (Singapore: NUS Press, 2013), p. 168.
[44] "What Makes the 4th Asean Summit Historic", *Straits Times*, 23 Jan. 1992.

Given the new focus on the globalization and regionalization of the world economy, a trend mentioned above, one of the key decisions of the Fourth ASEAN Summit was to establish an ASEAN Free Trade Area in 15 years. It was also at this summit that the idea of a security forum or forums was raised for future discussion. At the Post-Ministerial Conference in July 1991, Japanese Foreign Minister Taro Nakayama had proposed using the ASEAN Post-Ministerial Conference as a forum to discuss regional security.[45] This suggestion would eventually morph into the ASEAN Regional Forum (ARF) in 1993.[46] However, at the fourth summit, a reinterpretation of the relevance of ZOPFAN (Zone of Peace, Freedom and Neutrality) in the post-Cold War period as well as a formal endorsement of the East Asia Economic Caucus (discussed in chapter 3) were tactfully deferred, in typical ASEAN fashion, given the lack of consensus within the group. Still, as Koh noted, the ASEAN discussion of regional security with its dialogue partners for the first time at the ASEAN Post-Ministerial Conference in Manila (July 1992) showed that "ASEAN recognises that economics and security are linked" and "the security of Southeast Asia cannot be isolated from the security of the larger Asia Pacific region".[47]

The late Michael Leifer, recognized as one of the most distinguished scholars of Southeast Asian studies, in an essay marking the 25th anniversary of the association, judged that "its record of cooperation compares favourably with that of any other post-colonial regional grouping". He also noted that "like Britain which had lost an empire

---

[45] See Paul Midford, "Japan's Leadership Role in East Asian Security Multilateralism: The Nakayama Proposal and the Logic of Reassurance", *Pacific Review* 13, 3 (2000): 367–97.

[46] "Call to Set up Regional Security Forum", *Straits Times*, 19 Jan. 1992; "What Makes the 4th Asean Summit Historic"; Singapore Declaration, 28 Jan. 1992, http://asean.org/?static_post=singapore-declaration-of-1992-singapore-28-january-1992, accessed 18 Aug. 2016; "S'pore to Push for More Talks Among Members with Dialogue Partners", *Straits Times*, 27 July 1992. See also Peter Ho, "The ASEAN Regional Forum: The Way Forward?" in *ASEAN-UN Cooperation in Preventive Diplomacy*, ed. Sarasin Viraphol and Werner Pfenning (Bangkok: Ministry of Foreign Affairs, 1995), p. 252; Peter Ho, "Some Observations on the Regional Architecture in Southeast Asia", in *50 Years of ASEAN and Singapore*, ed. Tommy Koh, Sharon Seah Li-Lian and Chang Li Lin (Singapore: World Scientific, 2017), chapter 17.

[47] Koh, "ASEAN Charts a New Regional Order".

and not yet found a role", ASEAN in its 25 years "has lost a conflict and may not yet have found a regional security role".[48] In his view, "such a role had always been its prime ambition, despite its obvious attention to economic cooperation".[49] According to Leifer, ASEAN was "afflicted by a sense of drift over its security role". This was worsened by the "disturbing changes in the regional balance of power"—the disintegration of the Soviet Union, an ineffective Japan, and a United States that "appears to have turned a blind eye to China's creeping assertiveness in the Spratly Islands in the South China Sea".[50]

ASEAN was preoccupied with two major and concurrent projects in the 1990s and as it passed its 25th year: one had to do with its expansion, which according to Malaysian Foreign Minister Abdullah Ahmad Badawi "was inevitable" although "the pace towards full regional integration must not be forced".[51] The expansion of ASEAN would be completed almost a decade later, in 1999. We will discuss each stage of the expansion of ASEAN at the appropriate juncture of this narrative. From its inception in August 1967, ASEAN had the long-term goal of bringing all the countries in the Southeast Asian region together as one cohesive political, economic and social forum and making it a truly regional organization. This was not possible during the Cold War years. Thus, ASEAN, despite its name, was in fact a subregional association or organization until 1999. Brunei joined the original five members of ASEAN the day it gained independence in 1984. It would take another decade and a seismic change in the world order before Vietna became a member in 1995, followed by Myanmar and Laos in 1997 on the 30th anniversary of the formation of ASEAN; and finally, after a delay, Cambodia in 1999. As Nguyen Vu Tung put it:

> ASEAN was eager to enlarge the organisation to enable it to speak for the whole of Southeast Asia, Vietnam was a good starting point for

---

[48] In Leifer's opinion, ASEAN's diplomacy in the Cambodian conflict was effective in the 1980s but eventually "lost its edge when the United Nations Security Council assumed responsibility for resolving that issue".

[49] Michael Leifer, "ASEAN: Now for the Next 25 Years", *International Herald Tribune*, 12 Aug. 1992.

[50] Ibid.

[51] "Inevitable That Asean Membership Will Grow: KL Minister", *Straits Times*, 17 Jan. 1992.

> the subsequent entry of Laos, Myanmar and Cambodia ... Vietnam's membership of ASEAN seemed natural given the end of the Cold War and the resolution of the Cambodian problem.[52]

Indeed, the admission of Vietnam (and Laos) was uncontroversial compared to that of Myanmar and Cambodia.

In 1973, soon after the signing of the Paris Peace Accord, North Vietnam was invited to one of the high-level ASEAN meetings. Hanoi, however, rejected the invitation (from the Thai government, conveyed through the Indonesian Embassy in Hanoi) to take part in the meetings of the ASEAN foreign ministers in Pattaya (16–18 April 1973) because of "Thai involvement in the Vietnam War, and the Thai government's willingness to permit the existence of US military bases in Thailand".[53] Hanoi's mindset gradually changed because of its not too pleasant experiences with the Soviet Union and China during the 1980s. Soon after Gorbachev came to power in 1985, it became clear to the Vietnamese that being economically dependent solely on the Soviet Union might not be a good idea. In their effort to wean themselves from this dependency, the Vietnamese pursued simultaneously a two-pronged strategy. First was a "multi-directional orientation"—reaching out to the West, particularly the United States—which was spearheaded by Foreign Minister Nguyen Co Thach. Unfortunately for Thach, Washington was not ready to respond to Hanoi's overture and the Vietnamese leadership thus did not give his approach priority. Second was reaching out to China, the remaining pillar of socialism/Communism, an effort led by General Secretary Nguyen Van Linh, whose priority was defending the socialist state, especially in the wake of the Tiananmen Square Incident (June 1989) and the developments in Eastern Europe. In Vietnam's relations with foreign powers in the post-Cold War period, its relation with China remains the most difficult despite the normalization of relations. The Seventh National Congress of the Vietnamese Communist Party (1991) called for Vietnam to diversify and multilateralize its economic relations with all countries and economic organizations, and since then it has been successful. This strategy of multilateralizing and diversifying

---

[52] Nguyen Vu Tung, "Vietnam's Membership of ASEAN: A Constructivist Interpretation", *Contemporary Southeast Asia* 29, 3 (2007): 483–505.

[53] *Hanoi Radio*, 16 Apr. 1973, *BBC/SWB/FE*/4272/i.

its foreign relations would include joining ASEAN.[54] Vietnam (and Laos) acceded to the Treaty of Amity and Cooperation in Southeast Asia and obtained "observer country" status at the 25th ASEAN Ministerial Meeting in Manila in 1992. Subsequently, both the Vietnamese and Laotian foreign ministers attended the 26th ASEAN Ministerial Meeting in Singapore in July 1993 as observers[55] before becoming full-fledged members in 1995 and 1997 respectively.[56] Vietnam's ASEAN partners were pleasantly surprised by Hanoi's offer to host the Sixth ASEAN Summit in 1998, less than half a year after its admission into ASEAN in July 1995.[57]

Concurrent with the ASEAN expansion project was the formation of the ARF. The ARF was inaugurated in Singapore in 1993 and formally launched in Bangkok in July 1994. Although the ARF was a Japanese idea, ASEAN was the driving force from the outset. ASEAN played a leading role in establishing the ARF with the objective of fostering "multilateral dialogue on security matters".[58] Singapore played a "quietly nudging" role by providing the first drafts of two key papers on the structure, role and membership of the ARF that were later adopted at the ARF meetings in 1995 and 1996.[59] That said, the ARF would not have come about had there also not been a change of attitude towards regional security multilateralism by first the Japanese and then the

---

[54] Carlyle Thayer, "China and Vietnam: An Uneasy Modus Vivendi?" *Thayer Consultancy*, 6 July 2012.

[55] To facilitate the participation of Laos and Vietnam in the meetings of the functional committees and subcommittees, the fourth meeting of the 27th ASEAN Standing Committee held in Jakarta (June 1994) approved the "Guidelines for the Participation of Observer Countries in ASEAN Meetings".

[56] See Frank Frost (Foreign Affairs, Defence and Trade Group), "Vietnam's Membership of ASEAN: Issues and Implications", Department of the Parliamentary Library, Parliament Research Service (Australia), Current Issues Brief, Number 3, 1995–96; "Deputy Foreign Minister Vu Khoan's Exclusive Interview", *Vietnam Southeast Asia Today*, Special Issue, 25 July 1995.

[57] "Reaction to SRV Offer to Host ASEAN Summit", *The Nation*, 30 Nov. 1995, *FBIS-EAS*-95-231. Brunei, which had been a member since 1985, had not hosted a summit although it had hosted two annual ministerial meetings.

[58] Carlyle A. Thayer, *Multilateral Institutions in Asia: The ASEAN Regional Forum* (Hawaii: Asia-Pacific Center for Security Studies, Dec. 2000), p. 5.

[59] Presentation by Kishore Mahbubani, permanent secretary, Singapore Ministry of Foreign Affairs, at the policy forum organized by the Institute of Policy Studies, 20 Sept. 1996.

Americans in the early 1990s. Tokyo had been averse to multilateral security frameworks until the First Gulf War, when it was compelled to reassess its international security role.[60] Washington, too, was uninterested, preferring its hub-and-spoke approach to Asia-Pacific security. According to Paul Midford, the Nakayama proposal forced the Bush administration to reassess security multilateralism in East Asia; and at the Post-Ministerial Conference of July 1992 in Manila, during the discussion of regional security (apparently the first official discussion on regional security matters in an ASEAN post-ministerial meeting), US Secretary of State James Baker endorsed the initiative.[61] It was only in 1993 that the Clinton administration (which succeeded Bush in January 1993) "overcame a long-standing aversion to multilateral security institutions in Asia-Pacific by endorsing multilateralism and the ARF".[62] As for China, despite its reservations, Beijing, in the words of Leifer, "was reluctant to be excluded from such an extensive assembly of regional states, even if it did harbour the suspicion that such an assembly might be employed to 'gang up' on China".[63]

The first meeting held in Bangkok in July 1994 coincided with the 27th ASEAN Ministerial Meeting. Peter Ho (permanent secretary of the Singapore Ministry of Foreign Affairs) recalled that the creation of the ARF "was not pre-ordained" and "it would have unimaginable during the Cold War".[64] As described above, the end of the Cold War brought about a transformation in the security landscape.

The end of the Cold War also speeded up the process of globalization. With globalization came greater economic interdependence and a new host of issues, ranging from drug and human trafficking to environmental issues. Scholars described them as non-traditional security issues, as unlike traditional issues they could not be resolved by military means. For Southeast Asia, non-traditional security issues would become more

---

[60] For a discussion of Japanese decision making, see Midford, "Japan's Leadership Role in East Asian Security Multilateralism": 367–97.

[61] Midford, "Japan's Leadership Role in East Asian Security Multilateralism": 387–8.

[62] Thayer, *Multilateral Institutions in Asia*, p. 5.

[63] Michael Leifer, *The ASEAN Regional Forum*, Adelphi Paper 302 (London: IISS, 1996), pp. 26–7; Rosemary Foot, "China in the ASEAN Regional Forum: Organisational Processes and Domestic Modes of Thought", *Asian Survey* 38, 5 (May 1998): 425–40; Mahbubani, Institute of Policy Studies.

[64] Ho, "ASEAN Regional Forum", p. 251.

salient after 1997, as elaborated on in chapter 2. At the same time, traditional security issues such as the South China Sea dispute, the two Koreas, and Taiwan continued to plague the region. There was no framework to manage all these complex and interlocking issues.

"This sense of uncertainty," according to Ho, "inspired some serious thinking about a political and security framework in the Asia-Pacific." Ho revealed that ideas mooted in the early post-Cold War years by countries such as Australia, Canada and Japan, however, met with resistance because the major powers—the United States and China, in particular—were uncomfortable with any framework created by any one of them or their allies. ASEAN, too, felt that external parties were not sufficiently neutral to lead this project. Thus, almost by default, ASEAN (whose members also felt the "need to strengthen the network of linkages within the Asia-Pacific and in forging a predictable and constructive pattern of relationships") was perceived to be more or less neutral and could therefore assume a leading role. As Ho put it, "the ASEAN Regional Forum could be described as the culmination of almost two decades of steady ASEAN diplomacy" beginning in the 1970s with the introduction of "dialogue partnerships" with external powers.[65] In 1993 China and Russia had become regular guests at the annual ASEAN Ministerial Meetings; and Laos and Cambodia became observers of ASEAN coinciding with the establishment of the ARF.

The original ARF members (18 in total) included the six ASEAN members; ASEAN's dialogue partners—the United States, Japan, South Korea, the European Union, Canada, Australia and New Zealand; two guests of ASEAN—China and Russia; and the three observers of ASEAN—Vietnam, Laos and Papua New Guinea. Today ARF has 27 members—the ten ASEAN member states, ten ASEAN dialogue partners, one ASEAN observer (Papua New Guinea), as well as Bangladesh, Mongolia, North Korea, Pakistan, Timor-Leste and, the newest addition in 2007, Sri Lanka.

It is common knowledge that ASEAN's twin objectives for the ARF (though not explicitly mentioned) were: to "envelop" a rising China in this multilateral organization,[66] and to keep the unipolar power United States (absorbed by developments in Eastern Europe and elsewhere)

---

[65] Ibid.

[66] See Foot, "China in the ASEAN Regional Forum": 425–40.

engaged in the region within a multilateral framework. As Kishore Mahbubani observed, "the task of both restraining" the United States and China "while preserving at the same time their enthusiasm for the ARF is an inherently difficult task" even during the "propitious and relatively benign security environment" in the Asia-Pacific of the early 1990s. Singapore Prime Minister Goh Chok Tong cautioned that if Sino-US relations failed to stabilize, it would start a second Cold War, affecting the whole region.[67]

Mischief Reef and the South China Sea Dispute

From mid-1994, around the time the ARF was formed, the Chinese started occupying Mischief Reef, which was also claimed by the Philippines. This was the first time that China had occupied a reef claimed by an ASEAN country. Previous disputes had always been with Vietnam (which became an ASEAN member only in 1995). According to one source, the construction on Mischief Reef took place between June and December 1994. Manila found out about it only in February 1995. Elements in the People's Liberation Army Navy (PLAN) apparently carried out the construction without the sanction of the top leadership. Chinese officials reportedly told the Philippine government that this was the case. In addition, elements within the PLAN were involved in smuggling activities and piracy in the South China Sea. Sceptics, however, argue that even if it were true that the decision to occupy Mischief Reef did not come from the top civilian leadership, senior military leaders must have endorsed it.[68]

It would appear that Beijing had shifted its focus from Vietnam to the Philippines. Sino-Vietnamese ties had improved considerably since both countries normalized relations in November 1991. During Chinese President Jiang Zemin's visit to Hanoi in November 1994, both sides agreed to establish a joint working group to discuss the Spratlys issue. This was set up at the Third Vice-Ministerial Meeting of the two countries in July 1995. The first meeting took place on 13–15 November 1995 in Hanoi and the second on 2–7 July 1996 in Beijing.

[67] Mahbubani, Institute of Policy Studies.

[68] See Ian James Storey, "Creeping Assertiveness: China, the Philippines and the South China Sea Dispute", *Contemporary Southeast Asia* 21, 1 (April 1999): 95–118.

Until 1995, ASEAN had not taken a public position regarding the South China Sea. A series of unilateral Chinese actions from 1992, cited earlier, culminating in the January 1995 Mischief Reef occupation led to a change of stance. Two days before the bilateral talks between the Philippines and China in Beijing, on 18 March 1995, ASEAN for the first time adopted a united stand by issuing a statement calling for all parties concerned to adhere to the letter and spirit of the Manila Declaration on the South China Sea.[69] Jose Almonte (then national security adviser in the Ramos administration) recalled that Foreign Affairs Secretary Roberto Romulo and Undersecretary Rodolfo Severino proposed that ASEAN take a concrete step by drawing up a code of conduct on the South China Sea "that would, in effect, restrain China from flexing its muscles and encroaching into other countries' territories". A plan to install lighthouses in Scarborough Shoal as a legitimate and least costly way to establish a Filipino presence while waiting for the Philippines' baseline law to be passed was overruled by President Ramos for fear of provoking China to move into the shoal.[70] In March 1995 Ramos proposed the demilitarization of the South China Sea and the joint development of its resources for the benefit of the contiguous states.[71] China and the Philippines subsequently signed a "Joint Statement on PRC-RP Consultations on the South China Sea and on Other Areas of Cooperation". In 1996 ASEAN foreign ministers in a joint communiqué called for a code that would lay the foundation for long-term stability in the area as well as foster understanding amongst claimant states. At the Sixth ASEAN Summit in Hanoi in December 1998, the Philippines was assigned to draft the code of conduct.[72]

---

[69] 1992 ASEAN Declaration on South China Sea signed by the six ASEAN foreign ministers in Manila, 22 July 1992, https://cil.nus.edu.sg/rp/pdf/1992%20ASEAN%20Declaration%20on%20the%20South%20China%20Sea-pdf.pdf, accessed 21 Mar. 2017.

[70] Jose T. Almonte (as told to Marites Danguilan Vitug), *Endless Journey: A Memoir* (Quezon City: Cleverheads, 2015), chapter 28.

[71] For a list of Ramos' proposals, see Jose T. Almonte, "Coordinating Asean's Position on the South China Sea Issue", speech before the ASEAN Experts on the Law of the Sea Conference, 27–28 Nov. 1997, in Jose T. Almonte, *Towards One Southeast Asia* (Quezon City: Institute for Strategic and Development Studies, 2004), pp. 195–236.

[72] The above narrative is drawn from Ang, "South China Sea Dispute Revisited": 201–15.

The First Three Years of the ASEAN Regional Forum

Meanwhile, in 1995, the ARF adopted a three-stage roadmap: Confidence Building Measures, Preventive Diplomacy and, finally, Conflict Resolution—in that order but with no specified deadline to transition from one phase to the other. After more than two decades, the ARF is still hovering at phase 2, which perhaps is not surprising given that the ARF "has been racked from the beginning by differences between members on the pace of ARF's growth".[73] Mahbubani revealed that at the very first dinner in Bangkok on 24 July 1994, a vigorous debate broke out between Qian Qichen (Chinese foreign minister) and Gareth Evans (Australian foreign minister). The former wanted the ARF to focus on generalities, while the latter insisted on specific deliverables. Two camps emerged within the ARF: the fast (Western-style) track and the slow (Asian-style) track.[74] There was the feeling amongst the Western countries in the ARF, particularly Australia and the United States, that ASEAN was conceding too much to China, which in turn led to some unhappiness with ASEAN's central role in the ARF. Nevertheless, at the second ARF meeting held in Brunei in August 1995, it was agreed that the ARF should proceed at a pace comfortable to all its members. One concern Singapore and other ASEAN members had in 1995 was to prevent developments in the South China Sea from becoming the focus of the ARF discussions for fear of isolating China and inducing Beijing to adopt a hostile attitude towards the ARF. ASEAN saw a larger strategic interest in not adopting a tough stance against China on the South China Sea issue during the ARF Senior Officials Meeting in May 1995, a view that the Western powers concurred with.

From the beginning, there were two broad views about the ARF within the academic community: The "realist" view, best articulated by Leifer, argued that the ARF could at best perform an adjunct role in the management of the regional order in Asia-Pacific. The viability of the ARF depended on the "prior existence of a stable balance of power", but it was "not really in a position to create it". The ARF was thus "a complementary diplomatic activity" to be lauded but was "of the same nature as ASEAN and subject to the very same intrinsic limitations".[75]

[73] Mahbubani, Institute of Policy Studies.

[74] Ibid.

[75] Leifer, *ASEAN Regional Forum*, pp. 57–9.

The other, so-called liberal, view (represented by Yuen Foong Khong) argued that the ARF was "a mechanism for defusing the conflictual by-products of power balancing practices" and as such had a critical (rather than an adjunct) role. This was because "the Asia-Pacific has a surfeit of major and minor territorial disputes, a system of military alliances is already in place; and an arms buildup is occurring" and what the region needed were "ways and means to attenuate these destabilising factors, not more balancing tactics in search of the elusive equilibrium".[76] On hindsight, in the short term Khong was correct. When viewed from a much longer time frame, Leifer's perspective holds true.

The first three years were the teething years of the ARF. By the third ARF meeting in Jakarta in 1996, the group was beginning to discuss the criteria for admitting new members. It was agreed that the ARF should expand "carefully and cautiously" and that it would only admit participants that could "directly affect the peace and security of the region on which the ARF shall focus its peace-building and peace-making efforts".[77] The first two new additions to the original 19-member ARF were India and Myanmar, which both joined in 1996. Myanmar was granted observer status in ASEAN in 1996 (and was expected to join ASEAN in the near future), and as such, its entry into the ARF could be considered as procedural.

The admission of India requires some explanation. One of the reasons why India was not a founding member of the ARF was because during the Cold War years, particularly in the 1970s and 1980s, ASEAN's relations with India were somewhat strained. New Delhi supported the Soviet Union and Vietnam's occupation of Cambodia. As See Chak Mun (former Singapore high commissioner to India) recalled, the Indira Gandhi government's recognition of the Heng Samrin regime in July 1980 was seen by ASEAN countries as "a move which worked towards the interest of the Soviet Union and its proxy Vietnam" and "would undermine the initiatives by the ASEAN to find

[76] Yuen Foong Khong, "Making Bricks Without Straw in the Asia Pacific?" (Review Article), *Pacific Review* 10, 2 (1997): 296. See also David Dickens, "Lessening the Desire for War: The ASEAN Regional Forum and Making of Asia Pacific Security", Centre for Strategic Studies, Victoria University of Wellington, Working Paper 11/98.

[77] See "Chairman's Statement, The Third ASEAN Regional Forum, Jakarta, Indonesia, 23 July 1996", https://www.asean.org/uploads/archive/5187-9.pdf, accessed 5 Sept. 2016.

a durable solution to the Cambodian conflict".[78] New Delhi's position on the Cambodian issue, however, began to shift in 1987 towards supporting ASEAN's informal initiatives to resolve the almost decade-long issue. Relations between Singapore and India, both members of the Commonwealth, also slowly improved, beginning with Lee Kuan Yew reaching out to Indira Gandhi's son and successor, Rajiv Gandhi, in March 1988. The bilateral relations intensified under Singapore's Prime Minister Goh Chok Tong (who succeeded Lee) and India's Prime Minister Narasimha Rao (who succeeded Rajiv Gandhi) when they met at the Non-Aligned Movement Summit in September 1992. In September 1994 Rao visited Singapore and for the first time articulated India's new Look East Policy in a public lecture, which his successors followed. Singapore had advocated for and actively supported India's engagement—or perhaps re-engagement—in the region. India, which had been keen to join the ARF, became a full dialogue partner of ASEAN in December 1995. One other hesitancy with admitting India into the ARF earlier was the concern that New Delhi would bring the Kashmir issue into the infant ARF. According to Domingo Siazon (Philippine foreign affairs secretary), "clashes between India and Pakistan over Kashmir … are 'too big' and 'too advanced' for the ARF to handle 'right now'".[79] Pakistan eventually joined the ARF as the 24th member in 2004.

The view in 1996 was that with the admittance of Myanmar and India, the ARF should take a pause in accepting new members so that it could consolidate its confidence-building activities.[80] The chairman's statement issued at the end of the fourth ARF meeting in 1996 noted that the participants displayed "a high degree of comfort" in their interactions with each other and that the ARF was "progressing at a good pace". The hope was that this trend would continue, which would in turn "pave the way for agreements on substantive issues in the coming years".[81]

---

[78] The above is summarized from See Chak Mun, "Singapore-India Strategic Relations: Singapore's Perspective", in *The Merlion and the Ashoka: Singapore-India Strategic Ties*, ed. Anit Mukherjee (Singapore: World Scientific, 2016), chapter 3.

[79] "Korea and Kashmir Clashes 'Too Big' for ARF", *Straits Times*, 20 June 1999.

[80] "ARF Senior Officials Agree on Membership Criteria", *Straits Times*, 11 May 1996.

[81] "Chairman's Statement, The Third ASEAN Regional Forum, Jakarta, Indonesia, 23 July 1996".

CHAPTER 2

1997–99: Ripples of the Asian Financial Crisis

> *"... these days no one can argue successfully that security issues—whether national, regional or global—can somehow be quarantined or separated from economic developments, least of all in the Asia-Pacific region. Prosperity and security are increasingly intertwined."*[1]

The Establishment of the Asia-Pacific Economic Cooperation Forum

We would recall from chapter 1 that when the Cold War ended, there was considerable scepticism about ASEAN's future after the resolution of the Cambodia conflict. Nayan Chanda described the Vietnamese invasion of Cambodia as "a gift" to ASEAN—"an organization in search of a cause". He predicted a weakening of ASEAN post-Cambodia, with even ASEAN leaders being worried about "life after Cambodia".[2] Indeed, as Bilahari Kausikan recalled, Cambodia was "the greatest diplomatic success of ASEAN's first quarter century ... to the extent that it

[1] Alexander Downing (foreign minister of Australia) quoted in Graeme Cheeseman, "Asian-Pacific Security Discourse in the Wake of the Asian Economic Crisis", *Pacific Review* 12, 3 (1999): 333–56.

[2] See Nayan Chanda, "Vietnam's Withdrawal from Cambodia: The ASEAN Perspective", in *Vietnam's Withdrawal from Cambodia: Regional Issues and Realignments*, ed. Gary Klintworth (Canberra: Australian National University, 1990), chapter 8.

overshadowed the actual stagnation in progressing ASEAN's professed goals as set out in the Bangkok Declaration".[3] The organization appeared to be holding itself well until July 1997, when the Asian Financial Crisis hit the region. It is thus to the Asian Financial Crisis, which began in Thailand in July 1997 and culminated in the fall of the Suharto regime in Indonesia in May 1998, that we must now turn.

Ralph Smith rightly noted that "the most remarkable feature" of the East Asian region in the early post-Cold War years compared with the post-World War II years was the "rapid industrialisation and economic growth" that "contributed a good deal to the region's new found political stability". This was a process that began in the 1960s, led by Japan and followed closely by Taiwan and then South Korea, Hong Kong and Singapore—the last four popularly referred to as the four Asian Tigers. By the early 1990s, the other ASEAN economies—specifically Thailand, Malaysia and Indonesia (as well as China)—were also attracting the "attention of the world business community".[4] Until 1997, all these countries were widely regarded as "economic miracles".[5] The spectacular economic growth of these countries over the past few decades underpinned the region's fundamental cohesion and stability.[6] In a May 1990 speech, Lee Kuan Yew predicted that in the post-Cold War world future competition between industrialized countries would be "primarily economic, and this competition will be worldwide".[7] The subject of economics was a recurring theme of many post-Cold War speeches, and in his early-1990s remarks Lee was generally optimistic about the future of East and Southeast Asia barring tensions across the Taiwan Straits, in the Korean Peninsula and in Sino-American relations.[8] It was

---

[3] See Bilahari Kausikan, "The Ages of ASEAN", in *The Inclusive Regionalist: A Festschrift Dedicated to Jusuf Wanandi*, ed. Hadi Soesastro and Clara Joewono (Jakarta: Centre for Strategic and international Studies, 2007), chapter 34.

[4] R.B. Smith, *Changing Visions of East Asia, 1943–93: Transformations and Continuities* (London: Routledge, 2007), p. 203.

[5] Robert J. Barro, "The East Asian Tigers Have Plenty to Roar About", *BusinessWeek*, 27 Apr. 1998, p. 24.

[6] See Paul Dibb, "The End of the Asian Miracle? Will the Current Economic Crisis Lead to Political and Social Instability?" *SDSC Newsletter*, Summer 1998, p. 1.

[7] Ang, *Lee Kuan Yew's Strategic Thought*, pp. 72, 75.

[8] Ibid., chapter 4.

increasingly acknowledged, as Lee noted, that both stability and security were the "preconditions for economic growth".[9]

Indeed, many in the latter part of the 1980s already saw the importance of economics in world affairs. On 31 January 1989, Australian Prime Minister Bob Hawke pointed out in a speech in Seoul that the countries in the region were "essentially interdependent and their economic futures were interlinked".[10] He believed that the underlying reason for the strong economic growth of the Asia-Pacific countries was "the multilateral trading system operating under the rules of the General Agreement on Tariffs and Trade (GATT)", a system that was under threat.[11] He thus proposed a meeting of regional ministers to "assess attitudes in the region towards creating a more intergovernmental forum for economic cooperation". Nine months after his speech, the first ministerial meeting of APEC was held on 7–8 November in Canberra. The fact that it took just nine months from a speech to the establishment of APEC testifies to the significance of economics in the minds of the leaders then.

APEC being mooted by Australia, Richard Woolcott (then secretary of the Department of Foreign Affairs and Trade) travelled the region to explain the idea and ascertain support for it. On 26 April 1989 he reported that Japan, South Korea and the ASEAN states were all favourable, although there was concern on the part of some ASEAN states that the initiative "might in some way push ASEAN out of the driver's seat on regional economic issues". The agreement that every other APEC meeting would be held in an ASEAN city somewhat (but not completely) assuaged ASEAN's concern. It was, as Frank Frost noted, a recognition of ASEAN's "central role in regional cooperation".[12]

---

[9] Ibid., p. 75.

[10] "Speech by the Prime Minister, Luncheon of Korean Business Associations 'Regional Co-Operation: Challenges for Korea And Australia', Korea – 31 January 1989+", https://pmtranscripts.pmc.gov.au/release/transcript-7475, accessed 19 Mar. 2019.

[11] For a discussion of GATT and its limitations, see "GATT, Its Purposes, History, with Pros and Cons", https://www.thebalance.com/gatt-purpose-history-pros-cons-3305578, accessed 15 Aug. 2018.

[12] Frank Frost, *Engaging the Neighbours: Australia and ASEAN Since 1974* (Canberra: ANU Press, 2016), p. 83.

Woolcott further reported that there had been "considerable progress" in getting a consensus on the inclusion of the United States, Canada, China, Hong Kong and possibly Taiwan "subject to working out acceptable arrangements". Woolcott met Chinese Premier Li Peng in May 1989. While the Chinese were supportive of the initiative, they objected to the proposed inclusion of Hong Kong (then still a British colony) and Taiwan. Woolcott explained that Hawke's idea was a ministerial-level meeting of major economies of the region and not regional countries. The Chinese eventually agreed on the condition that "China's formal positions were not compromised". Hong Kong and Taiwan participated in the third APEC meeting in Seoul in 1991.

Washington was initially miffed that it had not been consulted on such a major regional initiative. Woolcott explained:

> [A]t this stage excessive American enthusiasm for the idea, and particularly any American attempt to add a political or security dimension to the economic nature of the proposal, would prejudice its prospects. Had a superpower like the United States, or the biggest Asian economy, Japan, pushed for an APEC forum it would probably have failed. It had more chance of success if it was promoted by a country like Australia, which was neither a major power nor economically dominant.[13]

This appeared to have appeased the Americans, and the Bush administration subsequently announced its support. The first leaders meeting of the APEC economies was held on Blake Island, Seattle, on 20 November 1993. The "1993 Leaders' Declaration" issued at the end of the "unprecedented meeting of the economic leaders of the Asia-Pacific Economic Cooperation forum" affirmed to "build a new economic foundation for the Asia Pacific" in order to strengthen cooperation and promote prosperity in the post-Cold War era".[14] Malaysian Prime Minister Mahathir Mohamad, who had strong reservations about APEC,

[13] Richard Woolcott, *The Hot Seat: Reflections on Diplomacy from Stalin's Death to the Bali Bombings* (Sydney: HarperCollins, 2003), chapter 16. For an account of the discussions leading to the first leaders meeting on Blake Island (1993), see Paul Keating, *Engagement: Australia Faces the Asia-Pacific* (Sydney: Macmillan, 2000), chapter 4.

[14] "1993 Leaders' Declaration", https://www.apec.org/Meeting-Papers/Leaders-Declarations/1993/1993_aelm, accessed 15 Aug. 2018.

was conspicuously absent from the meeting, which led to a souring of Malaysia-Australia relations for a period.[15] For a number of years, despite some internal differences within ASEAN concerning APEC, ASEAN "was able to main an effective united front and gave ASEAN a central decision-making role in APEC" (until the Asian Financial Crisis). It was not a coincidence that the second APEC meeting was held in Bogor, Indonesia. It was in this meeting, hosted by President Suharto, that a timetable to achieve a free market by 2010 for developed countries and 2020 for developing countries was agreed upon.[16]

Lee Kuan Yew spoke approvingly of the goals of APEC and of US President Clinton's informal summit of APEC leaders in Seattle as a "significant initiative" that would focus American and Asian thinking on the future of Asia-Pacific and "crystallize their ideas on how to get the economies of the region to be in greater harmony and synergy".[17] However, not long after, Lee noted that the largeness of spirit that the United States displayed after World War II had been replaced by "a certain meanness of spirit" in its treatment of Japan, Indonesia, Malaysia and China because of its own economic problems and domestic uncertainties. He was particularly critical of the United States in his 19 May 1994 speech to the Asia Society. "East Asia was disappointed that the US was so ready to abandon long term benefits and high moral ground for short term gains," Lee said.[18] In his speech Lee listed a number of American actions, such as pressuring Indonesia and Malaysia on their labour policies, accusing Japan of being guilty of unfair trade practices, and threatening to withdraw China's Most Favoured Nation status, amongst others. Washington, according to Lee, paid attention to the region only because of the tensions between China and Taiwan during the run-up to the Taiwanese elections in March 1996. As Lee put it, it "is not as if the US planned to bring about this renewal of its security interests. It happened by accident." He fretted that too much

[15] Frost, *Engaging the Neighbours*, pp. 85–7.

[16] Ibid., pp. 84–7.

[17] "Speech by Lee Kuan Yew, Senior Minister of Singapore for the Asahi Forum in Tokyo, 29 October 1993", http://www.nas.gov.sg/archivesonline/data/pdfdoc/lky19931029.pdf, accessed 20 Mar. 2019.

[18] Speech by Senior Minister Lee Kuan Yew at the Asia Society Conference, 19 May 1994, quoted in Ang, *Lee Kuan Yew's Strategic Thought*, p. 80. The United States was going through a brief recession in the early 1990s.

of what happened in US policy towards the region was "not thought and not planned" when it should have been.[19]

By 1998, APEC had expanded from its initial 12 economies to 21. China, Hong Kong (China) and Chinese Taipei joined in 1991; Mexico and Papua New Guinea in 1992; Chile in 1994; and Peru, Russia and Vietnam in 1998. During the critical years of the Asian Financial Crisis, APEC was convened in Vancouver (November 1997), Kuala Lumpur (November 1998) and Auckland (September 1999), where it commemorated its tenth anniversary. In the first half of 1990, as Lee Kuan Yew noted, APEC and the ARF were the only two settings in which ASEAN could engage China on issues of peace and security in Asia-Pacific.[20]

The Asian Financial Crisis

There was generally a sense of optimism in the first half of the 1990s. At the first general meeting of the Council for Security Cooperation in the Asia Pacific in June 1997, a month before the financial crisis broke out (beginning in Thailand), Tony Tan (then Singapore's deputy prime minister and minister for defence) made the following remarks, which epitomized the mood of the time:

> It is often said that the 21st Century belongs to the Asia-Pacific ... The Asia-Pacific countries are enjoying a period of rapid economic growth. By the year 2010, it is projected that East Asia alone will account for one-third of the global production growth. East Asian countries are also expected to generate up to 40% of the world's new purchasing power and demand for imports. The Asia-Pacific region is projected to out-perform other regions of the world in economic growth. The prospects are bright ...[21]

The key message of Tan's speech was, "countries cannot concentrate on economic development unless there is peace and stability".

[19] "US-Japan Move on Security 'Positive'", *Straits Times*, 3 June 1996; "US Needs Consistent Policy Towards Asia", *Straits Times*, 5 June 1996.

[20] Lee Kuan Yew quoted in Ang, *Lee Kuan Yew's Strategic Thought*, p. 80.

[21] Transcript of keynote address by Dr Tony Tan Keng Yam, deputy prime minister and minister for defence, at the first general meeting of the Council for Security Cooperation in the Asia Pacific, 4 June 1997, Singapore. The term "East Asia" includes Southeast Asia.

One month later, the financial crisis hit the region and very quickly turned the (economic) miracles into mirages—or, as Goh Chok Tong (prime minister of Singapore during the financial crisis) described, transformed the Asian Tigers into "Asian Kittens"[22] and forced a reassessment of the regional political and security environment, and even ASEAN itself. Until this time, the mantra was "prosperity and stability went hand in hand". Paul Dibb, David Hale and Peter Prince described the crisis as a "defining event of the post-Cold War international order" and further noted, "Not since the 1930s has the world witnessed such a massive economic dislocation."[23] Given the increasingly important role economics played in international politics in the 1990s, the failure of the "state-centred elements of the East Asian model"—once considered the key to East Asia's economic miracle but now perceived as the cause of the financial crisis[24]—badly affected ASEAN's credibility and standing.

Before August 1997, most would have agreed with David B.H. Denoon and Evelyn Colbert's view that "as 1997 and its thirtieth anniversary approached, the Association of Southeast Asian Nations (ASEAN) seemed to have every reason for unrestrained celebration ..."[25] But the euphoria soon gave way to gloom, although in July–August it was thought that the economic problem could be confined or limited. In his keynote address delivered on the occasion of the ASEAN Roundtable on 4 August 1997, Professor Jayakumar (Singapore's minister for foreign affairs and minister for law) even proclaimed, "Today, ASEAN has succeeded against all odds and expectations. ASEAN countries have experienced rapid economic growth. ASEAN stands out as a model of regional co-operation and the most successful such grouping among developing countries."[26]

---

[22] Edited transcript of Senior Minister Goh Chok Tong's TV interview with the BBC, "Financial Crisis, 10 Years On", *Straits Times*, 6 July 2007.

[23] See Paul Dibb, David D. Hale and Peter Prince, "The Strategic Implications of Asia's Economic Crisis", *Survival* 40, 2 (Summer 1998): 5–26.

[24] See Mark T. Berger, "Bringing History Back In: The Making and Unmaking of the East Asian Miracle", http://library.fes.de/pdf-files/ipg/ipg-1999-3/artberger.pdf, pp. 237–52, accessed 24 Oct. 2016.

[25] David B.H. Denoon and Evelyn Colbert, "Challenges for the Association of Southeast Asian Nations (ASEAN)", *Pacific Affairs* 71, 4 (Winter 1998–99): 505.

[26] Keynote address by Professor S. Jayakumar, minister for foreign affairs and minister for law at the ASEAN Roundtable 1997, "ASEAN in the New Millennium", 4 Aug. 1997, Singapore, http://www.nas.gov.sg/archivesonline/data/pdfdoc/sj19970804s.pdf, accessed 12 Apr. 2019.

The technical reasons for the Asian Financial Crisis need not delay us here. The consensus on hindsight is that the crisis was caused by a combination of excessive foreign short-term investment and inadequate financial regulations or supervision in those countries affected—or, as S.M. Thangavelu and Yong Yik Wei put it, "macro-economic and institutional weaknesses".[27] It was, as Mark Berger described, the result of "a financial panic which fuelled a dramatic and unnecessary shift in investor confidence and market expectation which led to the rapid movement of capital out of the region and the resultant currency collapses".[28] However, until late 1998 the causes could be boiled down to three words: corruption, cronyism and nepotism. These words were simple enough for the layman to understand and, rightly or wrongly, became the popularly remembered reasons for the 1997–98 Asian Financial Crisis.

Our narrative is more concerned with the strategic consequences and implications of the crisis for Southeast Asia. What interests us here is the impact of these supposedly domestic developments on the region, ASEAN, and ASEAN's external relations. As mentioned above, it started in Thailand on 2 July 1997. It was at first perceived to be a currency crisis confined to Thailand. However, it quickly spread beyond Thailand, which no one anticipated. On 8 July Malaysia's central bank had to intervene to defend the ringgit. On 11 July the Philippines devalued the peso and sought assistance from the International Monetary Fund, while Indonesia tried to fend off speculators in the rupiah. By October the contagion had spread to Hong Kong and South Korea.

The crisis led to changes in leadership in two Southeast Asian countries: in Thailand, Chuan Leekpai replaced Chavalit Yongchaiyut as prime minister in November 1997; and in Malaysia, Prime Minister Mahathir Mohamad managed to remain in power but sacked (and expelled from UMNO) his deputy, Finance Minister Anwar Ibrahim, because of differences over how to solve the crisis in the country. Anwar Ibrahim was a long-time political ally of Mahathir and was widely expected to succeed him. However, the most significant fallout from the

---

[27] In 2007 Thangavelu was the director of the Singapore Centre for Applied and Policy Economics at the National University of Singapore. Yong was a research fellow at the centre. See "Can S-E Asia Ride the Next FDI Wave?" *Straits Times*, 9 June 2007.

[28] Berger, "Bringing History Back In", p. 250.

crisis was the downfall of President Suharto of Indonesia in May 1998. Suharto had been in power since 1967. Indonesia was the linchpin of ASEAN. The downward slide of the Indonesian economy began on 11 July 1997, when Indonesia widened its trading band for the rupiah to ward off speculators. In August the government abandoned its fixed exchange rate against the US dollar. This led to the plunging of the rupiah, followed by IMF interventions in October 1997, January 1998 and February 1998, which brought about domestic upheaval in the country, eventually forcing Suharto to step down on 21 May 1998. Although, on hindsight, Indonesia's political transformation post-Suharto can be said to have been successful, George Yeo (then a cabinet minister in Singapore) recalled, "Indonesia's relatively smooth transition to a modern democracy could not have been foreseen" during the crisis, "when the vast country was in danger of breaking up".[29] Political upheavals in Indonesia and Malaysia affected Jakarta's and Kuala Lumpur's relations with Singapore. Wealthy Singapore, only lightly affected by the crisis, was perceived—rightly or wrongly—to be unhelpful towards its financially strapped neighbours. Thus, contrary to Jayakumar's claim on 4 August cited earlier, the financial crisis showed that ASEAN was not really a model of regional cooperation. Not only were ASEAN nations unable to help each other during the crisis, the crisis also showed that in periods of extreme stress latent tensions could resurface, as was the case with the three core ASEAN member states—Indonesia, Malaysia and Singapore—a reminder that "ASEAN has contributed much more to conflict avoidance amongst its members than to conflict resolution".[30] ASEAN unity might have been more superficial than real.

The priority of the unipolar power, namely the United States, best illustrates the primacy of economics in the post-Cold War period. David Rothkopf, in his account of the US National Security Council (NSC), noted, "America's foreign policy interests seemed to be turning on economic considerations." This was not just because the United States was interested in its own growth or because of globalization (a term that would come to be very much associated with the Clinton administration

---

[29] Speech by George Yeo, former minister for foreign affairs, Ninth S. Rajaratnam Lecture, 11 Nov. 2016, Singapore.

[30] Denoon and Colbert, "Challenges for the Association of Southeast Asian Nations": 506.

[1993–2001]) but, most important, because in every case "the new best tools in the foreign policy toolbox were economic". The newly established National Economic Council superseded in importance the NSC during the Cold War years.[31] EASI-III (February 1995), described in chapter 1, spelled out one of the three goals of US national security policy to be the promotion of democracy abroad. The Clinton administration held the strong view that democratic countries did not go to war with one another. Therefore, if more countries in the region were democratic, the reasoning went, the region and the United States would be more secure. This was not necessarily a view shared by the region.

As mentioned in chapter 1, ASEAN had been trying to keep the United States fully engaged in the region. However, the Asian directorate of the NSC had only two professional officers covering East and Southeast Asia. As Robert Suettinger (director for Asian affairs for the NSC from 1994 to 1997) recalled, "there was nobody at a senior level on the National Security Council who had the gravitas and the experience to deal with Asia in a sort of comprehensive and strategic way". This was true in the US Department of State as well.[32] The financial crisis compounded the difficulty of engaging the United States at a time when Southeast Asia needed the United States even more. The simplistic view that crony capitalism had brought about the Asian Financial Crisis, combined with the post-Cold War focus on human rights—particularly by the United States—thus exacerbated America's lack of interest in the region. Furthermore, during this difficult period in Southeast Asia, President Clinton was himself distracted by the Monica Lewinsky saga. The sex scandal almost led to his impeachment at the end of 1998. As one leading Asian politician reportedly told a senior American diplomat, "... the last thing we can afford at this point is an incapacitated president and Washington taking its eye off the ball out here".[33]

The crisis brought forth a degree of ambivalence in the ASEAN states' attitude towards the Americans—a mixture of worry and pique.

---

[31] See David Rothkopf, *Running The World: The Inside Story of the National Security Council and the Architects of American Power* (New York: Public Affairs, 2005), pp. 344–5, chapter 11.

[32] Ibid., p. 348.

[33] Quoted in Bill Powell, "Here's to a Rapid Recovery", *Newsweek*, 2 Feb. 1998.

On the one hand, Washington's prompt assistance to Mexico during the latter's economic crisis in 1993–94 and to Brazil and Russia in 1998 exacerbated "old fears of abandonment by the United States" and the perception that the ASEAN states—old allies of the US (except for Vietnam)—were no longer of sufficient (economic) importance to the United States.[34] On the other, as Berger noted, in the second half of 1997 "there has been a re-assertion of US hegemony in East Asia via the IMF". By 1998, however, the IMF was "increasingly seen to have failed, and/or aggravated a worsening situation".[35] As Dibb et al. noted, there were "anti-Western, anti-International Monetary Fund sentiments" directed "not least at the US".[36] Washington came across as generally unsympathetic to the plight of the Southeast Asian states and forcing its neo-liberal agenda by advocating "liberation and deregulation as the key to economic progress".[37] There was also the perception that the United States was benefiting the most given the massive outflow of international capital into the country because of the Asian crisis. Jeffrey Bartholet, in his 2 February 1998 essay in *Newsweek*, warned, "The harder the United States tries to impose its will on the region, the greater the potential for anti-American resentment ... Now, American, European and other foreign companies can buy Asian properties at fire-sale prices; that could make the foreigners seem like carpetbaggers."[38]

In contrast, Chinese actions during the crisis allayed some, if not all, fears of a rising China in the region. The Chinese economy, like the Southeast Asian economies, was powering ahead at an average rate of 10 per cent in the 1990s, which was much higher than most of all the Southeast Asian countries. However, as its economy was not fully open and free, China was able to avert a crisis. China's economic growth was helped by massive foreign investment, particularly from Taiwan and overseas Chinese in Southeast Asia, which more than compensated for the drop in Western and Japanese investments following the

[34] Evelyn Goh, *The Struggle for Order: Hegemony, Hierarchy, & Transition in Post-Cold War East Asia* (Oxford: Oxford University Press, 2013), p. 55.
[35] Berger, "Bringing History Back In".
[36] Dibb et al., "Strategic Implications of Asia's Economic Crisis": 5.
[37] See Berger, "Bringing History Back In".
[38] Jeffrey Bartholet, "Who Will Lead the East?" *Newsweek*, 2 Feb. 1998.

Tiananmen Square Incident (1989)/June 4 Incident.[39] Beijing did three things that enamoured the Chinese to the Southeast Asian states during this challenging period: (a) The Chinese refrained from repeating the "Corruption", "Cronyism" and "Nepotism" slogans; (b) Beijing did not devalue its currency to compete with some of the other Southeast Asian countries that had to devalue theirs during the crisis;[40] and (c) China did not intervene in the anti-Chinese violence in Indonesia in May 1998. Had Beijing done any of these three things, it would have brought back memories of the Cold War years. As Jeffery Sng and Pimpraphai Bisalputra put it:

> [A]s Southeast Asian business groups' operations in China became predominantly important, Southeast Asian governments naturally grew concerned, especially because ethnic Chinese controlled a disproportionate amount of national wealth in the host countries where they resided in. The old spectre of the divided loyalties of the overseas Chinese again reared its head, and the primary loyalties of the Chinese began to be questioned once again by their host governments.[41]

The financial crisis marked the beginning of a long honeymoon period in Southeast Asia-China relations, which lasted for almost a decade. As Ong Keng Yong recalled, "... until 2009, the Chinese policymakers held ASEAN in a different light and smooched ASEAN in a way the Westerners considered obscene".[42] The general view was that ASEAN, because of the financial crisis, was "in a much weaker position in dealing with the outside world, particularly in dealings with China on disputed islands in the South China Sea".[43] However, the Chinese response to the financial crisis gave the much-weakened ASEAN states a glimpse of hope that a rising China could contribute to the stability of the region.

---

[39] Jeffery Sng and Pimpraphai Bisalputra, *A History of the Thai-Chinese* (Singapore: Editions Didier Millet, 2015), pp. 413–5.

[40] "Asian Financial Crisis and China", *Hong Kong Ta Kung Pao*, 2 Nov. 1998, FBIS-CHI-98-310. The author pointed out that if China devalued the renminbi, it would set off a new round of currency devaluation in Asia and exacerbate the financial turmoil, hurting the entire region, including China. Prices of Chinese products on the international market were also already very low.

[41] Sng and Pimpraphai, *History of the Thai-Chinese*, p. 414.

[42] Ong Keng Yong, email correspondence, 5 Oct. 2016.

[43] Zakaria Haji Ahmad and Baladas Ghoshal, "The Political Future of ASEAN After the Asian Crisis", *International Affairs* 75, 4 (1999): 760.

Myanmar Joins ASEAN

August 1997 was still early days of what came to be called the Asian Financial Crisis. Prior to the crisis, the focus was on the expansion of ASEAN, which would cap its 30th anniversary celebrations with the admission of Laos, Myanmar and Cambodia, finally becoming a full-fledged regional association in its 30th year. Vietnam's admission in 1995 did not arouse any controversy, although it generated a lot of attention as it was a former foe and ostensibly still a Communist state. It was also the first country to join ASEAN since 1984. The admission of Laos was a quiet affair. Things became complicated in the case of Myanmar and Cambodia; much discussion and debate was triggered within the association of the relevance of one of its cardinal principles: non-interference, particularly in the post-Cold War setting.[44]

The admission of Myanmar into ASEAN, as Jose T. Almonte (then national security adviser in the Philippines' Ramos administration) recalled, was "the hardest" because of the position of the United States and the European Union, which argued that "incorporating it into the ASEAN would 'legitimise' an oppressive and undemocratic regime".[45] ASEAN's decision to admit Myanmar sparked a vigorous debate between ASEAN and the major Western/liberal governments that continued into the 2000s about how states should conduct their relationship with other states that violated human rights and ignored democratic norms. This was not a new issue, and had the admission of Myanmar taken place during the Cold War period it would perhaps not have been so contentious. A related disagreement was over what constituted a state's internal affairs and what constituted matters of international concern. The debate was most intense between 1995 and 23 July 1997, when Myanmar officially became a member of ASEAN. On one side was ASEAN's policy of "constructive engagement"; on the other was the policy of isolation and punitive action, particularly in the form of

[44] See Chua Teng Hoe, "ASEAN's Principle of Non-Interference: A Case of Indifference or Flexibility?" Master's thesis, Institute of Defence and Strategic Studies, Nanyang Technological University, 1999–2000.

[45] Almonte (as told to Vitug), *Endless Journey*, p. 293; Kenton Clymer, *A Delicate Relationship: The United States and Burma/Myanmar Since 1945* (Ithaca: Cornell University Press, 2015), chapter 13.

sanctions advocated and implemented by the United States and the European Union, which were also ASEAN's dialogue partners.

As Deepak Nair noted, Vietnam, Laos and Cambodia were keen to join ASEAN because they saw it as "a stepping stone for international integration". Myanmar, on the other hand, viewed membership of ASEAN as "a shield from the geopolitics of the post-Cold War period" —a buffer between Chinese influence and the pressures of Western liberalism.[46] In private, some ASEAN officials were critical of Myanmar's poor human rights record, but their attitude did not affect policy because if the Myanmar kettle was black, some of the ASEAN pots were not much cleaner. Before July 1997, ASEAN might have been able to effect change in the military government known as State Law and Order Restoration Council (SLORC). However, it was not prepared to. Human rights and security were not a priority for ASEAN. For example, the ASEAN governments did not adopt the ASEAN-ISIS suggestion of drawing up a roadmap for change in Myanmar in the social and political fields.[47] Once Myanmar became an ASEAN member, the window of opportunity was closed, as member states were constrained by ASEAN's cardinal policy of non-interference in the domestic affairs of its member countries. ASEAN has clung tenaciously to this policy despite some attempts to change it led by Bangkok, Manila and briefly Anwar Ibrahim when he was deputy prime minister of Malaysia. Before the onset of the Asian Financial Crisis in 1997, the view held by some in ASEAN—Jakarta in particular—was that with Myanmar in ASEAN the military junta, which had shown some interest in the Indonesian political model, could learn from the Indonesians how ABRI (Armed Forces of the Republic of Indonesia, now TNI) managed Indonesia. However, after 1997 the Indonesian military was in no position to mentor Myanmar.

In admitting Myanmar into ASEAN, the association showed that it would not succumb to pressure from the United States and the

---

[46] Deepak Nair, *Learning Diplomacy: Cambodia, Laos, Myanmar and Vietnam Diplomats in ASEAN*, Trends in Southeast Asia, No. 14 (Singapore: Institute of Southeast Asian Studies, 2016), p. 12.

[47] Jusuf Wanandi, "The ASEAN-10 and Its International and Regional Implications", in *A Pacific Peace: Issues and Responses: Papers Presented at the 11th Asia-Pacific Roundtable, June 5–8, 1997, Kuala Lumpur*, ed. Mohamed Jawhar Hassan (Kuala Lumpur: ISIS, 1998), pp. 197–203.

European Union. The admission of Myanmar had its cost. Termsak Chalermpalanupap (then assistant director of programme coordination and external relations in the ASEAN Secretariat) recalled that Western countries refused visas to the Myanmar leadership and officials, which "created inconvenience" in ASEAN's interactions with some of its dialogue partners. The United States could not host the 14th ASEAN-US Dialogue Meeting in 1998, as it would not issue visas to the Myanmar delegation. The ASEAN-EU Ministerial Meeting in Berlin in 1999 was also cancelled because Bonn would not issue a visa to the foreign minister of Myanmar. These are just two examples. There were many more cases of meetings that had to be aborted or reconfigured only after much negotiation because the inclusion of Myanmar was unacceptable in the eyes of the US and EU.[48] In 1999 and 2000, Washington refused to allow Myanmar's foreign minister into the US even to attend academic forums. Sanctions against Myanmar continued and expanded during the George W. Bush administration (2001–09).[49]

Continued isolation and sanctions by the United States and European countries made it extremely difficult, if not impossible, for Myanmar to reboot its economy. One report described a black market pervading the whole country.[50] Because the isolation was not complete and the sanctions were not as effective as they could have been, change in Myanmar did not materialize as envisaged. The United States and other like-minded countries continued to keep up the pressure believing that sanctions would eventually work. On its part, Yangon realized that investments from China and the ASEAN countries could not fully substitute for those from Western countries. Furthermore, there were perils to being over-reliant on any one country, in this case China. As for ASEAN, most of the member states (after 1997) were themselves experiencing difficulty attracting foreign direct investment because of the financial crisis. If Western countries did not lift their sanctions, it would be impossible for Myanmar to plug into and compete in the fast-changing and increasingly interconnected global economy. The issue of Myanmar is discussed further in chapter 3.

---

[48] Termsak Chalermpalanupap, "ASEAN 10: Meeting the Challenges", Plenary Session 5, 1 June 1999, 13th Asia-Pacific Roundtable, 30 May–2 June 1999, Kuala Lumpur.

[49] Clymer, *Delicate Relationship*, pp. 287–9.

[50] "Isolated Myanmar Driven by Black Economy", *Straits Times*, 21 May 2001.

Cambodia Joins ASEAN

Cambodia would have been admitted into ASEAN on 23 July 1997 during ASEAN's 30th Ministerial Meeting in Kuala Lumpur (at the same time as Myanmar), had it not been for the dispute between its then two co-premiers, Norodom Ranariddh and Hun Sen, which led to the ouster of the former in early July 1997. Cambodia lost its seat in the United Nations as a result. Because of the political uncertainty in Cambodia at the time, ASEAN on 10 July 1997 decided to indefinitely postpone its admission. A general election was held a year later, in July 1998, and in early December a new coalition government was established in Cambodia. Cambodia regained its seat in the United Nations and reapplied for admission into ASEAN. Thus, about two weeks before the Sixth ASEAN Summit in December 1998 in Hanoi, amidst more pressing issues brought about by the ongoing financial crisis, the nine members had to consider whether to admit Cambodia as the tenth and last member of the regional grouping at the summit. We do not know the full details of the deliberations amongst the foreign ministers who met on 12 December 1998 and the subsequent meetings of the heads of state. However, the leaders were candid in admitting that there were disagreements amongst themselves on the timing of Cambodia's admission into ASEAN.

Of the member states that supported Cambodia's immediate admission, Vietnam—given its proximity and historical relationship with Phnom Penh—was the most enthusiastic and vocal. For example, the Cambodian flag was hoisted alongside those of the ASEAN countries outside Ba Dinh Hall, the venue of the summit, even though a decision regarding Cambodia's admission into ASEAN had not been made. The Vietnamese also continued to rally behind the Cambodians despite the failure of the foreign ministers to reach a consensus. In the 14 December issue of *Vietnam News*, a headline read, "Cambodia Suited for ASEAN, Says Hun Sen".[51] At a press briefing after the meeting of the ASEAN foreign ministers on 12 December 1998, Vietnamese Deputy Prime Minister and Foreign Minister Nguyen Manh Cam reiterated Vietnam's preference for Cambodia's immediate admission into ASEAN.

[51] "Flag of Cambodia Joins Rest of Asean", *Straits Times*, 12 Dec. 1998. Also see interview with Jonathan Birchall of the *Financial Times* (from Hanoi) in BBC London, *East Asia Today*, 14 Dec. 1998.

He pointed out that the majority of foreign ministers shared this view. Singapore, Thailand and the Philippines had made public statements expressing their reservations.[52] As ASEAN operated on the principle of consensus and as there was no agreement amongst the foreign ministers, it was decided that the heads of state during the summit would reconsider the issue.[53] Until the afternoon of 14 December, the impression given was that there was still no agreement.[54] However, at an informal dinner that same evening, the heads of state decided to admit Cambodia but to announce it only after the summit. The leaders also agreed to hold the official ceremony marking its admission a fortnight to a month later in Hanoi. Indonesian President Habibie (who had succeeded Suharto in May 1998), who was scheduled to meet Cambodian Prime Minister Hun Sen after the informal dinner, was mandated to relay the news to him.[55] In his speech at the opening of the summit the next day, Malaysian Prime Minister Mahathir Mohamad hailed Phan Van Khai for his "skilful arrangement for Cambodia to be admitted in a special ceremony to be held in Hanoi soon".[56] Cambodian radio reported the ASEAN decision on 15 December. According to the report, Hun Sen welcomed ASEAN's decision. The report added that Thailand, Singapore and the Philippines had objected to the quick inclusion of Cambodia as a member, whereas the other six countries were happy with the decision.[57] A Vietnamese Foreign Ministry statement of 16 December confirmed the admission of Cambodia.[58] Cambodia became the tenth member of ASEAN on 30 April 1999, marking the beginning of the ASEAN-10 we know today.

---

[52] "Cambodia in Asean: Yes, but When", *Straits Times*, 10 Dec. 1998.

[53] *Voice of Vietnam*, 13 Dec. 1998, *SWB/FE*/3411/S1/2.

[54] "PM Urges Asean Action Plan", *Straits Times*, 15 Dec. 1998; *Kompas*, 15 Dec. 1998, *SWB/FE*/3411/S1/3.

[55] *Kompas*, 15 Dec. 1998, *SWB/FE*/3411/S1/3. For another account of the sequence of events, see Michael Vatikiotis, "Awkward Admission", *Far Eastern Economic Review*, 24 Dec. 1998, p. 17.

[56] *Vietnam TV*, 15 Dec. 1998, *SWB/FE*/3411/S1/1.

[57] *National Voice of Cambodia*, 15 Dec. 1998, *SWB/FE*/3412/S1/6.

[58] *Voice of Vietnam*, 16 Dec. 1998, *SWB/FE*/3413/S1/9-10; "Leaders Express Hope for Unified Cambodia", *Straits Times*, 17 Dec. 1998. For Habibie's confirmation of Cambodia's admission, see *Radio Republic of Indonesia*, 17 Dec. 1998, *SWB/FE*/3413/S1/10.

There was a China factor in the decisions to admit Myanmar and Cambodia with such urgency. Although it was never publicly expressed, various ASEAN officials confided that in deciding to accept Myanmar into ASEAN in 1997, concern over the growing influence of China was uppermost in their minds. Domingo L. Siazon Jr, then the Philippines' foreign secretary, pointed out that Myanmar's entry into ASEAN was not one-dimensional and that there were other strategic realities in the consideration.[59] Almonte recalled, "the urgency of making Myanmar part of ASEAN was its geography ... Because of the isolation of Myanmar, since sanctions had been imposed on it by the West, it became naturally very close to China ... If this continued for a longer period, it may have been difficult to wean Myanmar from China."[60] In the early 1990s there was the perception, albeit exaggerated, that Mandalay, the second-largest city in Myanmar, was turning into a Chinese city.[61]

Thus, admitting Myanmar into ASEAN was considered a strategic necessity in order to wean Yangon away from the tightening embrace of Beijing. It is therefore ironic that the one country that quietly benefited from the continuing policy disagreements was China. The reality was that after July 1997, Myanmar-China relations continued to strengthen while Myanmar's relations with Thailand remained problematic. The association not only failed to draw Yangon away from China, but in recent years almost all the ASEAN countries—most notably Indonesia, Malaysia and Thailand—adjusting to what they see as the rising Chinese power, have considerably improved their relations with Beijing. However, beneath the façade of closer ties, the ASEAN states remain wary of China.[62]

In the case of Cambodia, the urgency was perhaps not as acute compared to Myanmar in the early 1990s. It is, however, worth noting that China was increasingly becoming a major player in Cambodian politics. In April 1996 General Zhang Wannian, chief of the General

---

59 See "Thailand: Foreign Ministers 'Firmly' Support Burma's ASEAN Entry", *Hong Kong AFP*, 29 Apr. 1997, *FBIS-EAS*-97-119; "Thailand: Philippine Ambassador Defends Burma's ASEAN Entry", *Bangkok Post*, 11 June 1997, *FBIS-EAS*-97-162.

60 Almonte, *Endless Journey*, p. 293.

61 Ibid.; "Myanmar and China: But Will the Flag Follow Trade?" *The Economist*, 8 Oct. 1994, pp. 31–2.

62 See "China Steps in Where US Fails", *Far Eastern Economic Review*, 23 Nov. 2000, pp. 20, 22.

Staff Department, People's Liberation Army, visited Cambodia. It was reported that China granted $1 million in non-lethal aid to Cambodia and was considering providing training assistance to the Cambodian coalition government.[63] Both the Hun Sen-led Cambodian People's Party and the Ranariddh-led National United Front for an Independent, Neutral, Peaceful and Cooperative Cambodia (FUNCINPEC) were also courting Beijing. In mid-June 1996 Loy Simchheang, secretary-general of FUNCINPEC, met China's Premier Li Peng in Beijing.[64] During Vietnam's Eighth Party Congress, on 1 July 1996 in Hanoi, Wen Jiabao (acting leader of the Chinese Communist Party [CCP] Central Committee delegation, alternate member of the Politburo, and secretary of the CCP Central Committee secretariat) held separate talks with Chea Sim (chairman of the Cambodian People's Party and Cambodia's National Assembly) and Chhim Seakleng (leader of the FUNCINPEC delegation).[65] About a fortnight later, on 12 July, it was announced that Hun Sen had been invited to visit China from 18 to 22 July. There was no elaboration as to the purpose of the visit except that it was part of a friendship programme between the two countries. According to Hun Sen, the trip to China had been well planned.[66] The Chinese disclosed the visit shortly after Sihanouk left Beijing for Cambodia. When the news was announced, Hun Sen and Ranariddh were in Tokyo attending a consultative group meeting on financial aid to Cambodia for 1996 and 1997.[67] In China, Hun Sen met with Chinese President Jiang Zemin and Premier Li Peng and toured Zhuhai, one of China's special economic zones in Guangdong Province, as well as Shenzhen.[68] Beijing could have decided that in view of Sihanouk's age and poor health, it was prudent to cultivate Hun Sen.

According to a December 1997 report in the *Far Eastern Economic Review*, China was the second-largest Asian aid donor to Cambodia, next to Japan. Many of the most prominent investors in Phnom Penh were from mainland China. The Chinese had also been providing

[63] *Phnom Penh Post*, 23 Aug.–5 Sept. 1996, *FBIS-EAS*-96-167.
[64] *Reaksmei Kampuchea*, 10–11 July 1996, *FBIS-EAS*-96-137.
[65] *China Radio International*, 2 July 1996, *SWB/FE*/2656/B/3.
[66] *Reaksmei Kampuchea*, 20 July 1996, *FBIS-EAS*-96-141.
[67] *Reaksmei Kampuchea*, 14 July 1996, *FBIS-EAS*-96-137.
[68] For Hun Sen's visit to China, see *SWB/FE*/2668/B/3; *SWB/FE*/2669/G/1; *SWB/FE*/2670/G/1; *SWB/FE*/2673/G/3.

military assistance to Hun Sen in his fight against the Khmer Rouge.[69] According to one source, General Zhang conveyed Beijing's invitation to Hun Sen to visit China. Beijing was apparently upset with Ranariddh because of his overtures to Taipei, which included discussions on a possible direct air link between Phnom Penh and Taipei and the opening of a consular office in Phnom Penh.[70]

Hun Sen, too, like Sihanouk in the past, successfully cultivated the Chinese. In a conversation with Malcolm MacDonald in May 1962, Sihanouk said that he was most concerned about the South Vietnamese and the Thais, and that if push came to shove he would resort to Chinese assistance, which would then mean the end of Cambodia's policy of nonalignment.[71] We do not have the benefit of any record of conversation between Hun Sen and the Chinese officials whom he met on many occasions during this period, but one issue worth citing is the dumping of Taiwanese toxic waste in Sihanoukville. Hun Sen while in Beijing met Chinese officials for assistance to ship the toxic waste back to Taiwan based on the logic that Taiwan was a province of China.[72] One wonders what the Chinese could realistically have done, but what Hun Sen said must have been music to their ears. China-Cambodia relations continued to improve rapidly in the late 1990s. Hun Sen visited Beijing in February 1999 and secured low-interest commercial loans as well as aid grants from the Chinese. Defence ministers of both countries met at the end of March 1999 in Beijing, and a large Chinese trade delegation led by the Chinese deputy of the Ministry of Foreign Trade and Economic Cooperation visited Cambodia in April 1999. China had also been very forthcoming in helping the Cambodians kick-start their economy.[73] It is worth noting that Ranariddh somewhat belatedly also began to cultivate Beijing more assiduously.[74] In an interview with Xinhua on 16 June 1999 before visiting China, he was effusive in his

---

69 "Dancing with the Dragon", *Far Eastern Economic Review*, 11 Dec. 1997, pp. 26–7.

70 *Phnom Penh Post in English*, 19 Dec. 1997–1 Jan. 1998, *FBIS-EAS*-97-363.

71 *FO 371*/166667, DU 1022/5, 6 June 1962, "Notes on Conversation with Prince Sihanouk about Cambodia's Attitude to Present-Day South East Asian Problems".

72 "Cambodia Town on Rampage over Toxic Waste", *Straits Times*, 21 Dec. 1998.

73 For information on both visits, see *Xinhua News Agency*, 31 Mar. 1999, *SWB/FE*/3499/G/4, and 22 Apr. 1999, *SWB/FE*/3517/B/1.

74 See "Ranariddh to Woo Chinese Investors", *Business Times*, 18 June 1999.

praise for China and its importance to Cambodia.[75] According to a commentary in the Cambodian newspaper *Moneakseka Khmer*, both China and Japan were seeking political influence in Cambodia using aid, and China saw an opportunity to restore its strategic position and influence in Cambodia.[76]

Beijing's influence in the region was increasing, as was seen in its growing clout in Myanmar, Cambodia as well as Laos. Ralf Emmers noted that the financial crisis reduced Thai investments in Laos, which enabled Beijing to fill the gap and increase its influence in the country. China also helped Laos stabilize its currency in 1999 and gradually became the leading foreign investor in that country.[77]

The Hanoi Plan of Action

The mood of the ASEAN leaders during the Sixth ASEAN Summit was starkly different from during the build-up to the commemoration of the 30th anniversary of ASEAN formation in August 1997. At the Sixth ASEAN Summit in Hanoi on 15–16 December 1998, Singapore's Prime Minister Goh Chok Tong pointed out that ASEAN's "immediate priority" was "to demonstrate convincingly that we are seriously coming to grips with our present economic problems", a view shared by the other eight ASEAN members.[78] The summit was to show the world ASEAN's unity and resolve in overcoming the current crisis both as individual countries and as a group. The Hanoi Plan of Action (HPA)[79] was to be a testimony and demonstration of ASEAN's continued

[75] *Xinhua News Agency*, 16 June 1999, *SWB/FE*/3564/B/1.

[76] *Moneakseka Khmer*, 23 Mar. 1999, *SWB/FE*/3496/B/1.

[77] Ralf Emmers, "Regional Hegemonies and the Exercise of Power in Southeast Asia: A Study of Indonesia and Vietnam", *Asian Survey* 45, 4 (2005): 658.

[78] "Top Priority in Asean: Boost Confidence", *Straits Times*, 16 Dec. 1998.

[79] For the full text of the Hanoi Plan of Action, see *SWB/FE*/3413/S1/1-9. The action plan is divided into ten categories: (1) strengthen macroeconomic and financial cooperation, (2) enhance greater economic integration, (3) promote science and technology development and develop information technology infrastructure, (4) protect human resource development, (5) protect the environment and promote sustainable development, (6) strengthen regional peace and security, (7) enhance ASEAN's role as an effective force of peace, (8) justice and moderation in Asia-Pacific and in the world, (9) promote ASEAN awareness and its standing in the international community, and (10) improve ASEAN's structures and mechanisms.

relevance. As Prime Minister Goh said, "Let us have no illusions about where we stand if the Hanoi Summit does not live up to international expectations."[80] The deliberations over whether to admit Cambodia into ASEAN and Vietnam's antics to ensure Cambodia's admission (described above) unfortunately overshadowed the announcement of the HPA. In April 1999 Goh lamented, "ASEAN as a group is being seen as helpless and worse, disunited ... In our summits in 1997 and 1998, we failed to convince the outside world that ASEAN was tackling the crisis with determination and decisiveness to regain its high growth."[81]

A cursory reading of the comments made by both ASEAN leaders and political analysts from about 1998 to as late as 2001 would show the same sense of disappointment but not necessarily hopelessness despite such headlines as "Is ASEAN Dead?"[82] Khong Yuen Foong, who claimed he was agnostic about ASEAN's future growth rates, remarked, "... I agree with the consensual view that by and large, ASEAN's performance in the economic crisis has been disappointing. But I do not think this is decisive or fatal. Where the current pessimism about ASEAN's future errs is in its excessive reliance on economic criteria to assess ASEAN." Based on ASEAN's record of accomplishment, Khong pointed out, "ASEAN is less an anticipatory creature than a reactive one—it paces itself—too leisurely some say—but it has survived and prospered." In short, "ASEAN is down but not out."[83] Writing in the *Far Eastern Economic Review*, Thailand's Foreign Minister Surin Pitsuwan said, "What is clear after the nearly three years since the economic crisis descended upon us is that if ASEAN cleaves to the wisdom of its founders, then its future prosperity and greater influence will be that much better guaranteed ..." He was referring to "the need to foster greater cooperation among the countries of the region in an increasingly interdependent world", which the founding members of ASEAN highlighted in 1967.[84] The 1997 financial crisis was, as Zakaria Ahmad

---

[80] "Top Priority in Asean: Boost Confidence".

[81] Quoted in Ahmad and Ghoshal, "Political Future of ASEAN": 759.

[82] "Is ASEAN Dead?" *Sunday Times*, 20 Dec. 1998.

[83] Khong Yuen Foong, "Whither ASEAN?" in *Singapore: The Year in Review 1998*, ed. Ooi Giok Ling and Ramkishen Rajan (Singapore: Times Academic Press, 1999), pp. 88–101. See also Tommy Koh, "Grouping Will Emerge Victorious", *Sunday Times*, 20 Dec. 1998.

[84] "Heeding ASEAN's Legacy", *Far Eastern Economic Review*, 17 Feb. 2000, p. 29.

and Baladas Ghoshal described, "a shock and a catalyst"[85]—a catalyst for a revamp of the association in order for it to be able to "respond to the new challenges of globalisation".[86] ASEAN, according to Jusuf Wanandi, had to "set clearly her vision of the future, namely to build a community in Southeast Asia".[87]

Perhaps the most scathing criticism of ASEAN was by the International Institute for Strategic Studies. In its 2001 report, it described Southeast Asia as crippled by "institutional paralysis". It said ASEAN "is now, to an even greater extent than ever before, tied to the lowest common denominator in managing consensus" and had become "a unity that lacks political substance, and the group is decreasingly able to speak credibly with one voice".[88]

The Asian Financial Crisis, in the view of Singapore's Senior Minister Lee Kuan Yew, was "a considerable setback to what was an extremely promising trend of more growth and stability, increasing cooperation, freer trade and better international coordination". He expected individual countries to turn inwards as they grappled with their own economic and social problems. Lee was, however, optimistic that Asia would recover, although not all countries at the same pace,[89] and that after overcoming the crisis—perhaps two to five years later—ASEAN would again coalesce as a group to maintain the geopolitical balance in the region.[90] Asked whether the Pacific renaissance or the Age of the Pacific was ending even before it started because of the Asian Financial Crisis, Lee replied, "No, how can it be? You have the first typhoon and you see it is over. Typhoon is very unsettling but it brings a lot of rain, cleanse out the rivers. It will subside and new crops will grow."[91] On another occasion he described the Asian crisis as "a blip on a long-term trend".[92]

---

[85] Ahmad and Ghoshal, "Political Future of ASEAN": 776.

[86] Jusuf Wanandi, "Revamp Needed to Become a Community", *Sunday Times*, 20 Dec. 1998.

[87] Ibid.

[88] "South-east Asia's Influence Hurt", *Straits Times*, 17 May 2001.

[89] "Asia Will Recover, but Not at Same Pace: SM", *Straits Times*, 27 Mar. 1999.

[90] Ang, *Lee Kuan Yew's Strategic Thought*, p. 82; "SM Lee Fields Wide-Ranging Questions from CNN Viewers", CNN (English), Q&A Asia, 11 Dec. 1998 (transcript).

[91] Full transcript of interview with Senior Minister Lee Kuan Yew, Singapore, by Hong Seok Hyun (Publisher-President) and Kim Young Hie (Editor-at-Large), Joogang, Ilbo, Seoul, Korea, 23 Feb. 1998.

[92] "Asian Crisis 'a Blip on Long-Term Trend'", *Straits Times*, 11 Dec. 1999.

More significantly, the financial crisis made it even more difficult for the Southeast Asian countries to compete economically with China. ASEAN had no choice, as Lee explained:

> ... getting together was because we needed that added weight to deal on equal terms with big countries in the old days with the US, with Europe and with Japan. Now we've got to deal with China. One by one, the ten of us will be featherweights, I mean, against the scale of a country like China. Even the ten of us put together isn't of the same balance, but at least we'll have greater weight.[93]

Lee observed that after the severe financial and economic setback, none of the ASEAN countries had "time for ideological or expansionist issues".[94] He was right. ASEAN did recover, and faster than most predicted; and Indonesia did not break up as feared. Indeed, between late 1999 and early 2000, contrary to expectations, there were signs that the region would make a steep V-shaped economic recovery. By 2007—the tenth anniversary of the Asian Financial Crisis—the general view amongst economists was that the region had recovered better than most expected. S.M. Thangavelu and Yong Yik Wei were of the view that "driven by strong exports, regional countries' output growth rates have been converging to pre-crisis levels".[95] Elena Okorotchenko wrote, "Asia is well on its way to achieving pre-crisis creditworthiness" and "a number of their credit factors are better than in the pre-crisis period ..."[96]

---

[93] "SM Lee Fields Wide-Ranging Questions from CNN Viewers". See also "S-E Asia Will Have a Tough Time Against China", *Straits Times*, 27 Mar. 1999.

[94] "East Asia Peace Hinges on Ties Between US, Japan, China", *Straits Times*, 15 May 1999. Lee was alluding to the debate with ASEAN about the principle of non-interference and the South China Sea dispute amongst some ASEAN member states.

[95] "Can S-E Asia Ride the Next FDI Wave?" In their article, Thangavelu and Yong noted that belying the output recovery, there was a decline in the flow of foreign direct investment.

[96] "The Asian Financial Crisis: 10 Years On", *Straits Times*, 30 June 2007. In 2007 Okorotchenko was the Asia head of sovereign ratings at Standard & Poor's in Singapore. She, however, qualified her assessment by reminding readers that a resurgence of oil prices, a sudden and disorderly unwinding of imbalances in the American economy, as well as the state of the Chinese economy could stall, if not derail, the positive trajectory.

Enter Timor-Leste

The landscape of Southeast Asia pre-July 1997 was greatly different from that post-1997. Perhaps the most obvious difference was the emergence of a new state in Southeast Asia: Timor-Leste. Had there not been the financial crisis that brought down Suharto, who was briefly replaced by B.J. Habibie, Jakarta would not so easily have allowed its 27th province, commonly referred to as East Timor (which it invaded in 1975 ostensibly to eliminate a potential Communist threat in the region), to secede. Since the occupation of East Timor, a conflict between the separatists, particularly the Revolutionary Front for an Independent East Timor, and the Indonesian military had been ongoing despite the end of the Cold War. In January 1999 President Habibie offered a referendum to the East Timorese to have either autonomy or independence. The East Timorese (a large segment of whom had never accepted Indonesia's brutal rule in the last 23 years) chose the latter in a UN-organized referendum in August 1999. That was followed in September 1999 by a spate of violence, killings and flagrant human rights abuses involving the Indonesian military. Subsequently, a UN peacekeeping force (International Force East Timor, InterFET) led by Australia was set up in East Timor until the referendum result was approved.[97]

East Timor, renamed Timor-Leste, officially became an independent and sovereign state on 20 May 2002. The extraterritorial killings and human rights abuses brought Indonesia into confrontation with Australia as well as the United States. Jakarta was of the view that Canberra was putting "the Timor cart before the Indonesian horse" by championing the East Timorese cause. According to the Indonesian diplomat Hasan Wirayuda, Australia's preoccupation with East Timor was not shared by other countries such as Japan, China, India, ASEAN and even the United States, which "regarded the paramount issue in Southeast Asia as the successful transition of Indonesia to more stable representative government and the recovery of the Indonesian economy".[98] Indonesia-Australia relations and, by association, ASEAN-Australia relations were affected by the Timor-Leste episode for some years.

---

[97] For a first person account of this episode leading to InterFET, see Surin Pitsuwan, "How East Timor Reshaped ASEAN", *Bangkok Post*, 19 May 2002. Surin was the foreign minister of Thailand from November 1997 to February 2001.
[98] See Woolcott, *Hot Seat*, pp. 264–5.

Jose Ramos-Horta, then the chief foreign affairs spokesman for East Timor (he would become the country's first foreign minister), said that East Timor should give priority to joining ASEAN after formal independence, as "ASEAN is far more important for East Timor to join (compared to the South Pacific Forum), in terms of our security needs, trade, economic relations and investment."[99] This was in 1999. Ramos-Horta's position was, in Michael Richardson's words, "an about face" as he had previously criticized ASEAN for siding with Indonesia in its invasion and occupation of East Timor and for overlooking the human rights abuses perpetrated by the Indonesian military.[100] Indeed, the East Timorese leaders had opposed any Southeast Asian nation being in charge of the UN peacekeeping force for the same reasons.[101] This explains why Australia led the UN peacekeeping force. In 2002 Ramos-Horta, now the foreign minister, predicted that East Timor needed a decade to prepare for admission into ASEAN. We will continue this narrative in chapter 4.

From East Asian Economic Caucus to ASEAN Plus Three

The financial crisis gave Kuala Lumpur the opportunity to revive the idea of the East Asian Economic Group (renamed East Asian Economic Caucus [EAEC] in 1991) proposed by Malaysian Prime Minister Mahathir in 1990.[102] The main intention of the EAEG/EAEC, as explained by Seri Rafidah Aziz (then Malaysian trade and industry minister), was to provide a "loose consultative forum" for "East Asian countries on trade and economic issues which will dominate world affairs in the coming years".[103] Initially, fellow ASEAN members were not too enthusiastic about the idea. For example, Indonesia (always the most important voice in ASEAN) expressed concern that the EAEG "might be seen as a bid by ASEAN to drive a wedge between Japan and the United States" (which in the 1980s had had some differences

[99] "East Timor Now Looks to ASEAN", *International Herald Tribune*, 8 Dec. 1999.
[100] Ibid.
[101] "US Backs Aussies in E. Timor", *Straits Times*, 6 Dec. 1999.
[102] "East Asian Grouping Idea Revived by Malaysia", *Straits Times*, 22 Aug. 1998; "Mahathir: An Outspoken Asean Visionary", *Straits Times*, 30 Nov. 2000.
[103] "Programme of Action Will Be Proposed at Summit: Badawi", *Straits Times*, 22 Aug. 1992.

over economic issues). Whether named Group or Caucus, the new entity was seen to duplicate—if not torpedo—the incipient APEC and other ASEAN post-ministerial conferences with its dialogue partners. In addition, the exclusion of the United States from the EAEC was, in the words of an Indonesian official, "not helpful" and "unrealistic". Washington, backed by Singapore, was fiercely opposed to the EAEG proposal and reportedly exerted pressure on Japan and South Korea to reject it.[104]

ASEAN's position on the EAEC appeared to have shifted after 1997, although the term "EAEC" was never revived but appeared in the form of ASEAN Plus Three (China, Japan and South Korea). The arguments against the EAEC mentioned above appeared to be no longer relevant given the developments during the financial crisis. In the words of Termsak:

> [I]n order to reduce our heavy dependence on our traditional Western markets and sources of investments from the West, ASEAN has tried to develop its cooperation with other parts of the world to diversify its external relations. The flourishing ASEAN+3 framework is a good calculated move. It came at the right time when East Asia was and still is suffering from similar problems arising from the defects in the international financial architecture ...[105]

ASEAN Plus Three would also not duplicate APEC, because the general consensus was that APEC was impotent and fell short in mitigating the financial crisis. Some analysts would go even further to argue that APEC had "failed to adopt leadership positions on any regional or global key issues and has been marginalised" since.[106] In 1999 Termsak remarked:

> In APEC, it may already be too late for ASEAN to salvage the situation. Some ASEAN members preferred individual participation in APEC. ASEAN thus virtually gave up its leadership in what was actually ASEAN's own initiative. Consequently, US domination of the APEC process is inevitable. And the future of APEC depends very much on the US ...[107]

[104] "EAEC May Be Seen as an Attempt to 'Drive in a Wedge'", *Straits Times*, 23 Jan. 1992; "North-east Asia's Challenge", *Business Times*, 28 Nov. 2000.
[105] Termsak, "ASEAN 10: Meeting The Challenges".
[106] "APEC at 20: Still Relevant, but For How Long?" *Straits Times*, 31 Oct. 2009.
[107] Termsak, "ASEAN 10: Meeting The Challenges".

The financial crisis did not, as Tang Shiping pointed out, create ASEAN Plus Three (APT) but provided the catalyst.[108] Whether APT would have been a natural and inevitable outcome of an "ever-increasing independence" amongst the Southeast and East Asian economies can be debated. It is worth noting that ASEAN foreign ministers had already been meeting with their Northeast Asian counterparts informally at the ARF.[109] The first informal meeting of APT took place in Kuala Lumpur in December 1997, and the group was regularized/institutionalized in 1999 in Manila. APT would become the "main forum for the thirteen East Asian countries", but as Hadi Soesastro noted in 2000, "it is still a process and is perhaps at the very early stage of moving to become an institutional arrangement. This process has great symbolic significance, but it still is an empty process as it lacks substance."[110]

Non-traditional Security

The financial crisis affected all aspects of the states and societies in the region. It compelled the Southeast Asian governments to focus collectively and systematically for the first time on what we now commonly refer to as "non-traditional security" (NTS) issues. As Andrew Tan and Kenneth Boutin rightly noted:

> Globalisation has resulted in new security threats to communities and individuals that are transnational in character and are increasingly defined in social and economic terms. Southeast Asia's vulnerability to the consequences of globalisation was graphically demonstrated by the economic crisis ... The generally positive view of globalisation resulting from its perceived role in engineering the "Asian economic miracle" and enhancing regime legitimacy through what has been termed "performance legitimacy" has been supplanted by a much more nuanced view of globalisation as both an opportunity and a threat.[111]

---

[108] Tang Shiping, "Forging a Sense of Community", *Straits Times*, 2 July 2007.

[109] See Goh, *Struggle for Order*, pp. 54–7; Richard Stubbs, "ASEAN Plus Three: Emerging East Asian Regionalism?" *Asian Survey* 43, 3 (2002): 440–55.

[110] Hadi Soesastro, "East Asia Economic Cooperation: In Search of an Institutional Identity", Plenary Session Four, 4 June 2000, 14th Asia-Pacific Roundtable, Kuala Lumpur, 3–7 June 2000.

[111] Andrew T.H. Tan and J.D. Kenneth Boutin (eds), *Non-traditional Security Issues in Southeast Asia* (Singapore: Select, 2001), p. 5.

A combination of climate change and Indonesia's management inadequacy led to a serious environmental issue, commonly described as "haze", caused by fires (to clear land for oil palm plantations) in parts of Borneo and Sumatra. The fires affected not just Indonesia but also Malaysia, Singapore and Brunei, which in turn affected Indonesia's relations with its two immediate neighbours. The haze started in 1997 and since then has been an annual occurrence despite ASEAN's action plan drawn up in December 1997.

There has been "a keen interest in rethinking and refashioning the concept of security idea" since the Cold War ended.[112] The prevailing view in the 1990s was that security during the Cold War years was too narrowly focused on the state at the expense of the people/citizens. Thus the introduction of a new term, "human security". NTS (the preferred term of the Southeast Asian countries and China) was in fact human security by another name—the shifting of perspective from territory or government to people. One criticism of the concept was its remarkable breadth. Japan (under Keizo Obuchi's premiership) and Thailand (under Prime Minister Chuan Leekpai and Foreign Minister Surin) were supportive of the term "human security". On the other hand, Malaysia was concerned that it could create the impression that "the individual is more paramount than the state, meaning society as a whole".[113] As Amitav Acharya concluded, in Southeast Asia the state was still very much in control—the decision maker—in any securitization or de-securitization process, as civil society remained weak, underdeveloped or even suppressed by governments.[114]

At the fifth ARF meeting in July 1998 in Manila, US Secretary of State Madeleine Albright devoted a considerable proportion of her speech to issues such as AIDS, HIV infection, human rights, corruption, environmental protection and the fight against drugs. Albright could "think of no legitimate reason why we should not address them together,

[112] David Capie and Paul Evans, *The Asia-Pacific Security Lexicon* (Singapore: Institute of Southeast Asian Studies, 2002), p. 139.

[113] The above is summarized from Capie and Evans, *Asia-Pacific Security Lexicon*, pp. 139–46.

[114] Mely Caballero-Anthony, Amitav Acharya and Ralf Emmers (eds), *Non-traditional Security in Asia: Dilemmas in Securitisation* (London: Ashgate, 2006), chapter 11.

for they are issues as far as our people are concerned". "Many of the challenges we face today," Albright pointed out, "will require us to talk about matters that are usually seen as the domestic affairs of other nations ... The question we must ask is what we mean by interference, especially in an age of interdependence."[115] Albright specifically mentioned the situations in Cambodia, Burma as well as Indonesia. The issues she cited were not new, but they were issues that ASEAN leaders were unaccustomed to addressing publicly. Asked whether the non-interference policy should be put aside or moderated, Lee Kuan Yew's response was that it was "logical and intellectually irrefutable, but emotionally, it's not acceptable because it is still a sensitive issue".[116] The Chairman's Statement of the Fifth ASEAN Regional Forum noted that "the ARF had maintained its approach to security concerns in a comprehensive manner" and the ministers "welcomed the fact that while the focus of the ARF was on core military and defence-related issues, the ARF also addressed non-military issues, which would have significant impact on regional security".[117] There were apparently discussions on the challenges of an expanded ASEAN, human rights, governance and the environment during the first retreat (in an informal setting) of the ASEAN foreign ministers in Singapore in July 1999.[118]

In 1998 the Ford Foundation funded a research project on NTS in Asia essentially to advance the debate and understanding of such issues in the region. According to Andrew Watson (representative for China at the Ford Foundation), concepts of non-traditional or human security were already being discussed in other parts of the world during this time but "little was done in Asia".[119] Southeast Asian states

---

[115] "US Commitment to Security and Prosperity in Asia" (Secretary of State Madeleine Albright) (transcript), 1 Aug. 1998, US Department of State Dispatch, DSB 1, Vol. 9, No. 7, ISSN: 1051-7693, Factiva.

[116] "SM Lee Comments on ASEAN's Policy of Non-Interference", BBC London, *East Asia Today*, 25 Nov. 1998.

[117] See "Chairman Statement, the Fifth Meeting of the ASEAN Regional Forum, Manila", 27 July 1998, https://www.mofa.go.jp/region/asia-paci/asean/conference/arf98/forum.html, accessed 20 Mar. 2019.

[118] Jurgen Haake, *ASEAN's Diplomatic and Security Culture: Origins, Developments and Prospects* (London: RoutledgeCurzon, 2003), p. 195.

[119] Ralf Emmers, Mely Caballero-Anthony and Amitav Acharya (compiled), *Studying Non-traditional Security in Asia: Trends and Issues* (Singapore: Marshall Cavendish, 2006).

remained focused on "traditional concerns of sovereignty, political and military interdependence, and defence" despite the new challenges ranging from health to the environment and international crime, to name just a few examples.[120] Furthermore, the existing knowledge, particularly the dominant model concerning the management of NTS issues propounded by the Copenhagen School, was deemed to be "too Euro-centric in its approach ... based on European history and culture". As previously noted, the Southeast Asian states did not share the same view of human rights and democracy as the United States and European countries. The view in the region was that there was a need to improvise a variant model based on the Asian context and setting. The newly established Institute of Defence and Strategic Studies (IDSS) (now known as the S. Rajaratnam School of International Studies [RSIS]) was the leading driver of this study from 1999 to 2005.[121] Non-traditional security covers a range of issues such as health, food, water, natural disasters, internal conflict, forced migration, energy, transnational crime, cybersecurity and many others—"transnational threats which are primarily non-military in nature but also include the threat of state sponsored violence on its own population and the emergence of non-state armed actors".[122]

Second Mischief Reef Incident

Returning to the issue of the South China Sea dispute, recall that after the Mischief Reef incident in 1995, ASEAN adopted a united position vis-à-vis China, albeit because of pressure from the Philippines to act.

---

[120] Ibid., p. v.

[121] See Tan and Boutin, *Non-traditional Security Issues in Southeast Asia*, which is the first book published from the Ford Foundation-funded NTS project and covers the relationship between regional institutions and governance and NTS as well as environmental security; Caballero-Anthony et al., *Non-traditional Security in Asia*, which has chapters on migration, piracy, small arms and drug trafficking, health issues such as diseases and AIDS, and resource development; Mely Caballero-Anthony and Alistair D.B. Cook (eds), *Non-traditional Security in Asia: Issues, Challenges and Framework for Action* (Singapore: Institute of Southeast Asian Studies, 2013), which has chapters on health, food, water, natural disasters, internal conflict, forced migration, energy, transnational crime and cybersecurity.

[122] Caballero-Anthony and Cook, *Non-traditional Security in Asia*, p. 1.

After a brief respite, China seized the next opportunity to re-exert its claim when ASEAN was distracted by the fallout of the financial crisis. At the Sixth ASEAN Summit in Hanoi in December 1998, the Philippines was tasked to draft a code of conduct on the management of the South China Sea dispute. Soon after, in January 1999, the second Mischief Reef incident occurred. This time ASEAN was apparently unwilling to confront Beijing more strongly even though this was China's second transgression.

Manila was also unable to elicit any American commitment to assist it in the dispute. Indeed, at a House International Relations Committee (East Asia subcommittee) hearing on 12 February 1999, Stanley Roth, assistant secretary of state for East Asian affairs, reportedly told Congressmen the Chinese forces in the Spratlys were "not a major security threat". According to Roth, "it's the trend and the fact that China claims all this territory that's troubling, not the situation on the ground". The US assessment was that the situation on the ground did not indicate there was a massive build-up of Chinese military forces. The United States preferred to work with ASEAN, either through the Indonesian-led South China Sea Workshops or the ASEAN Regional Forum, to resolve the Spratlys issue. Filipino military chief General Angelo Reyes publicly stated that the Philippines could not rely on the United States for its defence, despite a mutual-defence treaty.

According to Lauro Baja Jr, Philippine foreign affairs undersecretary, Manila was not getting international community aid in protesting against China's continued occupation of Mischief Reef: "On Mischief Reef, we were left alone. The other countries said that while they sympathise and understand our situation, the issue is only a 'Philippine-China problem'."[123] Baja, in a speech to the Rotary Club on 15 April 1999, described the Philippines as "an orphan in its campaign" (referring to Manila's recent efforts to internationalize the South China Sea issue). He also said that the Spratlys had no immediate significance for Manila's "so-called friends in the international community". He added, "Even some of our ASEAN friends are either mute, timid or cannot go beyond espousal of general principle of peaceful settlement of disputes and polite words of understanding given in the corridors or meeting rooms."

[123] The following account is taken from Ang, "South China Sea Dispute Revisited".

At the ASEAN-China meeting in Kunming (4–8 April 1999), ASEAN only managed to obtain Beijing's agreement to give serious and earnest consideration to the Philippines' proposal of a new regional code of conduct with regard to the South China Sea. According to Baja, the code would include provisions prohibiting the use of force, maintaining the status quo and promoting cooperation. It was, however, unclear how different the proposed code of conduct would be from the ASEAN Declaration on the South China Sea (signed on 22 July 1992), which Beijing had expressed agreement with, or the Joint Statement on PRC-RP Consultations on the South China Sea and on Other Areas of Cooperation (signed on 10 August 1995) and the joint statement signed between ASEAN and China during the ASEAN Summit in December 1997. According to Philippine Foreign Affairs Secretary Domingo Siazon and ASEAN Secretary-General Rodolfo Severino, a code of conduct was stronger than a declaration, which was unilateral in nature. The proposed code of conduct could not be drafted in time for the July 1999 ASEAN Ministerial Meeting. Eventually, it was tabled at the Third ASEAN Informal Summit in November 1999 in Manila. However, Manila failed to muster a consensus to have it formally adopted. All that the parties could agree to was to continue discussion on the draft.

Although the Mischief Reef dispute was in the limelight in the second half of the 1990s, it is easy to forget that besides China, Vietnam and the Philippines, there were other claimants to the reefs, rocks and islands in the South China Sea. In the months leading up to the November meeting, the Philippines, Malaysia and Vietnam were disputing amongst themselves over some of the islands, which they each claimed belonged to them. The Malaysians were building structures on Investigator Shoal and Erica Reef, both claimed by the Philippines and Vietnam. The Vietnamese, on their part, were building structures on Cornwallis South Reef and Allison Reef, which the Philippines also claimed. There were reports of Vietnamese troops having fired at a Filipino reconnaissance plane over Pigeon Reef as well as a brief stand-off between Filipino and Malaysian fighter planes over the Investigator Shoal. Prior to the Manila meeting, the Chinese threatened to take action if the Philippines did not remove its grounded navy logistic support ship from the vicinity of the Second Thomas Shoal. Indeed, as Stanley Roth observed, China was not the only country to maintain military outposts in the South China Sea. It also did not have the largest number of outposts. Vietnam controlled the most islands and reefs in the area. In September 1998 Vietnam built structures on the Orleana and Kingston Shoals, which Beijing also claimed. Malaysia claimed 12, of which it occupied six. Brunei claimed two, but it did not station troops or put up any installations on them. Taiwan was also a claimant and occupied the largest of the Spratly Islands—Itu Aba. (Taiwan and the PRC generally shared the same attitude with regard to the South China Sea, and the PRC garrisons in the Spratlys received fresh water supplies from Taiwanese troops stationed on Itu Aba.) Within ASEAN, just to cite a few prominent examples, Vietnam and the Philippines occupied Amboyna Cay and Commodore Reef respectively, both claimed by Malaysia. Vietnam also occupied Barque Canada Reef, which was also claimed by Malaysia. Malaysia occupied Louisa Reef (Terembu Semarang), which Brunei also claimed. Of all the claimants, Brunei was the least active. Therein lay the complexity of the South China Sea issue. As Lee Kuan Yew noted, China's entry as a dominant claimant in the Spratlys "muted territorial quarrels between ASEAN states". ASEAN countries now felt the need to close ranks and negotiate together, "a natural defensive move".[124]

As ASEAN and Southeast Asia entered the new millennium, the association and the region faced multiple challenges that were vastly more complex and convoluted than those of the Cold War and early post-Cold War years.

[124] "East Asia Peace Hinges on Ties Between US, Japan, China", *Straits Times*, 15 May 1999.

CHAPTER 3

2000–06: Together into the New Millennium

> *"ASEAN must integrate to survive ... Asia has become a new focus for the great game of international relations ... However, we cannot take it for granted that this favourable state of affairs will persist. If ASEAN is disunited or ineffective, we will lose the privileged position of being courted by various players. Credibility begins from within."*[1]

> *"ASEAN must hang together or hang separately."*[2]

Post-Financial Crisis Introspection

ASEAN entered the new millennium blemished but still intact. Since the end of the Cold War, the association has been, in the words of Singapore diplomat Tommy Koh, "the driving force behind new ideas on cooperation and dialogue among the countries in East Asia".[3] This was possible because the association was able to stay united through the 1990s (despite the Asian Financial Crisis) and, perhaps more important, because the two dominant East Asian powers—China and Japan—could not cooperate. Whether ASEAN could remain in the driver's seat, and for how long, was (and still is) an open question. Peter Ho

[1] Prime Minister Lee Hsien Loong's ASEAN Day Lecture at the 40th anniversary celebrations of ASEAN. See "Asean: Still Attractive at 40", *Straits Times*, 8 Aug. 2007.
[2] "Reinventing ASEAN", *Straits Times*, 3 Nov. 2001.
[3] "Asean's Ideas the 'Driving Force' Within East Asia", *Straits Times*, 22 Feb. 2000.

provides perhaps the most succinct definition of "driver's seat": "it is a phrase used in ASEAN circles to mean that ASEAN is at the centre of the regional architecture and that it is setting the pace and leading the shaping of the regional agenda."[4] One thing was clear to all: If ASEAN wanted to be in the driver's seat in its expanding relations with other countries and the region, it would need to preserve its credibility as an organization.[5] At the start of the new millennium, the credibility quotient was rather low. It was a new ASEAN, no longer the ASEAN of the Cold War era, having become a full regional organization not too long ago. Political observers and analysts anticipated integration challenges given the differences in strategic culture and development level, amongst other factors, between the original and new members.

Another question was whether East Timor, which Jose Ramos-Horta described as "more or less on the borderline of Southeast Asia and the Pacific",[6] would eventually be the 11th member of ASEAN. As mentioned in chapter 2, East Timor had expressed its wish to join ASEAN after formal independence. At the start of the new millennium, the country was a UN-administered protectorate. The United Nations Transitional Administration in East Timor, tasked to help East Timor gain statehood, was expected to fulfil its mandate in May 2002. However, East Timor was not a priority issue when the ASEAN foreign ministers met for the first time in the new millennium.

What was foremost in the minds of the ASEAN leaders was how to ensure the ten Southeast Asian countries that made up ASEAN remain united and how ASEAN could retain its centrality in the international politics of the region, in short, recover the clout or shine it had lost because of the Asian Financial Crisis. Singapore Foreign Minister S. Jayakumar wondered why the region's quick recovery from the crisis did not translate into a "restoration of international confidence

[4] Ho, "Some Observations on the Security Architecture in Southeast Asia", chapter 17. For academic discussions on the meaning of being in the "driver's seat" or its equivalent term "ASEAN centrality", see Amitav Acharya, "The Myth of ASEAN Centrality?" *Contemporary Southeast Asia* 39, 2 (Aug. 2017): 273–9; See Seng Tan, "Rethinking 'ASEAN Centrality' in the Regional Governance of East Asia", *Singapore Economic Review* 63, 1 (2018), DOI: 10.1142/S0217590818400076.

[5] "Asean Bid to Build on Trade Ties", *Straits Times*, 30 Apr. 2001.

[6] "East Timor Seeks to Join Asean, S. Pacific Forum", *Straits Times*, 1 Aug. 2000.

in ASEAN".[7] The harshest description of ASEAN must have been that made by its secretary-general, Severino, who called it a "region whose economy had been weakened, its politics unstable, a region in disarray and rudderless", a self-criticism that no ASEAN minister challenged.[8]

As discussed earlier, the financial crisis as well as the expansion of the association forced the member states to be inward looking, strained the relationships of a number of member states, and led to a two-tier ASEAN. The unwillingness as well as inability of the member states to abandon the non-interference principle led to the introduction of the ASEAN Troika at the 33rd ASEAN Ministerial Meeting in July 2000 as a form of compromise. Thai Prime Minister Chuan Leekpai proposed the idea at the Third ASEAN Informal Summit in Manila on 28 November 1999. The ministerial-level troika (which would be chaired by whichever member state was the chair of the rotating ASEAN standing committee at that time) could initially be activated only with the consensus of all ASEAN members, but this was soon modified to empower the chair to activate the troika and to call an emergency meeting of ASEAN's ten foreign ministers.[9] In the words of Thai Foreign Minister Surin (who was the prime advocate of replacing the non-interference principle with flexible engagement—a euphemism for some kind of intervention in the domestic affairs of member states), "Non-interference is still the cardinal principle of ASEAN relations. It is going to remain but some issues will have to be redefined ... whether they are exclusively internal or they have potential for spilling over into neighbouring countries."[10] Jayakumar gave the example of the peace-keeping force for East Timor. If the troika mechanism had existed then, he argued, it could have been activated and ASEAN would have been able to quickly "pull our act together and liaise with the Secretary-

[7] "Regaining Asean's Lost Ground", *Straits Times*, 25 July 2000. Full text of remarks by Professor S. Jayakumar, Singapore minister for foreign affairs and law, at the 33rd ASEAN Ministerial Meeting, Bangkok, 24 July 2000.

[8] Rodolfo Severino quoted in "Asean Can Overcome Threat of Redundancy", *Straits Times*, 8 Aug. 2001.

[9] For a discussion of the limitations of the troika mechanism, see "Asean Sets up System to Promote Regional Peace", *Business Times*, 26 July 2000; "ASEAN Troika Given More Powers to Deal with Regional Security Matters", *The Nation*, 25 July 2000, *BBC/SWB/FE*/3902 B/2.

[10] "Asean Looks Set to Adopt Troika Plan", *Straits Times*, 24 July 2000.

General Kofi Annan" and avoid all the confusion.[11] In sum, the ASEAN Troika along with a "full-circle hotline" and increased frequency of ASEAN leaders meetings was thus the first of a series of strategies or measures ASEAN adopted in the new century to ensure it remained relevant on the international stage. The first retreat of the ASEAN foreign ministers not held in conjunction with the annual foreign ministers meeting took place in Yangon in April 2001.[12] Not everyone was persuaded that ASEAN had gone far enough to be relevant "not only to itself, but also to the outside world", dynamic and coherent.[13] Jayakumar described the troika as a "modest step".[14]

ASEAN Plus Three

Economics was never very far from the minds of Southeast Asian leaders. The strength and potential of their economies was a key factor in ASEAN's international image from the 1980s until 1997. It was also a key reason why the Indochina states chose to join ASEAN after the end of the Cold War. Despite the rather swift and impressive rebound of the economies of the countries affected by the Asian Financial Crisis, the annual report presented by ASEAN Secretary-General Severino revealed that foreign direct investment fell sharply in 1998–99 and did not return to the pre-crisis level. There was concern that the statistics "might bolster perceptions that their countries' economic recovery was at risk" and that if ASEAN continued to be seen as ineffective, it could

[11] Excerpts from Singapore Foreign Minister Prof. S. Jayakumar's remarks to the Singapore media at the close of the 33rd AMM/Seventh ARF/PMC meetings in Bangkok, 24–29 July 2000. For an account of the confusion leading to InterFET, see Surin, "How East Timor Reshaped ASEAN".

[12] "Asean Bid to Build on Trade Ties". The idea of an informal retreat was first tested in Singapore in 1999 and Bangkok in 2000. See also "Burmese, Vietnamese Foreign Ministers Hold News Conference on ASEAN Talks", *BBC Monitoring Global Newsline-Asia-Pacific Political*, 30 Apr. 2001.

[13] The Thai prime minister in his opening address at the 33rd AMM in Bangkok said, "Asean must evolve into a concert of relevance, dynamism and coherence—relevant not only to itself, but also to the outside world." See "Ties That Bind", *Far Eastern Economic Review*, 10 Aug. 2000. See also Jusuf Wanandi, "Asean's Future at Stake", *Straits Times*, 9 Aug. 2000.

[14] Excerpts from Jayakumar's remarks at the close of the 33rd AMM/7th ARF/PMC meetings in Bangkok.

be "marginalised" as a major trading partner.[15] Although economic integration was not the key issue on the agenda at the July 2000 ASEAN meeting, the leaders recognized that they "must respond to the decline in investment by speeding up economic integration". As Singapore Prime Minister Goh Chok Tong put it, "... image is reality in all too real a sense ... Size is not destiny, but unfortunately, FDI is, and ASEAN countries have little choice but to do what it takes to command their share."[16] Severino urged ASEAN "to maintain and strengthen" its commitment to the ASEAN Free Trade Area (AFTA) proposed at the 24th ASEAN Ministerial Meeting in 1991 and endorsed at the Fourth ASEAN Summit in 1992. The initial target year was 2008. In 1995 it was brought forward to 2003 and then to the beginning of 2002 in light of the financial crisis. The new members had between 2006 and 2010 to meet that goal.

The economic power was increasingly shifting towards Northeast Asia. Investors were looking away from Southeast Asia to Japan, South Korea, and particularly China, which was expected to join the World Trade Organization (WTO)—in Lee Kuan Yew's words, that would be a "watershed change"—in the not too distant future.[17] Indeed, some had predicted that the trend of FDI flows to China, which in 1999 had surpassed the total to all of ASEAN, would increase after China's entry into the WTO either at the end of 2001 or in early 2002.[18] In 2000 Hong Kong (which rejoined China in 1997) attracted four times the FDI of the ten ASEAN countries combined.[19] As one journalist put it, "While the Northeast is bubbling with excitement, post-Crisis

---

[15] "Investment in Southeast Asia Plunges", *International Herald Tribune*, 27 July 2000. Only Singapore showed a substantial rise in FDI in 1999. FDI in the region dropped from US$21.5 billion in 1997 to US$16.8 billion in 1998 and US$13.1 billion in 1999.

[16] "All Eyes on How Asean Can Restore Its Prestige", *Straits Times Interactive*, 22 Nov. 2000.

[17] "SM Lee Says Asean Must Get Its Act Together if It Must Cope with Other Challenges", CNBC (English), *Wall Street Journal Asia*, 24 Nov. 2000.

[18] "WTO Entry by China 'A Plus as Well as a Challenge'", *Straits Times*, 28 July 2001.

[19] "Big Investors Skipping Asean", *Straits Times*, 19 Sept. 2001. The year 2001 saw the sharpest decline in the GDP growth of ASEAN since its formation in 1967. See "Year Ender ASEAN Getting out of Low Ebb (Part 1)", *Xinhua News Agency*, 15 Dec. 2001.

Southeast Asia's image remains badly deflated."[20] What attracted much attention in July 2000 was the APT meeting—"the hottest topic in Southeast Asian policy circles".[21] The July meeting was the first formal meeting of the group to "discuss economic cooperation and ways to improve political stability in East Asia"[22] since its inaugural and informal meeting in December 1997. The APT had been described as "a dying ASEAN's new lifeline", and it was believed that "hitching its wagon to the 'plus three' could be the solution to its deepest woes".[23] In Michael Leifer's analysis, the initial significance of the APT seemed to be economic as a "reaction to the failure of APEC and the United States to respond effectively enough to the regional economic crisis" (as discussed in chapter 2).

The July 2000 meeting seemed to show that ASEAN was "looking to some wider East Asian grouping as a way of giving the Association a greater sense of substance and credibility, particularly in terms of speaking with a collective voice". That was the upside. The downside of this initiative was that it showed up "the limitations of ASEAN and the fact that ASEAN has been obliged to go outside of its Southeast Asian membership in the case of ASEAN Plus Three", just as in the case of the ASEAN Regional Forum, "in order to try and count collectively in the wider world".[24] In November 2000 it was reported that a study would be conducted to explore the possibility of developing the APT process into "some kind of an East Asian summit ... to evolve an East Asian community". According to Singaporean Prime Minister Goh, "the Northeast Asians are talking about an East Asian community and the Asean members are also beginning to nurture such an idea ..."[25] Goh predicted that it could take as long as ten to 20 years "to have firmer trust with one another to have a stable platform for future growth".[26]

---

[20] Alejandro Reyes, "Southeast Asia Adrift", *Asiaweek*, 1 Sept. 2000.

[21] Ibid.

[22] "The Grouping's 'To-Do' List", *Straits Times*, 26 July 2000.

[23] Reyes, "Southeast Asia Adrift".

[24] Interview with Michael Leifer, BBC London, *East Asia Today*, 25 July 2000. See also interview with Robert Templer (Strategic Intelligence), BBCTV (English), *Asia Business Report*, 22 Nov. 2000; "North-east Asia's Challenge", *Business Times*, 28 Nov. 2000.

[25] "PM Goh Sees Merit in Developing Asean Plus Three into East Asian Summit", TV3 (English), *Nightline*, 26 Nov. 2000. See also "North-east Asia's Challenge".

[26] "PM Says Asean Must Pull Its Act Together", *Straits Times*, 17 Jan. 2001.

The fear of a widening gap between Northeast Asia and Southeast Asia, resulting in ASEAN becoming a "marginal group within Asia", was a real concern. Once marginalized, Southeast Asia would become an "Asian backwater".[27] To prevent this, ASEAN had to first integrate all its member economies—"integration" became a commonly heard word for much of the 2000s. ASEAN leaders had identified integration as a priority goal; then moving into an East Asian Community with Japan, China and South Korea; and finally creating an East Asia Free Trade Area. If an East Asia Free Trade Area was not possible, then "there should at least be closer economic cooperation" between the three Northeast Asian countries and ASEAN, "with the latter benefitting from the growth in the North East". That was the ASEAN game plan, from the Singapore perspective. Goh revealed that he had initiated the idea of a Japan-Singapore Free Trade Area (FTA) with the late Japanese Prime Minister Keizai Obuchi in December 1999 "as a catalyst to seek changes to the Japanese economy as a result of an FTA with another country".[28]

With one eye on the APT and China, ASEAN's other eye was on the United States. Southeast Asia had not been a priority region for Washington since the end of the Cold War, and it dropped further in priority during the Asian Financial Crisis. That said, it is worth noting that in January 1998 Washington and Manila negotiated a Visiting Forces Agreement; Thailand remained an "important refuelling and transit point"; and Singapore, described as "Southeast Asia's leading advocate of a continued US military presence", in early 1998 announced that Changi Naval Base would become operational in the year 2000.[29] The military/defence sector aside, there is a general acknowledgement, including by the Americans (on hindsight, at least), that, in the words of Kurt M. Campbell (American assistant secretary of state for East Asian and Pacific affairs, 2009–13), "as the Cold War ended, and threat of Soviet hegemony in Asia disappeared, US policy in Asia was set adrift". There were concerns over "American purpose going forward", and "both the United States and its allies were in search of a rationale

---

[27] Singapore Trade and Industry Minister George Yeo quoted in "S'pore, KL 'Can Help Push Asean Forward'", *Straits Times*, 4 Mar. 2001.

[28] "PM Says Asean Must Pull Its Act Together".

[29] See "The United States Security Strategy for the East Asia-Pacific Region (EASR)", http://www.dod.gov/pubs/easr98/easr98.pdf, accessed 9 Nov. 2016.

for strategic cooperation in an uncertain period very different from the Cold War".[30]

Goh urged Washington "to work with Asean to ensure that its interests are taken into account as the process of greater East Asian cooperation evolves". He warned, "There was a danger if both sides took their relationship for granted, their ties would weaken through complacency and neglect".[31] One reason for this persistent interest in the United States was the region's fear of China, despite Chinese Foreign Minister Tang Jiaxuan's assurance (echoed by successive Chinese foreign ministers) that Beijing was ready to work with everyone to promote "prosperity and development in the Asia-Pacific" and advance "the cause of peace and progress for mankind".[32] As Yang Razali Kassim noted, ASEAN, for economic reasons, had so far "suppressed their latent anxieties about the security and military impact of Beijing's rise as an economic juggernaut ... Asean's dilemma is that it cannot treat China as a friend in trade and economics, but a foe in diplomatic and security relations."[33] ASEAN Secretary-General Severino put on a brave front when he said that he did not see it as a dilemma: "It is inevitable that China gains in strength economically and politically. The way Asean handles this is to form strong relationships with China. *That's the only way to go* [emphasis added]."[34]

A flurry of visits in August 2001 by the newly appointed leaders of Indonesia, the Philippines and Thailand—the founding member states of ASEAN—gave the impression and hope that the ASEAN countries were finally ready to look beyond domestic politics in the aftermath of the financial crisis and come together to restore the group's credibility. Perhaps most significant was the introductory visit to ASEAN countries by Indonesian President Megawati Sukarnoputri, who succeeded Abdurrahman Wahid after he was dismissed by the People's Consultative Assembly in July. The Indonesian foreign minister did not attend the

[30] Kurt M. Campbell, *The Pivot: The Future of American Statecraft in Asia* (New York: Twelve, 2016), pp. 144–5.
[31] "PM Warns Against Taking US-Asean Ties for Granted", *Straits Times*, 8 Sept. 2000.
[32] *Xinhua News Agency Domestic Service*, Beijing, in Chinese, 26 July 2001.
[33] "Asean Must Get Its Act Together Vis-à-vis China", *Business Times*, 24 July 2001.
[34] Ibid.

annual ASEAN meetings in July because of the political crisis at home. Dewi Fortuna Anwar (assistant minister/state secretary for foreign affairs during the Habibie administration, 1998–99) described Megawati's visit as "a very important signal that Indonesia is back in business. Asean has long been a cornerstone of Indonesia's foreign policy, which took a slide under Abdurrahman Wahid."[35] Lee Kuan Yew noted, "With Indonesia refocusing its efforts on Asean, the organisation's cohesion and international standing will improve."[36] Also making their introductory visits were President Gloria Arroyo of the Philippines, who succeeded Joseph Estrada after he was ousted in a popular uprising known as EDSA II in January 2001; and Thai Prime Minister Thaksin Shinawatra, who succeeded Chuan Leekpai in February 2001. Like Dewi Fortuna Anwar, the new leaders of the Philippines and Thailand also spoke of their aim to focus on and revitalize ASEAN.[37]

Even Malaysian Prime Minister Mahathir Mohamad, despite the poor relationship between his country and Singapore in the aftermath of the financial crisis, made a quick visit to Singapore on 10 September 2001, when he and Senior Minister Lee Kuan Yew both received the ASEAN Achievement Millennium Award, the annual award given by the ASEAN Business Forum. Mahathir in his acceptance speech spoke of the importance of ASEAN. Recounting how ASEAN was formed "to discuss largely the problems of managing relations between newly independent nations whose historical backgrounds were rather different", he noted:

> [T]he differences are still there but they have not hindered cooperation on economic matters and even on certain aspects of international politics. Much remains to be done but there is little doubt that ASEAN is a very real grouping that has benefitted the members in their dealings with each other and the rest of the world.[38]

---

[35] "Trips by Asean Leaders to Restore Group's Credibility", *Straits Times*, 18 Aug. 2001.

[36] Speech by Senior Minister Lee Kuan Yew at the ASEAN Business Forum's conferment of the ASEAN Achievement Millennium Awards, Singapore, 10 Sept. 2001.

[37] "Trips by Asean Leaders to Restore Group's Credibility".

[38] Speech by Dato' Seri Dr Mahathir bin Mohamad (Prime Minister) at the ASEAN Business Forum's conferment of the ASEAN Achievement Millennium Awards, Singapore, 10 Sept. 2001.

Despite their well-known disagreements over "most" issues,[39] both Lee and Mahathir in their respective speeches drew attention to the significance of ASEAN and the group's "capacity to recover". According to Lee:

> [R]ecent developments are promising. Indonesia has a steady president with a professional cabinet. The uncertainties over the government of Thailand have been dispelled by PM Thaksin being acquitted by the constitutional court. President Arroyo has consolidated her position and the situation in the Philippines is more stable. In Malaysia, PM Dr Mahathir is clearly in command.[40]

September 11 and Aftermath

Lee Kuan Yew's and Mahathir's speeches on 10 September 2001 covered the challenges of ASEAN and the region but did not contain a word about or reference to terrorism. There were also hardly any significant reports regarding terrorism in the newspapers in the months leading up to September. Two Asia-wide polls conducted in 2001 and reported in May and September showed that Asians were worried about the state of US-China relations and the economic slowdown. The report, published on the eve of 9/11, noted that the economic slowdown was the most significant threat to regional security.[41] Terrorist activities were, of course, not unknown in Southeast Asia, but they had been confined mainly within the territorial boundaries of the individual countries, and presumably the authorities believed that they were in control of things and terrorism was not an imminent threat. For example, before 9/11, the Thai military described the disgruntled Muslims in southern Thailand as "trouble-makers" rather than terrorists.[42]

---

[39] "Malaysia's Mahathir Mourns Singapore's 'Strong Leader' Lee", http://news.asiaone.com/news/singapore/malaysias-mahathir-mourns-singapores-strong-leader-lee, accessed 9 Jan. 2017.

[40] Speech by Senior Minister Lee Kuan Yew at the ASEAN Business Forum's conferment of the ASEAN Achievement Millennium Awards; Speech by Dato' Seri Dr Mahathir bin Mohamad (Prime Minister) at the ASEAN Business Forum's conferment of the ASEAN Achievement Millennium Awards.

[41] "Asians Generally Optimistic About Region's Future, but Two Worries Crop Up", *Straits Times*, 28 May 2001; "Asia's Top Threat: The Economy", *Straits Times*, 10 Sept. 2001.

[42] "Thai Soldiers See Southern Muslims as Trouble-makers", *Straits Times*, 13 Apr. 2001.

This changed after 11 September 2001 (9/11), with the aerial destruction of the twin towers of the World Trade Center in New York by members of Al Qaeda, a militant Sunni multinational organization founded in 1998 by, most prominently, Osama bin Laden.[43] The event reminded Americans of the Japanese sneak attack in December 1941 on Pearl Harbor but with many more casualties. There has been so much written on the subject of global terrorism, especially since 9/11—and the literature continues to grow—that the following will focus only on the Southeast Asian dimension and matters that impact Southeast Asia.[44]

Soon after 9/11, evidence emerged that there was a Southeast Asian extension of Al Qaeda known as Jemaah Islamiyah (JI). Though JI had "a regional agenda", it was "an important cog in the Al Qaeda network". Between December 2001 and August 2002, the Singapore, Malaysia and Philippine authorities arrested a number of JI members for planning attacks in their respective countries and beyond. The Singapore cell was the "major operational unit of the Southeast Asian JI network, tasked with planning and coordinating attacks"; the Philippine cell was the logistics hub; and the Malaysian cell, which was the largest, was everything rolled into one as well as the "major conduit between JI and Al Qaeda in Afghanistan".[45] Given that Indonesia has the largest Muslim population in the world, it is not surprising that a lot of attention was focused on the extent of Al Qaeda penetration into the country, especially after Singapore's and Kuala Lumpur's swift and successful action to sever the network in their countries. As Zachary Abuza noted, "many JI members fled to Indonesia where the JI network has consolidated its position and expanded".[46] This was also because the Indonesian authorities were slow to acknowledge the existence of the JI network in the country and the terrorist threat emanating from Indonesia, even though the Indonesian cleric Abu Bakar Bashir was exposed to be a

[43] A third plane deliberately crashed into the Pentagon and damaged part of the western side of the building.

[44] The following account is summarized from various sources, in particular: Zachary Abuza, "Tentacles of Terror: Al Qaeda's Southeast Asian Network", *Contemporary Southeast Asia* 24, 2 (Dec. 2002): 427–65; Kumar Ramakrishna and See Seng Tan (eds), *After Bali: The Threat of Terrorism in Southeast Asia* (Singapore: World Scientific, 2003).

[45] See Abuza, "Tentacles of Terror": 427–46.

[46] Ibid.: 456.

leader—if not the leader—of the JI network. Singapore and Malaysian authorities expressed "tremendous frustration" over Indonesia's lack of cooperation in dismantling the terrorist network.[47] For example, Senior Minister Lee Kuan Yew's comment that the masterminds behind the arrested JI operatives in Singapore were still moving freely in Indonesia angered the Indonesians, who accused Lee of interference and making unsubstantiated statements.[48]

Critics of ASEAN such as David Jones and Mike Smith pointed out that the organization's "rigid adherence" to the non-interference principle "seems particularly complaisant given the exposure of a sophisticated terror network" and "significantly, ASEAN had failed to recognise the forces of jihad in its midst".[49] It was, however, not just the Southeast Asian states that had failed; the Bush administration had not foreseen the imminent danger either. As David Rothkopf recounted, during the transitional US National Security Council briefings in January 2001, outgoing National Security Adviser Sandy Berger had told his successor, Condoleezza Rice, that the Bush administration would spend more time on terrorism and Al Qaeda in particular "than any other subject". There was a counterterrorism plan drawn up, but according to Richard Clarke (the chief counterterrorism adviser on the National Security Council during the Clinton administration, who also served under the Bush administration) it was "placed on the slow track" as the Bush foreign policy team educated themselves about Al Qaeda and where it fitted into US foreign policy. Indeed, after the end of the Cold War the United States showed little interest in Afghanistan and its Taliban leadership.[50] This changed almost immediately after 9/11. The United States attacked Afghanistan in October 2001 and

---

[47] Ibid.: 458–9.

[48] "Asean Talks Focus on Anti-terror Measures", *Straits Times*, 22 Feb. 2002.

[49] David Martin Jones and Mike L. Smith, "The Strange Death of the ASEAN Way", *Australian Financial Review*, 12 Apr. 2002, pp. 4–8. See also "Editorial: Security the Priority", *South China Morning Post*, 16 Jan. 2002. The editorial noted, "the threat of global terrorism has highlighted Southeast Asia's inability to tackle regional security problems". The predominantly Muslim populations of some countries, ASEAN's lack of cohesion, and the non-interference policy were cited as reasons.

[50] David Rothkopf, *Running the World: The Inside Story of the National Security Council and the Architects of American Power* (New York: Public Affairs, 2005), pp. 42–30.

subsequently invaded Iraq in 2003 as part of its global war on terror. The question of whether the two wars were justified and the controversies surrounding both wars need not delay us here. What is relevant to this study is the Southeast Asian response and, connected to this, US-Southeast Asia relations.

The key ASEAN states had finally found the political will to move forward in the new millennium. The fallout of 9/11 and the discovery of the global terrorism network in Southeast Asia threatened to derail ASEAN's efforts to "reinvent" itself after the Asian Financial Crisis, to paraphrase the title of a book published by the Institute of Southeast Asian Studies (Singapore) in November 2001.[51] The press statement issued at the end of the Seventh ASEAN Summit in Brunei the same month noted, "in the current climate of intense global uncertainty, Southeast Asia faces its biggest, if not the biggest, challenge" since 1967. It went on to say, "the two fold challenge of addressing a severe world economic slowdown while contributing to international efforts to combat terrorism is without precedent. Moreover, this new challenge has emerged as many of us were just starting to recover from the financial shocks of 1997 and 1998."[52]

Speakers at the launch of the book *Reinventing ASEAN* (Tay et al. 2001) were unanimous in their concern that domestic politics would hinder ASEAN's ability to respond strongly, as "three members are Muslim countries, while three others, including Singapore, have sizeable Muslims populations".[53] Despite this, the relevant countries were able to manage domestic reactions to the US military operations in Afghanistan.

---

[51] Simon S.C. Tay, Jesus P. Estanislao and Hadi Soesastro (eds), *Reinventing ASEAN* (Singapore: Institute of Southeast Asian Studies, 2001).

[52] Press Statement by the Chairman of the Seventh ASEAN Summit and the Fifth ASEAN+3 Summit, Brunei Darussalam, 5 Nov. 2001.

[53] "Reinventing ASEAN", *Straits Times*, 3 Nov. 2001. The issue of terrorism in Southeast Asia is more complex than some make it out to be. Giovanna Dell'Orto in *AP Correspondents in Action: World War II to the Present* (Cambridge: Cambridge University Press, 2016), pp. 56–7, notes how Indonesian terrorism was often misunderstood as the media struggled "to be willing to see it as something other than just al-Qaida and this is all linked to 9/11". See also John T. Sidel, "Other Schools, Other Pilgrimages, Other Dreams: The Making and Unmaking of Jihad in Southeast Asia", in *Southeast Asia over Three Generations*, ed. James T. Siegel and Audrey R. Kahin (Ithaca: Southeast Asia Program, Cornell University, 2003), pp. 347–81.

At the Seventh ASEAN Summit in Brunei in November 2001, the organization issued a Declaration on Joint Action to Counter Terrorism that "unequivocally condemn in the strongest terms" the terrorist attack on 11 September. The declaration labelled terrorism as a "direct challenge to the attainment of peace, progress and prosperity of ASEAN and the realisation of ASEAN Vision 2020" and pledged "all cooperative efforts to combat terrorism ..." The ASEAN Declaration notably rejected "any attempt to link terrorism with any religion or race".[54] Declaration aside, the general view was that ASEAN was slow to forge collective action against cross-border terrorism in the aftermath of 9/11 and consequently investors were shying away from the region.[55] As Singapore's high commissioner to Malaysia said, "Asean countries face a disastrous economic future if they fail to succeed in the fight against terrorism ... Already facing the strain of having to compete with China, it would be a sad day if Asean investments flow away in search of safer haven."[56]

Combating terrorism is not simply a matter of preventing attacks. That, of course, is an important aspect, but counterterrorism also encompasses issues such as money laundering, drug trafficking, cybercrime and other transnational crimes. It also requires "new approaches" in the way ASEAN states conduct their diplomatic ties with each other, according to Malaysian diplomat Razali Ismail (UN secretary-general's special envoy to Myanmar, 2000–05). Razali Ismail noted that although the policy of constructive engagement remained a sensitive issue within ASEAN, there had been "an intellectual shift" within the organization concerning counterterrorism.[57] Singapore's Deputy Prime Minister Lee Hsien Loong said at the Third ASEAN Ministerial Meeting on transnational crime, "Asean's efforts to deal with various forms of transnational crime ... will demonstrate the organisation's determination to work as a group and with the international community to enhance stability and security in the region and elsewhere." This, in turn, "would

[54] 2001 ASEAN Declaration on Joint Action to Counter Terrorism, Bandar Seri Begawan, 5 Nov. 2001.

[55] "Editorial: Asean Needs to Fight Terrorism Together", *Bangkok Post*, 23 Feb. 2002; "Unity Against Terrorism", *New Straits Times*, 24 Feb. 2002.

[56] "Failure to Fight Terrorism Could Be Disastrous for Asean Economy", Bernama, The Malaysian News Agency, 5 Apr. 2002.

[57] "Change Approaches in Dealing with Asean, Malaysia Urged", *New Straits Times*, 6 Apr. 2002.

strengthen international confidence in Asean, and help member countries to pick up the pieces from the Asian crisis and the current economic downturn, and work towards greater growth and prosperity".[58] The younger Lee acknowledged that conditions were difficult given that most ASEAN states were facing significant problems of their own, particularly Indonesia. The expansion of ASEAN to ten members added to the complexity. The Indochinese countries and Myanmar would "take a while to re-establish a common sense of purpose and vision". There were differences not just in the level of development in the various countries but also in the "approach to the global environment", as well as how each member state chose to "fit in" and "move forward". In his view, it would "take some time for Asean to recover its thrust".[59]

Between 9/11 and 12 October 2002, when the Bali bombing occurred, the ASEAN states—while taking preventive actions and generally cognizant about the international terrorism threat—on the whole perceived terrorism as "a continuing low-level threat that must be managed" but "not the defining (not even the most significant) security issue".[60] After all, there had been no successful terrorist attack by Al Qaeda and its affiliates in Southeast Asia so far. As Jim Roffe observed, "ASEAN states appreciate the US domestic and emotional impacts of terror, and are prepared to assist the United States in the war on terrorism, but they are agnostic to its present strategic necessity and sceptical as to its ultimate effectiveness."[61] This attitude changed after the bombing that destroyed two nightclubs and killed 202 Australian tourists in Bali on 12 October 2002. The tragedy "shattered an era of relative tranquillity in East Asia"[62] and "riveted international attention on the threat of radical Islamist terrorism in Southeast Asia".[63] The Bali

[58] "Close Ranks Against Terrorism: BG Lee", *Business Times*, 12 Oct. 2001.

[59] "DPM BG Lee Comments on Singapore's Opposition and Asean's Challenges", BBCTV (English), *Asia Today*, 8 Nov. 2001.

[60] See Jim Roffe, "Security in Southeast Asia: It's Not About the War on Terrorism", *Asia-Pacific Security Studies* 1, 3 (May 2002): 1–4.

[61] Ibid.: 2.

[62] Mark Hong, "A Turning Point for East Asia", *Straits Times Interactive*, 24 Oct. 2002.

[63] See Kumar Ramakrishna, "Terrorism in Southeast Asia: The Ideological and Political Dimensions", *Southeast Asian Affairs 2004* (Singapore: Institute of Southeast Asian Studies, 2004), pp. 54–9.

bombing was the first of a series of attacks in Indonesia and the Philippines that culminated in the bombing of the JW Marriott Hotel in Jakarta, which killed 11 people and injured 150 on 5 August 2003. JI was responsible for both the Bali and Jakarta bombings, and very quickly Southeast Asia became known as a "terrorist haven".[64]

Perhaps the most important development arising from 9/11 was its effect on the course of US-Southeast Asia relations. The Southeast Asian states felt that Washington was not paying sufficient attention to their region compared to during the Cold War years, and diplomatic efforts were made to persuade and remind the United States that the post-Cold War challenges required "greater cooperation between the US and ASEAN at the bilateral, regional and even global level".[65] When Singapore's Prime Minister Goh Chok Tong made that remark, he did not expect that it would take the tragedy of 9/11 to refocus US attention on the region, especially after the Bali and Jakarta bombings in 2002, when Southeast Asia became increasingly seen as the second front in the war against global terrorism. As James A. Kelly (US assistant secretary of state for East Asian and Pacific affairs) said, at the top of the US list of policy priorities was "waging the war against terror, a threat that respects no national border, but is most dangerous in Southeast Asia".[66]

The changed US attitude towards Malaysia and Indonesia, both considered moderate Muslim states, best illustrated the United States' renewed interest in Southeast Asia. The United States had been very critical of Mahathir's human rights record and his treatment of his deputy Anwar Ibrahim. The Malaysian court has since found Anwar guilty of sodomy. Anwar's supporters (who included some Western leaders) believed that the charges were politically motivated. US Vice President Al Gore infamously walked out of a dinner hosted by Mahathir as a gesture of support for Anwar during the APEC Summit of 1998. Also before 9/11, Washington considered Indonesia a pariah

---

[64] Ibid., p. 54.

[65] "PM Warns Against Taking US-ASEAN Ties for Granted".

[66] "An Overview of US-East Asia Policy", James A. Kelly, assistant secretary of state for East Asian and Pacific affairs, Testimony before the House Relations Committee, Washington DC, 2 June 2004, https://2001-2009.state.gov/p/eap/rls/rm/2004/33064.htm, accessed 19 Jan. 2017.

state because of the human rights abuses committed by the Indonesian military in East Timor. However, in May 2002 President George Bush met with Mahathir in Washington, and Kelly described Malaysia as "a beacon of stability" that "plays an important role in the global war on terror". Malaysia was one of the countries that "contributed support ranging from overflight, access and basing to escort, logistics, and troops on the ground" in Operation Enduring Freedom (the US war in Afghanistan).[67]

US Deputy Secretary of Defence Paul Wolfowitz was reportedly keen to expedite the resumption of a training programme for Indonesian military officers that had been cancelled because of the atrocities committed in East Timor.[68] The International Education and Training programme resumed in 2002. As one analysis noted, the significance of Mahathir's visit, his first meeting with a US president in Washington since 1994,

> lies not just in what it conveys about the appreciable warming of bilateral ties between Kuala Lumpur and Washington since September 11. The trip also serves to illustrate the more significant international profile now carried by the region as a whole with US policymakers and other powers. After years in the doldrums following the regional financial crisis, the stock of the 10-member Association of Southeast Asian Nations is again on the rise.[69]

Even Yangon allowed United States planes en route to Afghanistan to overfly Myanmar.[70] After 9/11, the United States and the Philippines enhanced their defence cooperation aimed at combating terrorism. The

---

[67] "US Security Policy in Asia and the Pacific: Restructuring America's Forward Deployment", Hearing before the Subcommittee on Asia and the Pacific of the Committee on International Relations, House of Representatives, 108th Congress, 26 June 2003, p. 38.

[68] "Asean Back in Spotlight as Big Players Come A-wooing", *Straits Times*, 26 Apr. 2002.

[69] "Turning Tide Brings Asean out from Spell in Backwaters", *South China Morning Post*, 3 May 2002; Pamela Sodhy, "US-Malaysian Relations During the Bush Administration: The Political, Economic and Security Aspects", *Contemporary Southeast Asia* 25, 3 (2003): 363–86.

[70] Robert H. Taylor, *Ne Win: A Political Biography* (Singapore: Institute of Southeast Asian Studies, 2015).

United States and ASEAN signed an anti-terrorism pact (ASEAN-US Declaration on Cooperation to Combat International Terrorism) in July 2002. Washington would provide technical and financial aid to ASEAN, including logistics and training. There would also be greater cooperation and sharing of intelligence. Some analysts were of the view that the United States benefited the most from this pact, which gave Washington "an intelligence military edge", while the benefits for the region were "debatable".[71]

The 9/11 event apparently led Washington to pay more attention to Southeast Asia. At the APEC Summit in 2002, President Bush announced the Enterprise for ASEAN Initiative (EAI), the objective of which was "to create a network of bilateral FTAs" which would increase trade and investment amongst them. Under the EAI, the United States and individual ASEAN countries would jointly determine when they were ready for FTA negotiations. Nobody expected a free trade pact between ASEAN and the US in the near future. As US Trade Representative Robert Zoellick said, a free trade pact was far in the future and it was "far too premature to talk about roadmaps".[72] Nevertheless, the EAI was a small step forward.

We often hear that 9/11 changed everything. This was true from the American perspective. Woolcott noted that during his encounters with Southeast Asian and American officials, he was "struck by the different perspectives on the war on terrorism". In Washington, he noted "an unquestioning moral preoccupation". In Southeast Asia, while the governments "supported the war on terrorism in principle, they were not as preoccupied with it as the United States … High on their agenda was how to respond to the growing strength of China as well as dealing with their domestic problems." Kuala Lumpur and Jakarta in particular were of the view that the American wars in Afghanistan and Iraq posed "a greater danger than terrorism itself". The Americans may have been winning militarily, but they were not winning "regional public

[71] "Asean Agrees on Pact with US to Fight Terrorism", *Straits Times*, 27 July 2002; "US, ASEAN in Pact to Combat Regional Terrorism", *Australian Financial Review*, 2 Aug. 2002; "Double-Edged Deal", *South China Morning Post*, 2 Aug. 2002.

[72] "Bush Announces Trade Initiative with ASEAN", *Kyodo News*, 27 Oct. 2002; "Asean-US Free Trade Pact Still a Long Way Off", *Straits Times Interactive*, 6 Apr. 2002.

opinion"[73] and, most important, not defeating the ideology. Both Kuala Lumpur and Jakarta opposed the American war with Iraq that started in March 2003. Mahathir was particularly critical of the invasion.

Soon after 9/11, in October 2001, John Chipman (director of the International Institute for Strategic Studies) declared that a "new strategic era has dawned". He predicted (and accurately so) that there would come "a point at which the campaign against terrorism becomes routine, part of the sinews of international relations" and "like the Cold War, the campaign will be punctuated by special crises, and hot conflicts, yet characterised by a long, determined effort to ensure victory". The main difference would be that "with a hard-to-find enemy, the new battle will be even harder to win than the Cold War".[74] We will return to the issue of terrorism and the evolution of the terrorist threat in chapter 8.

Towards Greater ASEAN Integration

Counterterrorism aside, the focus of ASEAN for the next five years (2003–08) was how to bring about greater regional integration, which many believed would be a very challenging task.[75] One key area was AFTA. According to the noted Japanese financial analyst Kiyoshi Hasegawa (Singapore president of *Nihon Keizai Shimbun*), AFTA "must work if Asean is to survive the growing economic might of China".[76] Indeed, Singapore's Trade and Industry Minister George Yeo noted that ASEAN member states found it easier to invest and trade with China than amongst themselves because "we have been too leisurely in our internal liberalisation process".[77] The adoption of the "10 minus X" principle in certain areas was described as a break from the ASEAN tradition. The objective was "to speed up market-opening and keep up with growing competition from powerhouses like China". It was a positive start given that the pace of economic integration, according

[73] The above is from Woolcott, *Hot Seat*, pp. 298–300.
[74] "New World Order Is in the Making", *Straits Times*, 20 Oct. 2001.
[75] "S'porean 'To Be Next Secretary-General'", *Straits Times*, 6 June 2002.
[76] "Analyst Stresses Need for Asean to Integrate in Meeting Threat from China", *Radio Australia* (English), Correspondent's Report, 7 July 2002.
[77] "Landmark Agreement on Asean Trade Plan", *Straits Times*, 7 July 2002.

to outgoing Secretary-General Severino, had slowed and the member states were hazy on what form of integration ASEAN should aim for.[78] At the Eighth ASEAN Summit in November 2002, Singapore's Prime Minister Goh Chok Tong proposed the establishment of the ASEAN Economic Community (AEC) by 2020. The proposal was strongly supported by Thai Prime Minister Thaksin Shinawatra. It was described as "a logical extension of the Asean Free Trade Area".[79] (It was agreed that the original five ASEAN members would work towards eliminating import tariffs by 2010, and the new members by 2015.) Severino, however criticized Asean as lacking direction and being "stuck in framework agreements, work programmes and master plans".[80] Critics pointed out that it was much easier for Singapore to push free trade agreements and a common market, as it was a small and open economy and had more to gain than lose compared to other Southeast Asia countries. Other obstacles towards a common market included competition between member states, such as Malaysia and Singapore; the different levels of development amongst member states, such as Singapore and Laos; and Indonesia's sluggish economy and political problems.

Following up on its proposal made in 2001 at the Eighth ASEAN Summit, China signed a framework agreement with ASEAN to work towards a free trade pact by 2010. Japan proposed an ASEAN-Japan Economic Partnership. India, too, in its first summit meeting with ASEAN offered to negotiate a free trade area with ASEAN.[81] Australia and New Zealand also expressed interest in forming closer formal economic links with ASEAN. The ball was now in ASEAN's court. The question was whether these initiatives, and the US-proposed EAI,

[78] "ASEAN Breaks with Tradition to Liberalise Markets", *Reuters News*, 6 July 2002; "A Slow and Wobbly Club", *Today*, 6 Nov. 2002.

[79] "Singapore Plan for Single Asean Market", *Straits Times*, 5 Nov. 2002. For an early analysis of the AEC proposal (which was not elaborated on at the ASEAN Summit), see Denis Hew, "Towards an ASEAN Economic Community by 2020: Vision or Reality", *ISEAS Viewpoints*, 16 June 2003. In Hew's words, "at the end of the day, it could very well be the political dimensions of forming an economic community that would pose the greatest challenge for ASEAN".

[80] "A Slow and Wobbly Club".

[81] ASEAN and India signed a framework agreement to begin formal negotiations to set up a free trade area (Asean-India Regional Trade and Investment Area) within ten years in November 2003.

would compel the region to overcome the obstacles and inertia. As Ong Keng Yong, who succeeded Severino as ASEAN's secretary-general in 2003, said on his inauguration, "given the very strong potential for economic growth in East Asia and South Asia, if we don't put ourselves on the radar scope of investors and businessmen, by default people would just go to Northeast Asia and South Asia".[82] It was clear that under his five-year tenure as secretary-general, the focus would be on strengthening economic ties within ASEAN and doing so in "an integrated manner, and not in a way where some countries grow quickly while others languish behind". "Instead of simply competing against each other, Asean countries need to combine resources to get investors in to the region as a whole," he added.[83]

After Singapore's proposal of the AEC in November 2002, during the ASEAN Foreign Ministers informal summit in Phnom Penh in June 2003 Jakarta planted the idea of an ASEAN Security Community (ASC) by 2020. Indonesian Foreign Minister Hassan Wirayuda said that the ASC would be Jakarta's "main agenda" when it assumed the rotating chair of ASEAN at the Ninth ASEAN Summit in Bali in October. The ASC was to be a defence pact to prevent regional disputes from escalating into armed conflict. Rizal Sukma (then a security analyst at the Centre for Strategic and International Studies, Indonesia, who played a role in conceptualizing the idea) said, "A security pact would enhance economic partnership and integration in the region." He added that "since the 1997 economic crisis, Asean has been floating without a clear sense of purpose" and therefore working towards achieving the "condition" of a security community will allow the grouping to be "more cohesive".[84]

Both the AEC and ASC, if achieved, would certainly benefit ASEAN. The AEC, according to the economist Rahul Sen, would "provide a combined market of 500 million people and provide greater market access and investment opportunities for businesses with Asean ... The combined market would also be more attractive for foreign

[82] "At the Helm: Ong Starts as Asean Chief", *Today*, 1 Jan. 2003.

[83] "New Asean Chief Calls for Closer Economic Ties", *Straits Times*, 7 Jan. 2003.

[84] "Jakarta to Moot Asean Security Community", *Straits Times*, 21 July 2003. For a discussion of ASEAN as a "security community", see Amitav Acharya, "Asean Needs New Tools for New Threats", *Straits Times*, 6 Apr. 2003; Leonard C. Sebastian and Chong Ja Ian, "Towards an Asean Security Community", *Straits Times*, 7 Oct. 2003.

investors."[85] As for the ASC, Amitav Acharya (deputy director of the Institute of Defence and Strategic Studies) noted that two concepts had to be closely linked and that it was a chicken-and-egg situation of which should come first. There could not be an economic community without a security community: "If you have conflicts and warlike situations between states, you can't have economic cooperation."[86] Logic aside, Jakarta did not have enthusiastic support from its fellow ASEAN members. Barry Wain reported that even though the member states accepted the general principles of the ASC, Jakarta's "energetic promotion" of the ASC was perceived as "a blatant and unacceptable bid to reassert itself over the rest of the region".[87]

At the Ninth ASEAN Summit in Bali in October 2003, in the typical ASEAN give-and-take way, the organization committed to working towards not only establishing the AEC by 2020 but the ASC and the ASEAN Socio-Cultural Community (ASCC) as well. These were the three pillars of the ASEAN Community.[88] The ASC, in particular, attracted considerable attention from political observers and questions from journalists. Ong's reply was that "most of us agreed that progress had to be made on two legs, not one. We can't have economic integration without a secure Southeast Asia."[89] In August 2004, the original five ASEAN members brought forward the AFTA deadline from 2010 to 2007 and the four new members from 2015 to 2012. The deadline for achieving the AEC was advanced from 2020 to 2015 at the ASEAN Summit in December 2005.

Meanwhile, Jakarta's proposal of an ASEAN Peacekeeping Force (a component of the ASC), described by the political scientist Paul Evans as "an important aspiration" albeit "perplexing operationally", was politely rejected as an idea ahead of its time.[90] In summary, the central focus of ASEAN, particularly since the 1996 financial crisis, was ASEAN integration. Writing in December 2004, former ASEAN

[85] "Productive Sentosa Retreat for Leaders", *Straits Times*, 9 Sept. 2003.
[86] "Asean's Bali Boost", *Straits Times*, 15 Sept. 2003.
[87] "Jakarta Jilted", *Far Eastern Economic Review*, 10 June 2004.
[88] See Declaration of ASEAN Concord II (commonly referred to as Bali Concord II), signed on 7 October 2003.
[89] "ASEAN Summit: Taking the Helm", *Far Eastern Economic Review*, 16 Oct. 2003.
[90] "Peacekeeping Role Not for Asean for Now: Jaya", *Straits Times*, 5 Mar. 2004; "Jakarta Jilted".

Secretary-General Severino noted, "In tangible terms, however, the centrepiece of the Asean enterprise today is regional economic integration." "The path to Asean economic integration," he recalled, "has been strewn with good intentions that have not been fulfilled, by general statements that have not been reduced to binding, effective commitments." He warned that unless ASEAN leaders ensured that their agreements were carried out, "the Asean economy will continue to be fragmented and thus left behind by the more integrated economies of larger nations and groups, and Asean's role in the world will diminish in effectiveness and importance".[91]

The "Myanmar Problem"

ASEAN was unlikely to achieve its goal, particularly that of the ASCC, as well as its much-craved-for standing in the international community if it did not resolve the "Myanmar problem". Thus, it is to this issue that we must now turn. The admission of Myanmar into ASEAN in 1997 was controversial and immediately created difficulties for ASEAN with its Western dialogue partners, particularly the EU and the United States. The ASEAN-EU ministerial meeting was suspended, and an attempt in December 2000 to revive it came to naught. Many joint ASEAN-EU projects were unable to proceed after 1997. The EU also refused to lift its political restrictions, for example, a visa ban on Myanmar officials, unless Yangon took steps to move towards "democracy, national reconciliation and the rule of law". The first steps would be to release all political prisoners and begin reconciliation talks with the National League for Democracy (NLD) leader Aung San Suu Kyi. The Myanmar military regime, known as the State Law and Order Restoration Council (SLORC), had annulled the 1990 general elections won by the NLD. Aung San Suu Kyi, the daughter of the Burmese independence hero Aung San, became the internationally recognized icon of Myanmar's struggle for democracy and "the cornerstone of the West's policy towards Myanmar".[92] According to EU President Louis Michel, human "rights and democracy would be given priority

[91] "Is Asean Serious About Economic Integration?" *Straits Times*, 9 Dec. 2004.

[92] Kyaw San Wai, "Myanmar's Foreign Policy Responses to Western Sanctions", master's thesis, Nanyang Technological University, 2012–13, p. 7.

to underline the emphasis the EU gave to civil society and the rule of law". ASEAN, on the other hand, maintained that the EU must not discriminate against Myanmar in the context of ASEAN-EU relations. Even though both sides understood that the ASEAN-EU relationship should not, in the words of EU Commissioner for External Relations Chris Patten, "be held hostage to Myanmar's political stalemate", both sides were unable to reach any agreement on this issue.[93] The EU was important to ASEAN. As Eric Teo reminds us, "a seldom-realised fact" was that the 13 countries in ASEAN+3 had more trade with the 15 members of the EU than with the United States, although "the latter's shadow looms larger over this region".[94] ASEAN, which in this period had the weaker hand relative to the EU, had to do something more as its constructive engagement policy with Yangon had clearly not been effective in steering Myanmar towards democratic change.

Aung San Suu Kyi, who won the Nobel Peace Prize in 1991 and became "an international symbol of peaceful resistance", had been under house arrest for stretches of time from July 1989. In May 2003, after pro-junta groups clashed with her supporters from the NLD, she was again imprisoned. According to Myanmar Foreign Minister Win Aung, there was no time frame for her release.[95] This led to international outrage and condemnation, and more economic and political sanctions from the US and the EU. Thus, not surprisingly, her imprisonment was a major issue that overshadowed other matters for discussion at the 36th ASEAN Ministerial Meeting in Phnom Penh the following month. As Malaysia's Foreign Minister Syed Hamid Albar said, "There's a need for Asean to be able to explain it in a credible manner so that the reputation and image of Asean will not in any way be questioned."[96] Its hand forced, ASEAN put aside its long-held policy of non-interference

---

[93] "EU Sees Myanmar Situation as a Hurdle", *Straits Times*, 28 July 2001; "EU's Interest in Asean Waning", *Straits Times*, 9 Apr. 2002.

[94] "Asem: A Forum to Balance US Power", *Straits Times*, 2 Oct. 2002.

[95] For a timeline, see "Timeline: The Life of Aung San Suu Kyi", https://www.weforum.org/agenda/2016/02/timeline-the-life-of-aung-san-suu-kyi2/, accessed 1 Feb. 2017. For the SLORC perspective, see "Suu Kyi 'Being Protected from Assassins'", *Straits Times*, 16 June 2003; "Darts Fly at Myanmar Minister", *Straits Times*, 20 June 2003.

[96] "Junta's Detention of Suu Kyi Tests Asean Credibility", *Straits Times*, 17 June 2003.

in member countries' domestic affairs and told Yangon that it had to accept United Nations mediation in seeking a resolution to its political impasse. Singaporean Foreign Minister S. Jayakumar pointed out that "we could not have done this 10 years ago. But now, we've reached a comfort level that allows us to talk frankly with each other on a sensitive issue."[97]

The Phnom Penh meeting issued a joint statement calling upon the Yangon regime to release Aung San Suu Kyi, unprecedented in ASEAN's history. Malaysia's outspoken Prime Minister Mahathir Mohamad went so far as to say Myanmar might have to be expelled from ASEAN if the Yangon regime continued to defy world pressure to release Aung San Suu Kyi, "as a last resort". Mahathir further explained:

> [W]e don't criticise member states unless what one state does embarrasses us, causes a problem for us. We are thinking about ourselves as Asean, we are not criticising Myanmar for doing what is not related to us but what they have done has affected us, our credibility. Because of that, we have voiced our views.[98]

It was significant that Mahathir made the remark. He had fought the hardest to admit Myanmar into ASEAN in 1997, when Kuala Lumpur was the chair of ASEAN. Patten noted that ASEAN's recent criticism of Myanmar was an "impressive gesture" that had been welcomed in Europe.[99] There was a tacit acknowledgement on both sides that neither ASEAN's quiet diplomacy nor Europe's policy of sanctions had worked. As one EU diplomat confessed, "Frankly no one knows exactly which recipe to follow when it comes to the Myanmar generals."[100] In August 2003, the Yangon junta unveiled a seven-stage roadmap. The military regime also released Aung San Suu Kyi from prison in September 2003 but kept her under house arrest. The EU continued to refuse to engage in bloc-to-bloc talks so long as she remained under house arrest. A meeting in July 2004 failed to resolve the issue of Myanmar's participation in

[97] "Asean Urges Myanmar to Accept Role of the UN", *Straits Times*, 17 June 2003.
[98] "Expel Myanmar", *Today*, 21 July 2003.
[99] "EU Sets out to Halt Drift in Asia Relations", *Straits Times*, 23 July 2003.
[100] "Asean-EU Ties May Yet Enter New Era", *Straits Times*, 25 July 2003; "EU and Southeast Asia: Stronger Ties in the Making?" *South China Morning Post*, 29 July 2003; "Asean Unease: Myanmar Must Act", *Straits Times*, 9 Apr. 2005.

the coming Asia-Europe Meeting (ASEM). ASEAN was insistent that Myanmar must be included if the EU attended the approaching summit as an expanded community of 25 members.[101]

Javier Solana (the EU's high representative for foreign and security policy) did not think the EU could change its position. The Myanmar regime had to change. In his words, "as we have said many times, we are not asking for preconditions, like the country has to change upside down in 24 hours. Nobody is asking for that. We want to see things go in a certain direction."[102] In the end, the EU agreed to a compromise whereby Myanmar would attend the Fifth ASEM Summit in Hanoi but its representation would be below the head of state level. This was only because EU officials saw ASEM as an important vehicle to maintain political and economic ties with the region, particularly China.[103] The next issue concerned Myanmar taking over the rotating chair of ASEAN in 2006 after Malaysia. Allowing Myanmar to be the chair would risk the United States and the EU, amongst others, not attending the 2006 meetings. However, ASEAN could not allow "the threats of boycott by non-Asean countries" to dictate ASEAN's long-held procedure, as Indonesian Foreign Minister Marty Natalegawa pointed out.[104] Resolving this dilemma took up much of the first half of 2005. The optimal solution was for Myanmar "to take a rain check on the chairmanship and then proceed at a pace the junta is comfortable with in the constitutional process".[105] Myanmar's Foreign Minister Nyan Win

[101] "Asean-EU Dialogue Falters over Myanmar", *Straits Times*, 2 July 2004.

[102] Ibid.; "Asean and EU Thrash out Myanmar Problem", *Straits Times*, 3 July 2004.

[103] See 5th ASEM Summit (ASEM5), "Further Revitalising and Substantiating the Asia-Europe Partnership", Hanoi, 8–9 Oct. 2004, http://www.aseminfoboard.org/events/5th-asem-summit-asem5, accessed 1 Feb. 2017. Not all members of the EU shared the same view of how to manage the Myanmar issue and ASEAN. Myanmar along with Cambodia and Laos officially joined the ASEM process in 2004, the first enlargement of ASEM since its establishment in 1996, which saw ten new EU states and the three ASEAN states.

[104] "Asean May Need Face-Saving Solution to Myanmar Issue", *Straits Times*, 24 Mar. 2005.

[105] "Don't Push Myanmar into a Corner", *Straits Times*, 23 May 2005. Written by Singapore's former ambassador to Cambodia, Verghese Mathews, this was the first indication that Yangon was waiting for an appropriate time and forum to pass up its turn as chair after Malaysia.

informed his ASEAN counterparts of this at the ASEAN Ministerial Meeting in July 2005, giving the reason that Myanmar "could focus its full attention on its ongoing reconciliation and democratisation process".[106] With that decision, ASEAN once again wriggled out of its conundrum. As the former Singapore diplomat Verghese Mathews noted, "Myanmar gave up its right to chair Asean not because of Asean persuasiveness or EU pressure. It was because it was in its own national interest to do so."[107]

After 2003 ASEAN became more vocal in its criticism of Myanmar for its sluggish pace of democratization and release of Aung San Suu Kyi.[108] ASEAN Secretary-General Ong summed it up well when he said that Myanmar's political situation had resulted in an "undesirable scrutiny" of ASEAN by the international community, and Yangon needed to act and "extricate" ASEAN from that spotlight.[109] As mentioned above, in August 2003 the Yangon junta unveiled a seven-stage roadmap. It would take another seven years, until November 2010, before the State Peace and Development Council held its first elections in Myanmar since 1990; and the 2010 elections were widely condemned as "neither free nor fair".[110] The military-backed party known as the Union Solidarity and Development Party, led by a former general—Thein Sein—not surprisingly won by a landslide. Thein Sein became the prime minister, and one week after the elections Aung San Suu Kyi was eventually released from house arrest. In those seven years, the Myanmar issue continued to frustrate ASEAN and test the patience of the organization, which led another outspoken Southeast Asia leader, this time Singapore's Minister Mentor Lee Kuan Yew, to call the Myanmar generals "dumb" and predict that they would "not be able to survive indefinitely".[111]

---

[106] "Myanmar Gives up Asean Chair", *Straits Times*, 27 July 2005.

[107] "Myanmar Still Keeps Europe Wary of Asia", *Straits Times*, 15 Oct. 2005.

[108] See, for example, "Asean Foreign Ministers Press Yangon for Reforms", *Straits Times*, 16 Dec. 2005.

[109] "Asean Unease: Myanmar Must Act", *Straits Times*, 9 Apr. 2005.

[110] Kyaw San Wai, "Myanmar's Foreign Policy Responses to Western Sanctions", p. 45.

[111] "Myanmar Generals Cannot Survive Indefinitely, Says MM", *Straits Times*, 10 Oct. 2007; Stephen McCarthy, "Burma and Asean: Estranged Bedfellows", *Asian Survey* 48, 6 (Nov./Dec. 2008): 911–35.

East Asia Summit

The Myanmar problem was an irritant and a distraction. As Ong explained, while ASEAN needed to take a "strong stand" on the issue to maintain its "credibility", there were other "pressing issues".[112] Coping with a China that was growing more powerful and dominant by the day was one key issue. In fact, it had always been the central concern. Recall that the idea of developing APT into an East Asia Summit to nurture an East Asian Community was floated in early 2000 by the Northeast Asians and was slowly gaining traction with the Southeast Asians. Singapore's Prime Minister Goh Chok Tong in 2001 thought that it would take a decade or two to realize such a community. Seizing the initiative, ASEAN took the first step in 2004 by proposing that an EAS be convened in Malaysia in 2005.[113] The EAS was to be "open, outward-looking and inclusive" and, most important, "*with ASEAN being the driving force* [emphasis added]".[114] In the words of Singapore's Foreign Minister George Yeo, "Asean will be the focal point of the East Asia Summit, which will create a framework for peace and cooperation and hasten economic integration in Asia."[115]

There was always the fear that ASEAN would be diluted into a much bigger grouping. Jakarta apparently preferred to consolidate ASEAN before establishing the EAS. There were also differences in views within ASEAN as to whether the EAS should include members beyond the original three Northeast Asian countries. Jakarta was keen to include India, Australia and New Zealand. Indonesia-Australia relations were on the mend since Susilo Bambang Yudhoyono became president of Indonesia in 2004, whereas Kuala Lumpur had reservations despite

---

[112] "Asean's Myanmar Sidestep", *Today*, 20 Nov. 2006.

[113] See Point 10, "Chairman's Statement of the Eighth ASEAN+3 Summit", Vientiane, 29 Nov. 2004, http://asean.org/?static_post=chairman-s-statement-of-the-8th-asean-3-summit-vientiane-29-november-2004, accessed 7 Feb. 2017. For a brief account of the origins of the EAS idea, see Rodolfo Severino, "How Many Voices Should East Asia Have?" *Straits Times*, 11 Apr. 2005. The EAS was one of the recommendations of the East Asia Vision Group, established in 1998.

[114] See Point 56, "Joint Communique of the 38th ASEAN Ministerial Meeting", Vientiane, http://asean.org/joint-communique-of-the-38th-asean-ministerial-meeting-vientiane/, accessed 7 Feb. 2017.

[115] "Remake Asean to Ride on Asia's Boom", *Straits Times*, 7 Sept. 2005.

Prime Minister Abdullah Badawi's visit to Canberra—he was the first Malaysian prime minister to visit Australia since 1984. Malaysia's relations with Australia were on the mend, albeit much slower than Indonesia's, since Badawi succeeded Mahathir in 2003. Kuala Lumpur and Canberra could not agree over Australia's policy of pre-emptive strikes against terrorist cells across Asia enunciated in 2002.[116] Australia's interest in participating in the EAS was largely because of the China factor. Its initial reluctance to sign the Treaty of Amity and Cooperation, one of the three criteria for EAS membership, unlike India, was thus an impediment. Canberra eventually signed the non-aggression pact.[117] As Australian Foreign Minister Alexander Downer said, "we've come to the conclusion that the best thing for Australia's long-term interests is to be a key player in the East Asian summit".[118]

It was said that the origin of the EAS dated back to Mahathir's idea of an EAEG in 1990, although Mahathir was critical of the participation of Australia and New Zealand in the EAS. In his view, the two countries were "neither Asian nor from the East".[119] Mahathir believed that the East Asian countries must band together to manage their own affairs, not unlike the European Union and the North American Free Trade Agreement. As recounted in chapter 2, this did not materialize, because of objections from some ASEAN member states as well as the United States. Washington was then concerned that the EAEG would affect the newly formed APEC. From 9/11 until APEC 2005 in Busan, the United States used APEC to promote its anti-terrorism agenda

---

[116] For a peek into the different views within ASEAN regarding the EAS, see "E. Asia Summit's Birthing Pains", *Straits Times Interactive*, 22 Feb. 2005; "KL Wants Summit to Exclude India, NZ, Australia", *Straits Times*, 18 Mar. 2005. For Australia's relations with Indonesia and Malaysia, see "New Page in Aussie Ties with KL, Jakarta" and "Yudhoyono, Howard Set to Mend Matters", *Straits Times*, 2 Apr. 2005; "KL and Canberra Can't Quite Bridge the Gulf", *Straits Times*, 8 Apr. 2005; "Howard's Closer Ties Get Big Thumbs Up", *Straits Times*, 11 Apr. 2005.

[117] "Howard's Asean Headache", *Straits Times*, 4 May 2015; "Australia Set to Sign Non-aggression Pact", *Straits Times*, 21 May 2005.

[118] "Australia to Sign Asean Non-aggression Treaty", *Straits Times Interactive*, 28 July 2005. New Zealand confirmed in May that Auckland would sign the treaty.

[119] "Mahathir Criticises East Asia Summit", *Straits Times Interactive*, 8 Dec. 2005. Mahathir predicted that the EAS would be ineffective and its views diluted to accommodate the wishes of Europe and the United States.

rather than discuss regional economic issues.[120] In typical ASEAN style, Mahathir's idea was not jettisoned but renamed as a "caucus". It eventually became the APT and finally the EAS. Not surprisingly, Malaysia was the venue of the inaugural EAS in December 2005.

Equally unsurprising was that the United States did not have a place in the inaugural EAS. Some critics argued that any regional structure that did not include the United States and other key players would be "worse than meaningless".[121] In the words of US Deputy Secretary of State Richard Armitage, this was "a thinly veiled way to make the point that the United States is not totally welcome in Asia ... If the summit leads to the creation of an East Asian Community, then it would be the first stage of that process."[122] To the United States, the EAS was a "'black box' whose future character is unknown except that it is expected to fall under the sway of China".[123] Washington still harboured hopes of being invited to the summit. If not, it hoped that some of its regional allies would "help check the growing influence of China, which it fears will dominate the proceedings".[124]

Washington did not help its own cause when Rice, who assumed the position of US secretary of state in January 2005, decided to miss the ASEAN Post-Ministerial and ARF meetings in Laos in July 2005, sending her deputy instead. She was the first US secretary of state to miss the ARF since its inception in 1994. Not going to Laos, although she visited China, Japan and South Korea, confirmed the view of those who felt that the United States was ignoring the region. Dana Dillon,

---

[120] "Growing Regional Cooperation Threatens US Influence in E. Asia", *Straits Times*, 19 Nov. 2005; Jane Skanderup, "APEC 2005: Economics Takes Center Stage", *PacNet #50*, 23 Nov. 2005. President George Bush met the seven ASEAN APEC members in Busan, and the outcome was a joint vision statement for an ASEAN-US Enhanced Partnership. One item of the partnership was a plan for a region-wide ASEAN-US Trade and Investment Framework Agreement.

[121] See, for example, Jonathan Eyal, "Who's in, Who's out: That's the Issue", *Straits Times*, 14 May 2005. For an insider account of the US attitude towards the EAS, see Victor D. Cha, *Powerplay: The Origins of the American Alliance System in Asia* (Princeton: Princeton University Press, 2016), pp. 1–4, 207–8, 219. Cha was the director of Asian affairs at the National Security Council from December 2004 to 2007.

[122] "No Invitation in Sight for Washington", *Straits Times*, 14 May 2005.

[123] "West Is Welcome in Asean Plus 3: China", *Straits Times*, 1 Nov. 2005.

[124] "No Invitation in Sight for Washington".

senior policy analyst at the Heritage Foundation in Washington, commented that Rice's absence would demonstrate that she "doesn't care much" about Southeast Asia. Rice had also indicated that she might boycott future ASEAN meetings if Myanmar assumed the chair of the group in 2006.[125] Although the United States hoped to be part of the EAS, and the APT countries had all indicated that they would welcome the United States in the future, Washington, like Australia earlier, would still first need to fulfil the criterion of signing the Treaty of Amity and Cooperation, which it had so far refused to do. In the words of Tan See Seng, "if the US were to sign, it would be restricting itself from the right to speak on issues in the region, or take action that could be deemed unfit according to the treaty. Its war on terrorism, for example, could be a point of contention."[126]

In the end, Washington adopted a wait-and-see attitude towards the EAS. After the initial anxiety over being left out, the view was that the EAS might not amount to much after all given the existing bilateral problems between some of its members, for example China and Japan. There was thus "little chance" that the EAS could develop into an Asian security apparatus or a powerful bloc. Indeed, a row between China and Japan over Japanese Prime Minister Junichiro Koizumi's visit to the Yasukuni Shrine in October 2005 erupted and threatened to derail the EAS in December. Beijing was apparently also unhappy that India, Australia and New Zealand were included in the EAS.[127] Singapore Minister Mentor Lee Kuan Yew said:

> [T]he formation of the East Asian Community does not depend upon whether China and Japan agree or do not agree with each other ... It is driven by globalisation that results from technological advances. Therefore, it makes sense for the Asean region to come together. I believe the key countries in Asia will come together economically, though not politically.[128]

---

[125] "Rice's No-Show in Laos Will Be Seen as a Snub", *Straits Times*, 22 June 2005; "Rice Skipping Asean Meeting", *Straits Times*, 1 July 2005; "Rice's Asia Test", *Straits Times*, 9 July 2005.

[126] "China Opens Door to Possible US Role", *Straits Times*, 2 Dec. 2005.

[127] "EAC: More an East Asian Cacaphony", *Straits Times*, 3 Jan. 2016.

[128] "Economy First for East Asian Bloc: MM Lee", *Straits Times*, 10 Dec. 2005.

When it came to economics, the United States had other forums for engaging with Asian countries, such as APEC. As for Southeast Asia, Rice had met with the ASEAN foreign ministers in New York in September 2005, and the outcome was a joint vision statement for an ASEAN-US Enhanced Partnership. One item of the partnership was a plan for a region-wide ASEAN-US Trade and Investment Framework Agreement. In July 2006 both sides agreed to work on a five-year action plan for US-ASEAN cooperation in politics, security, trade and investments.[129]

Last but not least, Washington had friends in the EAS and many Southeast Asian countries who were "not eager to replace US leadership with Chinese hegemony".[130] Indeed, not long after the first EAS, it was announced that an annual US-ASEAN summit would be inaugurated in late 2006 (although it did not take place until 2009). The general view was that many, if not all, of the ASEAN countries wanted to keep the US engaged in the region in order to balance China. ASEAN Secretary-General Ong clarified that the emerging East Asian Community would not exclude the United States even as China sought a larger role in Southeast Asia.[131] Washington, too, wanted to balance China's rising influence.[132] Eric John, deputy assistant secretary of state for East Asian and Pacific affairs, described 2006 as a "big year" for the US and Southeast Asia, "both in bilateral engagements and particularly in multilateral engagements, specifically with Asean".[133] Coincidentally, it was Singapore's turn to be the country coordinator for ASEAN-US Dialogue relations in 2006–09.[134] Singapore was (and remains) one of the staunchest supporters of a US presence in the region. Myanmar, however, continued to hinder ASEAN-US relations. For example, the

[129] "US, Asean Agree on Five-Year Plan for Closer Ties", *Straits Times*, 28 July 2006.
[130] "But US Adopts Wait and See Attitude", *Straits Times*, 2 Dec. 2005; "Building Block", *Newsweek*, 12 Dec. 2005; "Asean Ministers Upbeat After Talks with Rice", *Straits Times*, 14 Sept. 2005; "Americans Building on Strong Ties with Asean", *Straits Times*, 23 Sept. 2005.
[131] "Asean Chief Says E. Asia Community Will Not Exclude US", *Straits Times*, 17 June 2006.
[132] "US, Asean to Boost Ties with Yearly Summit", *Straits Times*, 3 Feb. 2006.
[133] "US Poised to Take Asean Ties to New Level, Says Bush Aide", *Straits Times*, 11 Feb. 2006.
[134] "US Keen to Boost Asean Trade via S'pore", *Straits Times*, 3 Apr. 2006.

proposed ASEAN-US Trade and Investment Framework Agreement had to be renamed as an "arrangement" to avoid the need for congressional approval. As Ong explained, "many people in Washington want to jam US ties with Asean because of Myanmar ..."[135]

At the inaugural East Asia Summit on 14 December 2005, it was agreed that the EAS with ASEAN would be an "integral part of the overall evolving regional architecture"—a "forum for dialogue on broad strategic, political and economic issues of common interest and concern with the aim of promoting peace, stability and economic prosperity in East Asia". The realization of the East Asian Community would remain the role of the APT process.[136] Severino was of the view that the EAS would be "valuable enough" as a forum for confidence building and developing mutual understanding. However, as Tan See Seng and Ralf Emmers noted, the experience of Asian regionalism had shown that institutions with no other aim except confidence building did not go far.[137] When the dust has settled, the EAS "will probably be judged less on the basis of grand strategic calculations than on the nuts-and-bolts issues that promise to deliver economic growth".[138] ASEAN indicated that it intended to remain in the driver's seat. As Malaysian Deputy Prime Minister Najib Tun Razak pointed out, ASEAN would remain key to the emerging East Asian Community despite the rapid growth of China and India; and "within the context of the creation of the Asian community ... we see very much the emergence of the East Asia community should be and will be Asean driven".[139] All future EAS would be held in Southeast Asia. The Philippines would host the Second EAS in 2006.[140]

---

[135] "US, Asean to Sign Scaled-Down Trade Arrangement", *Straits Times*, 20 Aug. 2006.

[136] "Kuala Lumpur Declaration on the East Asia Summit Kuala Lumpur", 14 Dec. 2005, http://asean.org/?static_post=kuala-lumpur-declaration-on-the-east-asia-summit-kuala-lumpur-14-december-2005; "Chairman's Statement of the First East Asia Summit", Kuala Lumpur,14 Dec. 2005, http://dfat.gov.au/international-relations/regional-architecture/asean/Pages/chairmans-statement-of-the-first-east-asia-summit.aspx, accessed 8 Feb. 2017.

[137] "Some Proposals for the East Asia Summit", *Straits Times*, 19 Nov. 2005.

[138] "Building Block".

[139] "Asean Chief Says E. Asia Community Will Not Exclude US".

[140] Beijing offered to host the Second EAS.

CHAPTER 4

2007–10: A Few Steps Forward, a Few Steps Backwards

"ASEAN, once dismissed as a sinking ship of bickering leaders, seems to be finding a second wind in recent years."[1]

"Its [ASEAN's] priority should really be to get its own act together."[2]

"The size of China makes it impossible for the rest of Asia, including Japan and India, to match it in weight and capacity in about 20 to 30 years. So, we need America to strike a balance."[3]

ASEAN at 40

The year 2007 marked the 40th anniversary of ASEAN. It had been more than 15 years since the Cold War ended. This is, therefore, a good point to briefly pause and review how much Southeast Asia had evolved since 1990, how well the region had met its challenges, and to what extent the region as a whole had achieved its aims, before continuing the narrative.

The most obvious point is that whereas in 1990 Southeast Asia comprised the ASEAN 6, the three Indochina countries and Myanmar, in 2007 Southeast Asia was almost synonymous with ASEAN 10 and Timor-Leste, which has on a number of occasions expressed aspirations

[1] Goh Sui Noi, "A Second Wind for Asean?" *Straits Times*, 21 Jan. 2007.

[2] Ong Keng Yong quoted in "Asean Revamp: From Family Business to Global Player", *Straits Times*, 12 Jan. 2007.

[3] Quoted in Peh Shing Huei, "Can US Squeeze into the 'Chinasean' Bed?" *Straits Times*, 15 Mar. 2010.

of becoming the 11th member of the organization.[4] For a few years after 1997, ASEAN was Southeast Asia and Southeast Asia was ASEAN, but after 2002—if one considers Timor-Leste as a Southeast Asian state[5]—ASEAN returned to becoming a subregional organization, although a much bigger outfit than it was pre-1997. Nevertheless, one should not forget that Southeast Asia is more than ASEAN even if the ten countries combined dwarf Timor-Leste. Timor-Leste, as its president, Jose Ramos-Horte, admitted in 2010, was unable to achieve its self-imposed target for ASEAN membership by 2012.[6] However, in March 2011 it formally applied for ASEAN membership. Jakarta and Bangkok supported the application, but there was no ASEAN consensus to admit the country.[7] Singapore was particularly forthright in its opposition, arguing that the admission of Timor-Leste would jeopardize ASEAN's goal to create an ASEAN Economic Community by 2015.[8]

The next point to note is that the Southeast Asian states did not want to be merely a peripheral dimension of global politics. Since the Cold War ended, one goal that all ten members, old and new, were in complete agreement on was the strategic importance of "ASEAN centrality". Michael Vatikiotis recalled that ASEAN was "at its peak at the end of the Cold War when superpower rivalry was at its nadir", which allowed the organization "to steer its own economic and security policies and get the feel for regional cooperation".[9] ASEAN almost lost its perch in the aftermath of the 1997 Asian Financial Crisis.

Since then, the organization has been struggling to recover its image through greater integration, with some success, though not everyone

[4] "Jakarta Backs Timor Leste's Asean Bid", *Straits Times*, 26 July 2006. Tan See Seng noted, "Timor has arguably seen itself not as part of Asean, but more as part of the Pacific Forum group of states in the South Pacific"; see Tan See Seng, "Saving Timor: Responsibility Belongs to All", *Straits Times*, 14 June 2006.

[5] For the various views, see Tan, "Saving Timor"; Yang Razali Kassim, "Timor as a Failed State: A Slap in the Face of ASEAN?" *PacNet* #29, 22 June 2006.

[6] "Timor Leste Behind in Bid to Join Asean", *Straits Times*, 17 July 2010.

[7] "Timor Leste's Bid to Join Asean Faces Objections", *Straits Times*, 20 Mar. 2011.

[8] For details of which countries supported and which did not support Timor-Leste's admission into ASEAN, see Barry Wain, "Closing the Asean Door on Timor Leste", *Straits Times*, 5 May 2011; "S'pore Rebuts Article on Its Timor Leste Stance", *Straits Times*, 18 Nov. 2011.

[9] Michael Vatikiotis, "Asean Is Having a Hard Time Breathing", *Straits Times*, 3 May 2007.

is satisfied with the pace. In the words of former Philippine President Fidel Ramos, "Asean is now at a critical point. There is no guarantee that it can maintain its relevance in the coming decades."[10] Myanmar remained both an embarrassment and an obstacle, but the reality was that ASEAN had little leverage over Myanmar. As ASEAN Secretary-General Ong explained, ASEAN's trade ties with Myanmar were "insignificant". Also, Myanmar was not part of the global economy and could depend on China as well as India, which had refused to join the US and EU in imposing economic and political sanctions. Ong further revealed that some of the ASEAN leaders felt they had made their stand clear. He said:

> When we discuss Myanmar, we talk about it behind closed doors … we settle this among ourselves. It will be discussed, but it won't be the centrestage issue … It does not do Asean any good if we cannot move in our cooperation with the rest of the world. If they don't settle this, it's going to hamper our cooperation and relations with other countries.[11]

The only way was to allow political developments in the country—the junta's seven-step roadmap—to run their course. The European Union perhaps realized that that was "the only way", although it did not articulate it as such. Both the US and the EU renewed sanctions against Myanmar, first introduced a decade ago.[12] At the same time, in May 2007 ASEAN and the EU agreed to launch the ASEAN-EU FTA negotiations, "a breakthrough after more than two years of wrangling" over Myanmar's human rights record.[13]

Connected to the focus on centrality was the pursuit of a unified post-Cold War security design, arrangement or, the oft-used word, architecture, with ASEAN playing the central role. This was seen in the structure of the ARF as well as APT and EAS. Hadi Soesastro described APEC and the ARF as the "two pillars of a regional order" and "the main elements of an emerging institutional architecture" for Asia-Pacific.

---

[10] "Asean Advisers Call for Radical Policy Change", *Straits Times*, 9 Dec. 2006.

[11] "Asean's Myanmar Sidestep", *Today*, 20 Nov. 2006; "Sanctions on Myanmar Won't Work: Asean Sec-Gen Ong", *Today*, 12 June 2007.

[12] See "Until Suu Kyi Is Freed, US Ban on Myanmar Stays", *Today*, 26 July 2007.

[13] "Asean and EU to Start Free Trade Talks", *Straits Times*, 5 May 2007; "Free Trade Pact with US Unlikely: Asean Chief", *Straits Times*, 24 July 2007.

They were subsequently complemented by newer "regional institutions and processes", namely the APT and EAS, which came about because of the Southeast Asian states' disillusionment with APEC.[14] The EAS held its inaugural meeting in Kuala Lumpur in 2005. The intention was for the second EAS meeting to take place in Cebu in December 2006, during the annual ASEAN summit. Because of Typhoon Utor, the meetings were postponed to January 2007. The EAS was very much in its infancy.

ASEAN Regional Forum Reviewed

The ARF in 2007, on the other hand, had been around for 13 years. Recall from chapter 1 that ASEAN played a leading role in the formation of the ARF. It began with 18 members, and in the course of 13 years the membership grew to 27. Sri Lanka, which joined in 2007, was the newest member. The ARF had a three-stage roadmap beginning with Confidence Building Measures (CBM), followed by Preventive Diplomacy (PD) and finally Conflict Resolution. Starting with CBM was a logical and understandable first stage in the early post-Cold War period. From the very beginning, there were differences amongst members with regard to the pace of growth of the forum.

In 2000 Barry Wain noted that the ARF in its seventh year was still in the "talking stage" and "unable to move beyond confidence-building measures to preventive diplomacy, much less advance to the final phase where the settlement of disputes is contemplated. While patience is required in passing judgment on what is bound to be a long-term enterprise, it is hard to be upbeat about its prospects."[15] Wain was not alone in expressing his pessimism about the future of the ARF.[16] One reason why the ARF found it difficult to move to the second stage was "member countries' disparate interests regarding security issues".[17]

---

[14] Hadi Soesastro, "ASEAN Plus Three, East Asia Summit and APEC: Ensuring Productive Synergy", 21st Asia Pacific Roundtable, Kuala Lumpur, 4–8 June 2007.

[15] "Slow Progress on Asian Security", *Wall Street Journal Asia*, 17–19 Sept. 2000.

[16] See, for example, "Replace Asean", *Wall Street Journal Asia*, 3–5 Aug. 2001; "Regional Perspective: Making the ARF Relevant Post-September 11", *The Nation*, 8 July 2002.

[17] "Asia-Pacific Ministers Set to Strengthen Regional Forum Chairman's Role", *Kyodo News Service*, Tokyo, in English, 14 July 2001.

But as argued by Singapore's Foreign Minister S. Jayakumar, who in 2001 was the longest-serving ASEAN foreign minister and one of the only two who were present at the inception of the ARF, the ARF was "the only regional forum in which sensitive issues can be discussed ..." While the ARF could not solve all the security issues, it could help "cushion tensions and manage difficulties" and "minimise their impact". Chinese Foreign Minister Tang Jiaxuan described the ARF as "the most important venue" for discussing and resolving security issues in Asia-Pacific.[18]

At the 2001 ARF meeting, the forum finally moved to discuss an appropriate time to shift from CBM to the Preventive Diplomacy stage.[19] The members also agreed to develop the forum as "Asia's premier forum to promote regional peace and security". To achieve that, the ARF adopted three proposals: the development of the concept and principles of PD, enhancement of the ARF chair, and the creation of a register of eminent persons to make recommendations to the ARF when called upon. Finally, yet importantly, ASEAN would remain the "driving force" of the ARF.[20]

One year later, however, there was still no agreement to move to the PD stage. According to Kavi Chongkittavorn, while most members thought there was enough mutual trust to move beyond CBM, China did not agree. The ARF was at risk of obsolescence if it did not quickly move forward. Furthermore, ASEAN's fear of losing control of the ARF "if the chair falls into the hands of non-Asean members" could "drive away active non-Asean members demanding a stronger sense of belonging".[21] A June 2002 report of the Institute of Defence and Strategic Studies (Singapore) Project on the Future of the ARF noted that transition to PD "has proved immensely difficult owing to the resistance of some member states, such as China". PD measures were "still at a formative stage", and the measures being developed were "primarily peacetime, not crisis-time responses". The scope of PD was

---

[18] "Top Security Role for Asean Regional Forum" and "Security Partners 'Can Now Discuss Sensitive Issues'", *Straits Times*, 26 July 2001.

[19] *Voice of Vietnam text website*, Hanoi, in Vietnamese, 18 May 2001. Vietnam: ASEAN Regional Forum Preparatory Session Opens in Hanoi.

[20] "Top Security Role for Asean Regional Forum".

[21] "Regional Perspective". See also Barry Desker, "Is the ARF Obsolete? Three Moves to Avoid Irrelevance", *IDSS Commentaries*, 20 July 2006.

"limited to dealing with disputes and conflicts *between* rather than *within* states".[22]

In its tenth year, in 2003, the ARF retained its status; however, Cambodian Foreign Minister and ARF Chairman Hor Namhong noted that as "the principal consultative and cooperative forum for political and security matters in the Asia-Pacific",[23] it was still stuck at the CBM phase, which Indonesia's Foreign Minister Marty Natalegawa described as "the most elementary form of interaction among this type of grouping".[24] The Tenth ARF (in June 2003) was sidetracked by the issue of Myanmar, specifically the rearrest of Aung San Suu Kyi by the Myanmar junta in May, shortly before the ASEAN ministerial meetings. It is worth quoting Khong Yuen Foong here. In 1994 Khong argued that by the year 2000, "if the ARF is still around, if most East Asians feel as secure as they do today, if the ARF has helped prevent rivalry in the South China Sea from degenerating into warfare and if the ARF-sponsored confidence-building mechanisms have checked an arms race, then it may be proclaimed a success". On the other hand, "If the ARF dies—as did the Association of Southeast Asia, Maphilindo and Seato—or if diplomats consider it nothing more than an annual three-hour venting of national spleens, and if arms racing has become a permanent feature of the East Asian military landscape ... then one must conclude that the ARF had failed."[25] Revisiting the subject in 2005, based on his 1997 yardstick (chapter 1), Khong argued that the ARF had been a success. However, he noted, "the biggest blight on the ARF is its glacial pace in moving beyond confidence-building to preventive diplomacy".[26] In 2005 the ARF was reportedly ready to move on to the Preventive Diplomacy phase.[27] However, in 2007, the 40th anniversary of ASEAN, the "primarily ASEAN-led ARF" had still not

[22] See "Reassessing Multilateralism: A New Agenda for the ASEAN Regional Forum: A Report of the IDSS Project on the Future of the ASEAN Regional Forum", Institute of Defence and Strategic Studies, June 2002.

[23] "Jaya: Go Beyond Regional Matters to Global Issues", *Straits Times*, 19 June 2003.

[24] Indonesian Foreign Minister Marty Natalegawa quoted in "ARF Set to Move on from Building Trust", *Straits Times*, 29 July 2005.

[25] See Khong Yuen Foong, "Predicting the Future of the ASEAN Regional Forum", *Trends, Business Times*, 30–31 July 1994.

[26] "Amity Treaty Shows ARF Not Just Talk Shop", *Straits Times*, 29 July 2005.

[27] "ARF Set to Move on from Building Trust", *Straits Times*, 29 July 2005.

moved beyond the CBM stage. In addition, the emergence of new arrangements such as the APT and the EAS had given rise to the perception that "there might be competing conceptions of multilateralism and regionalism in Asia". It was unclear how the ARF fitted in.[28] In August 2007 Ong said that the ARF was "just starting" to go into PD. The ARF was still creeping towards PD in 2010.[29] (Eight years on, in 2018, the ARF was still stuck between stages 1 and 2.) Furthermore, the establishment of the ASEAN Defence Ministers Meeting (ADMM) and ADMM-Plus (described below) "meant that the lion's share of functional security cooperation has shifted to these processes". Thus, there was a need "for the ARF to reinvent itself to remain relevant".[30]

ASEAN Defence Ministers Meeting and ADMM-Plus

Meanwhile, ASEAN introduced a new initiative in the form of the ASEAN Defence Ministers Meeting (ADMM), which was held for the first time in May 2006 in Kuala Lumpur; it was the first meeting of ASEAN defence ministers since 1967. Analysts saw this inaugural meeting as "historic" and "representing a major shift in the regional grouping's focus from political and economic issues to security, and a significant step in bolstering military ties". The inaugural meeting discussed cooperation in tackling terrorism, piracy, disaster relief and transnational crime.[31] The idea was to first create an atmosphere of security dialogue and cooperation in "non-traditional security" issues before initiating substantial military cooperation. The ADMM was in line with the ASEAN Security Community (ASC) idea. Jakarta had pushed for the ASC, and ASEAN had committed to establishing it along with the ASEAN Economic Community and ASEAN Socio-Cultural

---

[28] Ralf Emmers, "ASEAN Regional Forum: Time to Move Towards Preventive Diplomacy", *IDSS/RSIS Commentaries*, 25 Oct. 2007. See also Ralf Emmers and See Seng Tan, "The ASEAN Regional Forum and Preventive Diplomacy: Built to Fail?" *Asian Security* 7, 1 (2011): 44–60.

[29] See Tan See Seng, "ARF: Ad Hoc Regional Forum?" *Straits Times*, 30 July 2010.

[30] Tang Siew Mun, "Rethinking the ASEAN Regional Forum", *ASEAN Focus* 5 (2018): 11.

[31] "First Meeting of Asean Defence Ministers", *Straits Times*, 8 May 2006; "Asean Reaffirms Security Community", *Straits Times*, 10 May 2006.

Community (by 2020) at the Ninth ASEAN Summit in October 2003. The idea of adding a military dimension to ASEAN was not new but for various reasons never implemented, although there was intelligence coordination and sharing as well as bilateral military exercises between some ASEAN member states.[32] Thus, like the ASEAN Charter (see next section), the ADMM was an idea whose time had come.

Soon after, at the Second ADMM held in Singapore in 2007, the ASEAN leaders approved a concept paper to extend the ADMM into ADMM-Plus in 2010. The "Plus" referred to the eight ASEAN dialogue partners, making it a total of 18 countries, nine fewer than the ARF.[33] Whereas the ARF was (and still is) essentially a "foreign ministry-dominated structure", the ADMM-Plus principally involves the defence ministers.[34] Unlike the ADMM, which is held annually, the ADMM-Plus, which convened for the first time in Hanoi in October 2010, is held biennially.[35] The ADMM-Plus has been compared to the Shangri-La Dialogue, which is another security dialogue mechanism of the Asia-Pacific countries, helmed by the London-based International Institute for Strategic Studies and held in Singapore since 2002. Brendan Taylor notes that the Shangri-La Dialogue has been the "de facto meeting of Asian defence ministers" since its inception. The difference between the ADMM-Plus and the Shangri-La Dialogue is that the former focuses principally on non-traditional security issues[36] whereas the Shangri-La Dialogue is "one of the few regional mechanisms that broaches more traditional security challenges—such as burgeoning military modernisation, alliances, great power politics and military

---

[32] Bhubhindar Singh and See Seng Tan (eds), *From "Boots" to "Brogues": The Rise of Defence Diplomacy in Southeast Asia* (RSIS Monograph No. 21, 2011), pp. 5–9, 40.

[33] The eight dialogue partners are Australia, China, India, Japan, New Zealand, South Korea, the Russian Federation and the United States.

[34] See "Towards a Better Security Framework", *Straits Times*, 15 June 2010; Barry Desker, "A Step Closer to Security Community", *Straits Times*, 20 Oct. 2010.

[35] For discussions on the ADMM and ADMM-Plus, see Singh and Tan, *From "Boots" to "Brogues"*; Tomotaka Shoji, "ASEAN Defense Ministers' Meeting (ADMM) and ADMM Plus: A Japanese Perspective", *NIDS Journal of Defense and Security* 14 (Dec. 2013): 3–17, 70–131.

[36] The focus of the ADMM-Plus is in the following six areas: maritime security, counterterrorism, humanitarian assistance and disaster relief, peacekeeping operations, military medicine, and humanitarian mine action; see "Roundtable: The ADMM-Plus and the Future of Defense Diplomacy", *Asia Policy* 22 (July 2016): 72.

transparency ..."[37] The plan was that over time, the ADMM-Plus would be able to "provide a platform for practical cooperation between Asean and its partners on key security issues, especially on non-traditional and transnational challenges".[38] Another key difference is that the Shangri-La dialogue is particularly useful for its "bilateral discussions and consultations" mostly on the side of the conference, while the ADMM-Plus is "multilateral and regional".[39]

Critics or sceptics of ASEAN and ASEAN-driven arrangements such as the ARF and the ADMM-Plus doubted whether the ADMM-Plus would be any more effective than the ARF, which had often been dismissed as a "talk shop" and "incapable of addressing regional security affairs".[40] One often-heard criticism was that ASEAN's preference for conducting affairs in the "ASEAN Way"[41] constrainted and limited the development of any initiative driven by the organization, ASEAN included. Malcolm Cook (programme director for Asia and Pacific, Lowy Institute) claimed that ASEAN leadership of the ARF undermined its institutional strength and likened it to "the tail wagging the dog".[42] Xu Jin noted that by 2013 the ARF had "developed and enforced" 51

[37] Brendan Taylor, "The Shangri-La Dialogue: Thriving, but Not Surviving?" in *From "Boots" to "Brogues"*, ed. Singh and Tan, pp. 59–60.

[38] "DPM Teo Signs Asean Joint Declaration", *Straits Times*, 12 May 2010.

[39] Siew Mun Tang, "ASEAN and the ADMM-Plus: Balancing Between Strategic Imperatives and Functionality" in "Roundtable: The ADMM-Plus and the Future of Defense Diplomacy": 77.

[40] Emmers and Tan, "ASEAN Regional Forum and Preventive Diplomacy": 48. The article argues that the ASEAN Way was not the most important reason for the failure of the ARF to move from CBM to PD.

[41] Amitav Acharya notes that the term is "vague and contested" (*Constructing a Security Community in Southeast Asia: ASEAN and the Problem of Regional Order*, 2001). S. Jayakumar (former foreign minister of Singapore), however, provides a few descriptors of the ASEAN Way in various sources: informality, organization minimalism, inclusiveness, intensive consultations leading to consensus and peaceful resolutions of disputes. See Shaun Narine, "The English School and ASEAN", *Pacific Review* 19, 2 (June 2006): 204. See also Jurgen Haake, "The Concept of Flexible Engagement and the Practice of Enhanced Interaction: Intramural Challenges to the 'ASEAN Way'", *Pacific Review* 12, 4 (1999): 581–611; Samuel Sharpe, "An ASEAN Way to Security Cooperation in Southeast Asia?" *Pacific Review* 16, 2 (2003): 231–50.

[42] "Security Panel and Charter Top Asean Agenda in Manila", *Straits Times*, 28 July 2007.

confidence-building programmes. After that, it "has stopped making further progress … because members of the ARF are unable to reach agreements on preventive diplomacy, whereas ASEAN requires all members to move to the next stage. Meanwhile, on issues of regional security, the ARF members only consult instead of taking measures to respond."[43] Xu concluded that it was "conceivable that sticking to the ASEAN way of reforming the ARF or ADMM-Plus on the premise of maintaining ASEAN's central role will lead to one outcome: making minor fixes to the existing mechanisms, mainly in the form of promoting low-level pragmatic cooperation in some non-sensitive areas …"[44] (In 2018, the 25th anniversary of the ARF, the general view was that there was a need to relook at the role of the ARF and streamline the foci and activities of the ARF and ADMM-Plus.[45])

ASEAN Charter

Many, including those within the establishment who had staunchly defended the "ASEAN Way" publicly, shared Xu Jin's view. There was a tacit acknowledgement by ASEAN leaders that ASEAN must transform its loose organizational structure into a rule-based one for it to remain relevant and effective in the long term. In the words of Singapore's Defence Minister Teo Chee Hean, "In order to be able to play a useful role, Asean will have to broaden and deepen its integration. Only then can Asean influence the development of constructive relationships which enhance regional security."[46] Thus the introduction of an ASEAN Charter, the next topic of discussion. Before that, note that there were two related initiatives with one common objective—to ensure ASEAN remained relevant and to ensure that ASEAN remained in the driver's

[43] See Shao Binhong (ed.), *Looking for a Road: China Debates Its and the World's Future* (Leiden: Brill, 2017), chapter 3, p. 57.
[44] Xu Jin, "China's Future East Asian Security Policy Framework: A 'Four-Wheel' Structure Design", in *Looking for a Road*, ed. Shao (Leiden: Brill, 2017), chapter 3, p. 57.
[45] See Termsak Chalermpalanupap, "State of Play of the ARF@25"; Alice D. Ba, "The ARF's Elusive Pursuit of Preventive Diplomacy"; Tang Siew Mun, "Rethinking the ASEAN Regional Forum", all in *ASEAN Focus* 5, Oct. 2018, https://www.iseas.edu.sg/images/pdf/ASEANFocus%20Oct%202018.pdf, accessed 12 Apr. 2019.
[46] "Asean Must Help Shape Security in the Region", *Straits Times*, 20 Feb. 2006.

seat in the unpredictable post-Cold War environment. This would require the building of a strong ASEAN identity—thus the first initiative, developing an ASEAN Community (chapter 3). One challenge related to developing an ASEAN Community or identity was how to bring the idea of ASEAN to the ordinary people as well as the younger generation living in various Southeast Asian countries. It is common knowledge that most inhabitants in the region perceive ASEAN to be an elitist organization and are not aware of how ASEAN decisions affect their lives. As ASEAN Secretary-General Ong pointed out, "What often springs to mind when people think of ASEAN are images of meetings, high-powered talks and gatherings of leaders from the region and beyond. So it's very hard for the young to relate to what Asean is all about."[47] As former Foreign Minister of Thailand Surin (who would succeed Ong as ASEAN secretary-general on 1 January 2008) put it, "How are we going to bring the fruits of integration to people at the village and kampong level?"[48]

The development of an ASEAN Community was obviously necessary but not sufficient. Therefore, there was a need for a second and related initiative, to borrow Samuel Sharpe's words, "a strong degree of institutionalisation legally binding members to agreements", that is, the ASEAN Charter.[49] The intention to develop an ASEAN Charter—"a constitutional framework of what the grouping wants to become"—was broached at the ASEAN Ministerial Meeting in June 2004. The idea of a charter, in fact, went back to as early as 1992. Brunei Sultan Hassanal Bolkiah recalled that the idea of shaping ASEAN's identity began at a leaders' summit Singapore hosted in 1992: "We were wondering what the future held for the association. We left with a dramatic sense of vision. It was there that Asean set the goal of widening and deepening ties among members and working towards economic

[47] "Asean Not Yet a United Entity for S'poreans", *Straits Times*, 24 Feb. 2007. See also Simon Tay, "Asean Integration Also About Mindset", *Straits Times*, 10 Sept. 2008; "Sex up the Image, Asean", *Straits Times*, 12 Sept. 2008; "People to People Ties Vital in Asean", *Straits Times*, 17 Apr. 2009.

[48] "Regional Integration Will Be a Challenge to Asean: Surin", *Straits Times*, 19 May 2007.

[49] See Rodolfo C. Severino, "Why Asean Should Have a Charter", *Straits Times*, 5 Dec. 2005.

integration."[50] It was thus an idea whose time had come. Paragraph 6 of the 2004 ASEAN communique pertaining to the ASEAN Charter is worth quoting. The charter would

> ... reaffirm ASEAN's goals and principles in inter-state relations, in particular the collective responsibilities of all ASEAN Member Countries in ensuring non-aggression and respect for each other's sovereignty and territorial integrity; the promotion and protection of human rights; the maintenance of political stability, regional peace and economic progress; and the establishment of effective [*sic*] and efficient institutional framework for ASEAN.[51]

An Eminent Persons Group comprising senior ASEAN statesmen, one from each member country, with former Malaysian Deputy Prime Minister Musa Hitam as the chairman, was formed in 2005. The panel was to produce a set of recommendations by the time of the 11th ASEAN Summit in Cebu initially scheduled for December 2006 (but subsequently postponed to January 2007 because of Typhoon Utor).[52] At the Cebu Summit, it was decided that the draft ASEAN Charter should be completed by the 40th Anniversary ASEAN Summit in November 2007.

It would not be an easy task. From the very beginning, there were two views: on one side were those who wanted simply to codify "the existing principles, norms, values and objectives of Asean"—thus Malaysian Prime Minister Abdullah Badawi's remark that the proposed charter "need not be an overly ambitious project". On the other side were those who saw it as "a golden opportunity for Asean to reinvigorate itself... as a forward-looking organisation"—thus the remark by Singapore Prime Minister Lee Hsien Loong, who described

---

[50] "Brunei Sultan Lauds S'pore's Efforts on Asean Charter", *Straits Times*, 28 June 2007.

[51] Joint Communique of the 37th ASEAN Ministerial Meeting, Jakarta, 29–30 June 2004, https://asean.org/?static_post=joint-communique-of-the-37th-asean-ministerial-meeting-jakarta-29-30-june-2004-2, accessed 14 Apr. 2019.

[52] See 2004 Joint Communique of the 37th ASEAN Ministerial Meeting, paragraph 6, https://asean.org/joint-communique-of-the-37th-asean-ministerial-meeting-jakarta/, accessed 2 Mar. 2017; "Jaya Picked to Join Senior Leaders on Asean Charter Panel", *Straits Times*, 8 Aug. 2005; "ASEAN's Vision 2020", *Straits Times*, 12 Dec. 2005; "Work on Asean Charter Gets Rolling" and "Rewriting the ASEAN Way", *Straits Times*, 13 Dec. 2005.

the objective of the charter as being to "set a clear and ambitious long-term direction for Asean".[53] There was also the Myanmar issue, which remained unresolved.[54] All parties, however, concurred that EU-style institutionalization was not on the cards.[55]

Speaking on the eve of the 11th ASEAN Summit, ASEAN Secretary-General Ong revealed:

> [H]alf of the Asean countries are prepared to compromise on this thing called the charter. They feel that we have to use this charter to instil a certain regional ego; instil the discipline in implementation and to provide a very clear message to all the non-Asean people out there, whether our dialogue partners or others, that we are serious about our organisation. Because the sense is that if you are not serious, then who wants to be serious with you?

The emphasis appears to have been on the economic aspect. Indeed, the original intent of the charter was to establish a legal foundation for the AEC. On more than one occasion, Ong referred to the economic dimension when speaking about the charter. According to him, "right now, the only way that we can remain competitive is to work together as one single market ... This charter should be facilitating the establishment of this single market as soon as possible."[56] On another occasion, Ong also revealed that in the discussion on drafting the human rights provision in the charter, "it was not Myanmar" that was obstructionist. He revealed that four countries had reservations: "two of them were most vocal, and they did not include Myanmar."[57]

---

[53] Amitav Acharya, "Challenges for an Asean Charter", *Straits Times Interactive*, 24 Oct. 2005; Rizal Sukma, "Asean: New Challenges, New Horizons, New Targets", 20th Asia-Pacific Roundtable, Kuala Lumpur, 29 May–1 June 2006.

[54] "Asean Slams Myanmar for Lack of Democracy", *Straits Times*, 30 July 2007.

[55] See Ong Keng Yong, "EU's Lessons for Asean", *Straits Times*, 11 June 2008.

[56] "Asean Revamp: From Family Business to Global Player". See also "Interview with ASEAN Secretary-General Ong Keng Yong: Moving away from Family Way", *Straits Times*, 24 Feb. 2006.

[57] "Progress Made on Asean Charter", *Today*, 7 Aug. 2007. Vietnam was initially unwilling to support the charter and agreed only when ASEAN scrapped the proposed punitive measures for errant members. The final agreed charter continued the policy of upholding the principle of non-interference in the internal political affairs of member states. See "Vietnam Ratifies Asean Charter", *Straits Times*, 20 Mar. 2008.

At the 40th Anniversary Summit in Singapore in November 2007, the ten members signed the ASEAN Charter, which committed ASEAN to become a "rules-based legal organisation".[58] The charter would come into effect only after all ten countries had ratified it, and they were given a year to do so. ASEAN's new secretary-general, Surin Pitsuwan (who succeeded Ong on 1 January 2008), acknowledged that the task of getting the charter ratified would be a "delicate" one as "some member states had expressed reservations out of respect for their parliamentary and constitutional processes".[59] Jakarta and Manila had already expressed their reluctance to ratify the charter unless ASEAN took a firmer stand against Myanmar. The junta's crackdown on the street protests described as "the largest ... in two decades against Myanmar's military rulers" in September 2007,[60] known as the "Saffron Revolution" because it involved monks, complicated matters further. Singapore was the first member state to ratify the charter in January 2008. In February 2008 Laos, Malaysia, Brunei and Vietnam ratified it. Myanmar did so in July (even as it continued to keep Aung San Suu Kyi under house detention). The last two countries to ratify the charter were the Philippines followed by Indonesia, both in October. It is worth noting Miriam Santiago's (head of the Philippines Senate foreign relations panel) explanation for the ratification. She said, "We wish it were a more perfect document ..." However, "the emergence of China and India as economic powerhouses has created new realities for Asean. The Asean economic community will keep the Philippines competitive alongside these Asian giants."[61]

US-ASEAN Relations

One development that somewhat marred ASEAN's 40th year was US-ASEAN relations. It was announced in May 2007 that US President George W. Bush would visit Singapore in September to attend the ASEAN-US commemorative summit marking 30 years of relations.[62]

---

[58] "Charter Turns Asean into Rules-Based Legal Organisation", *Straits Times*, 8 Jan. 2008.

[59] "Surin to Urge Asean Members to Ratify Charter", *Straits Times*, 8 Jan. 2008.

[60] "Monks' Protest Is Challenging Burmese Junta", *New York Times*, 24 Sept. 2007.

[61] "Manila Ratifies Asean Charter", *Straits Times*, 8 Oct. 2008.

[62] "Bush to Visit S'pore for Asean-US Summit", *Straits Times*, 5 May 2007. Singapore's Prime Minister Lee Hsien Loong in a speech marking the 40th anniversary of ASEAN and 30 years of US-ASEAN ties disclosed it.

However, in July it was reported that Bush would not be coming to Singapore after all and that the meeting of ASEAN leaders would be rescheduled "for a later date". Compounding the disappointment, Secretary of State Condoleezza Rice also decided to skip the ARF meeting in July because of developments in the Middle East that required her attention. Her deputy, John Negroponte, would represent her. Rice had last missed the ASEAN Post-Ministerial and ARF meetings in July 2005. Not surprisingly, the reaction of the Southeast Asian countries was that they were, to quote Surin, "being marginalised, ignored and given little attention" by Washington while other dialogue partners were "moving firmly and systematically to cultivate a closer and stronger relationship in the Asean region".[63] The reaction was very much a reflection of the importance of the US presence in the region in the eyes of the Southeast Asian countries.[64] The Southeast Asian leaders were concerned that the US was distracted by developments in the Middle East, terrorism and North Korea, thus allowing China to "raise its profile quietly and be more assertive".[65]

On both occasions, in 2005 and 2007, Rice was represented by her deputies Robert Zoellick (in 2005) and Negroponte (in 2007), both with strong credentials and knowledge of the region. Rice's absence was certainly a "dampener". "Domestic and international pressures" undoubtedly distracted the Bush administration. However, as Ong said, "the web of links and interactions" between the United States and ASEAN in general were "actually very dense and very impenetrable". The partnership was thus on "solid ground".[66] As Ralph Cossa put it, "unfortunately, when it comes to US-ASEAN relations, form has not matched substance".[67] At the APEC meeting in September 2007,

---

[63] "Bush No-Show 'Sends Asean the Wrong Signal'", *Straits Times*, 21 July 2007; "Condoleezza Rice to Skip Asean Forum in Manila", *Straits Times*, 25 July 2007.

[64] "Asean Sees Vital Role for US in Region: PM", *Straits Times*, 8 Sept. 2007.

[65] "Bush No-Show 'Sends Asean the Wrong Signal'".

[66] "Free Trade Pact with US Unlikely: Asean Chief", *Straits Times*, 24 July 2007; "Rice's No-Show a 'Dampener' But ...", *Today*, 24 July 2007.

[67] "ASEAN at 40: Coming of Age or Mid-Life Crisis?" *PacNet* #33, 5 Sept. 2007. See also interview with Christopher Hill (US assistant secretary of state for East Asian and Pacific affairs), *Straits Times*, 1 Aug. 2007. Hill said the perception that the US was uninterested in the region was "to some extent an anachronism" stemming from a view that Washington was not engaged during the 1997 financial crisis. The United States' focus on the Middle East did not mean it was neglecting ASEAN.

President Bush attempted to make up for the aborted meeting with ASEAN leaders in Singapore by inviting them to a meeting at his Texas ranch on a date convenient for all. Bush apparently reserved such invitations "as a diplomatic plum for close allies", but in the end the meeting did not take place because of scheduling difficulties and disagreements over Myanmar. Bush also announced that Washington would appoint an ambassador to ASEAN "so that we can make sure that the ties we've established over the past years remain firmly entrenched".[68] However, there remained the feeling that these actions were an afterthought. As Surin noted, "Over the last 30 years of US-ASEAN relations, there has been no US-ASEAN summit. In contrast, China, Japan and Korea have played an active part in initiating various meetings with ASEAN through ASEAN-Plus-Three modules."[69]

The year 2008 was the tail end of the Bush administration. A new administration led by Barack Obama took office in January 2009. Many in Southeast Asia hoped that the United States under Obama would pay attention to their region.[70] In July 2009 the United States finally signed the Treaty of Amity and Cooperation. Secretary of State Hillary Clinton announced, "I wanted to send a very clear message that the United States is back, that we are fully engaged and committed to our relationships in South-east Asia ... This treaty seals our commitment to work in partnership with the nations of Asean to advance the interest and values we share."[71] Many interpreted this declaration to be "a clear signal that the Americans were looking to challenge Chinese influence in South-east Asia". Analysts were, however, of the view that the immediate geopolitical concerns of the United States—developments in Afghanistan, Pakistan, Iran and Iraq—were "largely unchanged" from the Bush period. Thus, although US officials made all the right noises and gestures, including convening the inaugural US-ASEAN summit

[68] "Asean Leaders Get an Invite to Texas from Bush", *Straits Times*, 8 Sept. 2007; "Plans for Bush-Asean Summit Hit Brick Wall", *Straits Times*, 20 Dec. 2007. The first US envoy to ASEAN was Scot Marciel, who was concurrently deputy assistant secretary of state. In his senate confirmation hearing, he said he would focus on the Myanmar issue. See "US to Confirm 1st Asean Envoy", *Today*, 11 Apr. 2008.

[69] Surin Pitsuwan, "US-ASEAN Cooperation", *PacNet* #15, 3 Apr. 2008.

[70] See, for example, Simon Tay, "Asean Needs an Obama Policy", *Straits Times*, 25 Feb. 2009.

[71] "Clinton Declares: US back in Asia", *Straits Times*, 23 July 2009.

(known as US-ASEAN Leaders Meeting) in Singapore on the margins of the APEC meeting in November 2009, there was no guarantee that its engagement with ASEAN would not be "relegated to a form of 'drive-by diplomacy'".[72] As one political observer wondered, "... with two wars to fight and a groaning economy to tend", would it not be "a case of a willing heart but tiring flesh for the Americans"?[73] In short, it was too early to tell. This issue will be addressed in chapter 5.

Intra-ASEAN Relations

Most analysts agree that ASEAN has indeed achieved much in the last 40 years. The last ten years have been particularly challenging. Since 1997, "the battle-cry has been for all ten ASEAN members to pull together as one team, one market and one organisation".[74] There were two key tasks ahead for the organization and the region beyond 2007 and as ASEAN headed into its fifth decade. One would be "strengthening its three support pillars, that is, economic integration, regional security and socio-cultural ties" underpinned by the ASEAN Charter.[75] All ten member states agreed that regional integration was the prerequisite for ASEAN to remain in the driver's seat. However, there were differences regarding the pace of change. The process of economic integration seemed to be moving relatively faster. However, as George Yeo pointed out, "if only economic integration binds the grouping together, we can only go so far ... diversions of national interest will pull us apart ... If security and socio-cultural (ties) were not strengthened simultaneously, then the pillars will crack."[76] Two, the organization and the region needed to remain neutral or not take sides with one or the other of the major powers. Bilahari Kausikan, then second permanent

[72] "US 'Committed to Asean for Long Haul'", *Straits Times*, 2 Nov. 2009. The Second US-ASEAN Leaders Meeting took place in New York on 24 September 2010 on the margins of the annual 65th UN General Assembly.
[73] Peh, "Can US Squeeze into the 'Chinasean' Bed?"
[74] Yang Razali Kassim, "ASEAN at 40: The End of a Two-Speed Grouping?" *RSIS Commentaries*, 6 Sept. 2007; Simon Tay, "It's Time for Asean to Deliver", *Straits Times*, 16 July 2008.
[75] "Singapore Sets Itself Three Challenges as New Asean Chairman", *Straits Times*, 21 Aug. 2007.
[76] Ibid.

secretary at the Singapore Ministry of Foreign Affairs, explained the real meaning of the oft-repeated refrain "Asean in the driver's seat": "the complexity and sensitivity of relationships among major powers meant that Asean played an essential role in providing *a relatively neutral platform* for an East Asian architecture [emphasis added]."[77]

As ASEAN entered its fifth decade, its focus on the pursuit of an ASEAN-centred regional order remained unchanged. Addressing the Munich Security Conference on Security Policy in February 2008, Singapore's Defence Minister Teo Chee Hean pointed out that ASEAN, "which lies at the heart of many multilateral groupings such as the Asean Regional Forum, the East Asia Summit and the Shangri-La Dialogue, was well placed to play a unique role in the evolving Asian security architecture ..." He added that even as the US remained "pre-eminent and important as a stabilising force in Asia, new players and resurgent powers are jostling for influence, access to markets and strategic resources ... Southeast Asia is an important crossroads where this great game is being played."[78] ASEAN's determination not to lose its central position in any new regional order can be seen from its chilly response to Australian Prime Minister Kevin Rudd's proposal for a new Asia Pacific Community outlined in a June 2008 speech to the Asia Society Australasia. In his speech, Rudd proposed a new regional institution that could engage "the full spectrum of dialogue, cooperation and action on economic and political matters and future challenges related to security". Although he claimed that this new institution would not diminish any of the existing regional bodies, the ASEAN countries were clearly concerned that it would. Most of the existing economic and security platforms in the region are ASEAN-centred. ASEAN has always been acutely sensitive of being sidelined. Barry Desker (dean of the government-funded S. Rajaratnam School of International Studies) described the proposal as "dead in the water right from the very beginning". Indonesian President Yudhoyono reportedly told Rudd that it was an "interesting idea" but Indonesia's priority was "in strengthening

[77] "Asean 'Holds Key to Building Stable East Asian Region'", *Straits Times*, 23 Aug. 2007.

[78] "Singapore Sees Crucial Role for Asean in Shaping Asian Security", *Straits Times*, 12 Feb. 2008.

ASEAN and not supporting a new forum".[79] George Yeo, who was then Singapore's foreign minister, recalled his meeting with Rudd: "When I met PM Rudd I thanked him for helping to catalyse the thinking of Asean. So now there are two possibilities, either an EAS expanded for Russia and the US or a separate Asean plus eight (including the US and Russia) configuration."[80] Although Rudd's proposal failed to take off, it helped catalyze the thinking of ASEAN on broadening the EAS, which saw the inclusion of the United States and Russia into the EAS in 2010.[81]

Overall, ASEAN had made all the right moves since the shock of the 1997 financial crisis. However, as Singapore Deputy Prime Minister S. Jayakumar said, "just as within a country, it is easy to promulgate a law, the real test comes in the implementation, so it will be after the charter has been promulgated, whether members individually and Asean collectively have the political resolve to discharge their commitment to the charter both in letter and spirit".[82] Vatikiotis put it most eloquently:

> Here lies the heart of the problem: In many ways, the Asean Charter sets standards far higher than what is achievable in many member states, where democracy is flawed or imperfectly developed, freedom is

[79] Both Barry Desker's and Yudhoyono's quotes are from "Rudd's Asia-Pacific Plan Lost at Sea?" *Crikey*, 31 May 2010, https://www.crikey.com.au/2010/05/31/rudds-asia-pacific-plan-lost-at-sea/, accessed 14 Mar. 2017. The report noted that Vietnam and the Philippines were apparently supportive, while Singapore, Indonesia and Malaysia were sceptical. The proposal was also controversial within Australia. See also Rodolfo C. Severino, "What's the Point of a New Asia-Pacific Architecture?" *Straits Times*, 7 Jan. 2009. Rudd attempted to promote his idea in his Singapore lecture in August 2008 by adding that ASEAN would "remain the absolute core of the region's architecture". Rudd spoke of his idea again at the Shangri-La Dialogue in June 2009. See "Rudd Makes a Plug for his Asia-Pacific Vision", *Straits Times*, 13 Aug. 2008; "With ASEAN at Its Heart ...", *Today*, 13 Aug. 2008; Tommy Koh, "Australia Must Respect Asean's Role", *Straits Times*, 24 June 2009. By the time Rudd resigned his prime ministership in 2010, his Asia Pacific Community proposal had been quietly put aside due to lack of support, particularly from the ASEAN countries and, according to WikiLeaks, the United States as well. See https://www.wsws.org/en/articles/2010/12/rudd-d31.html, accessed 14 Mar. 2017.

[80] Quoted in Greg Sheridan, "An Inclusive Vision for the Asia-Pacific", *Straits Times*, 22 June 2010.

[81] Ibid.

[82] "S'pore Seeks 'Strong and Cohesive' Asean", *Straits Times*, 13 Jan. 2007.

> still constrained and human rights for many people a distant dream. That's not to say the Charter exercise is futile. The challenge is to find the best way to persuade governments to adhere to these lofty norms and principles.[83]

This called for political leadership. As Pavin Chachavalpongpun pointed out, "Leadership of Asean is key to success."[84] Analysts such as Pavin, however, were of the view that a leader was unlikely to emerge from within ASEAN in the near future. In his words, "at the most critical time for Asean ... some of the possible candidates have failed to stand out as the group's leaders, in fact since charismatic figures have left the regional scene, including Indonesia's Suharto, Singapore's Lee Kuan Yew and Malaysia's Mahathir Mohamad".[85] Indeed, there had not been any clear leadership in ASEAN since 1997 as most of the ASEAN leaders were preoccupied with domestic politics. Indonesia, being the largest country in Southeast Asia, was the natural leader, and until 1997 it was treated as the first amongst equals within ASEAN. However, from 1997 to 2004 its leadership of ASEAN was undermined by "political instability, economic hardship and internal security threats".[86]

The turning point came with the appointment of Susilo Bambang Yudhoyono (popularly known by the acronym SBY) as Indonesia's first directly elected president in September 2004. According to Dino Djalal, who was President Yudhoyono's former adviser and spokesman, SBY took great interest in world affairs and "wanted Indonesia to be

[83] Michael Vatikiotis, "Asean Charter Hangs in the Balance", *Straits Times*, 9 Jan. 2008. See also "Indonesian Thinker Takes Asean Charter to Task", *Straits Times*, 9 Jan. 2008. For a concise debate of the charter, see book review by William Choong of Tommy Koh et al. (eds), *The Making of the Asean Charter* (Singapore: World Scientific, 2009), *Straits Times*, 10 Mar. 2009; and the rejoinder, Tommy Koh, "Why You Shouldn't Yawn at Asean", *Straits Times*, 29 Apr. 2009.

[84] "Key Grouping Central to Regional Balance", *Straits Times*, 10 Apr. 2010.

[85] "One ASEAN Issue: No Clear Leader", *Today*, 30 May 2008. For an insider's revelation of the pecking order within ASEAN, see Dominic Faulder, *Anand Panyarachun and the Making of Modern Thailand* (Singapore: Editions Didier Millet, 2018), pp. 264–7. See also "Letter from Najib's Office Sent to CIA Belittling S'pore as Too Small to Make an Impact in Southeast Asia", https://www.theonlinecitizen.com/2018/07/20/letter-from-najibs-office-sent-to-cia-belittling-spore-as-too-small-to-make-an-impact-in-southeast-asia/, accessed 4 Jan. 2019.

[86] John McBeth, *The Loner: President Yudhoyono's Decade of Trial and Indecision* (Singapore: Straits Times Press, 2016), p. 111.

influential and relevant in international affairs". He wanted to be a "regional leader" and "statesman". According to John McBeth, who wrote a biography of SBY, "he moved the country's foreign policy away from its previous meandering path to one where it played a more prominent role in international relations and organisations … and reclaimed Indonesia's leadership of ASEAN …" Most important, he was keen on giving ASEAN "a larger global profile".[87] However, in the lead-up to the 2009 presidential election, SBY too was distracted by politics at home. Consequently, Indonesia's foreign affairs were "treated with little significance, including the country's role in Asean".[88] There was also an emerging view in Indonesia that the country had been too dependent on ASEAN as "the instrument of its foreign policy", understandably and necessarily so. That was the past. Looking ahead, if ASEAN could not move "beyond its lowest denominator, as defined by Laos or Myanmar", Indonesia would likely seek "to become more independent from ASEAN". "For the future", as Jusuf Wanandi put it, Indonesia "needs to pursue its own national interest, on top of its loyalty and solidarity with ASEAN". A younger generation of strategic thinkers such as Wanandi's protégé Rizal Sukma had urged Indonesia to break with ASEAN on issues concerning "freedom and human rights". Indonesia, in his words, needed to "begin formulating a post-Asean foreign policy".[89]

Thailand, too, was absorbed by its internal politics. The ouster of Prime Minister Thaksin Shinawatra in a military coup in September 2006 led to a clash between the Red Shirts (supporters of Thaksin) and the Yellow Shirts (supporters of the conservative establishment and purportedly the Thai royalty). The latter was also known as the People's Alliance for Democracy, or PAD. The clash culminated in a military dictatorship in 2014 that remained in force in 2017. A consequence of the political crisis was that it fuelled a dispute between Thailand and Cambodia over a 4.6-kilometre piece of land near the Preah Vihar

[87] Ibid., pp. 111, 117.

[88] "One ASEAN Issue: No Clear Leader", *Today*, 30 May 2008.

[89] Rizal Sukma, "Indonesia Needs a Post-ASEAN Foreign Policy", *Jakarta Post*, 30 June 2009. See also Jusuf Wanandi, "Indonesia's Foreign Policy and the Meaning of ASEAN", *PacNet* #27, 16 May 2008; "Indonesia May Be Outgrowing Asean", *Straits Times*, 11 July 2009; Barry Desker, "Is Indonesia Outgrowing Asean?" *Straits Times*, 29 Sept. 2010.

temple in July 2008, which threatened to impact ASEAN's integration efforts. While there were disputes of one sort or another between ASEAN member states, this one culminated in a military standoff.[90] The Thai-Cambodian border conflict was "primarily an internal Thai conflict in which the army is seeking to demonstrate its continuing ability to pursue its own foreign policy goals".[91] The PAD and Democrat Party "fuelled" the border dispute "to support their vulnerable political situations by igniting nationalism against each other" and to "discredit the Samak government's foreign policy".[92] Cambodian Prime Minister Hun Sen, on the other hand, was also exploiting the dispute "to gain popularity and political advantage" in the run-up to elections at home.[93] Clashes between the two sides continued sporadically until 2011. ASEAN's efforts spearheaded by Indonesian Foreign Minister Marty Natalegawa in early 2011 failed to help resolve the bilateral dispute.[94] In April 2011 Phnom Penh requested the International Court of Justice to interpret the 1962 judgement on the temple. This took two years. In November 2013 the ICJ ruled in favour of Cambodia, thus requiring Thailand to withdraw its troops completely from the area. This ended the saga.[95] Answering his own question of whether Thailand was ready to lead the organization as it geared up to establish the ASEAN Community by 2015, Pavin Chachavalpongpun's answer was that "it has shown no sign thus far that it is".[96]

---

[90] The International Court of Justice in 1962 awarded the temple to Cambodia, but the 4.6 square kilometres of land remain disputed. See also Tim Huxley, "Grasp Nettle of Security Problems", *Today*, 22 July 2008; Michael Vatikiotis, "The Faltering Asean Way", *Straits Times*, 28 Oct. 2008; K. Kesavapany, "ASEAN in Disarray?" *Straits Times*, 29 Oct. 2008.

[91] Duncan McCargo quoted in Veasna Var, "Cambodia-Thailand Sovereignty Disputes: Implications for Cambodia's Strategic Environment and Defence Organisation", *Strategic Analysis* 41, 2 (2017): 157.

[92] Samak Sundaravej, who became prime minister after the ouster of Thaksin Shinawatra in 2006, was seen as pro-Thaksin. Pavin Chachavalpongpun quoted in Veasna, "Cambodia-Thailand Sovereignty Disputes": 158.

[93] Veasna, "Cambodia-Thailand Sovereignty Disputes": 162.

[94] For a concise account of the Preah Vihar dispute, see Veasna, "Cambodia-Thailand Sovereignty Disputes": 152–72.

[95] "Preah Vihear Temple: Disputed Land Cambodian, Court Rules", *BBC Asia*, 11 Nov. 2013.

[96] Pavin Chachavalpongpun, "Bangkok May Not Be Ready to Lead Asean", *Straits Times*, 18 Nov. 2008.

Malaysia's Prime Minister Abdullah Badawi was also under pressure, no less from his predecessor, Mahathir Mohamad, for presiding over the worst result in the political history of the United Malays National Organisation and its National Front since independence. Over in the Philippines, President Gloria Arroyo was under intense pressure to step down because of corruption allegations even as she vowed not to relinquish power until her term ended in 2010. In fact, she had been under pressure to resign since allegations that she had rigged the May 2004 presidential election. According to Pavin, "although Singapore's leadership has enjoyed stability, the country is often perceived to be too small to lead Asean ... Singapore is comfortable with taking on a coordinating role, while acknowledging its policy constraints partly because of its close ties to the United States." As for the other ASEAN member states, they had "made known their preference to support, rather than guide, the organisation, possibly because of their own legitimacy vulnerability".[97]

The 14th ASEAN Summit in December 2008, hosted by Thailand, had to be postponed to February the following year and its venue changed because of the Thai political crisis that saw a weeklong takeover of Bangkok's two airports by protesters. It was originally to be held in Pattaya but had to be aborted (when the regional leaders were either already in Pattaya or arriving) because of the resurgence of the unrest in Thailand. The unrest eventually ended with the appointment of Abhisit Vejjajiva as the new prime minister. Many analysts predicted that the "respite from political instability would likely be short-lived".[98] Thailand was sufficiently stable to host the ASEAN Summit from 27 February to 1 March 2009 in Hua Hin. The meetings among dialogue partners that normally followed the meeting of the ten member states was shifted to April 2009 (because of scheduling reasons). In the eyes of many, the whole episode was a loss of face for the organization.[99]

---

[97] "One ASEAN Issue: No Clear Leader", *Today*, 30 May 2008. See also "Asean Charter a No-Go in Jakarta?" *Straits Times*, 26 July 2008. It was reported that several Indonesian legislators were upset by Singapore Prime Minister Lee Hsien Loong's remarks on members' slow ratification, with one quoted as saying, "we are still examining the Charter but Lee's remarks have negatively affected us".

[98] "Asean Summit Now Set for Feb. 24", *Straits Times*, 16 Dec. 2008; "Thai Opposition Leader Becomes PM", *The Guardian*, 15 Dec. 2008.

[99] See "It Seemed Like a Bad Dream", *Straits Times*, 14 Apr. 2009; Donald K. Emmerson, "ASEAN's Pattaya Problem", *PacNet* #30, 23 Apr. 2009.

The summit, as expected, reaffirmed ASEAN's commitment to achieve a single market by 2015 and ASEAN Community by 2015.[100] A roadmap that charted the path to achieve those goals was drawn up. The summit also saw the first draft of the terms of reference of an ASEAN Human Rights Body (as specified in Article 14 of the recently ratified ASEAN Charter). The ASEAN Inter-Governmental Commission on Human Rights was inaugurated in October at the 15th ASEAN Summit. Critics panned it as "toothless to act against member-states with poor human rights records", such as Myanmar.[101] Former diplomat and Director of the Institute of Southeast Asia Studies S. Kesavapany made the following observation:

> [S]ome believe that strengthening the human rights mechanism in the Asean Charter would help to bring recalcitrant countries like Myanmar to heel. However, others believe that spreading the virtues of democracy to Myanmar will help to bring about changes there, as they have in their own countries. To my mind, these are simplistic hopes. In the final analysis, change will come about in Myanmar as a result of internal pressures ...[102]

As mentioned in chapter 3, in August 2003 the Myanmar junta announced a seven-stage roadmap to democracy. In 2008 the draft constitution, which ensured that the military would continue to wield power, was finally completed; it was put to a referendum in May 2008 and subsequently adopted. A general election followed on 7 November 2010, the first since the election in 1990 (which was never implemented because of disagreement between the NLD, which won the election, and the military/SLORC). Thein Sein, a retired general, was appointed president. The political dynamic looked very much like that of Indonesia during the Suharto era. One week after the election Aung San Suu Kyi,

[100] The ASEAN Community date was brought forward to 2015 from 2020 at the 12th ASEAN Summit in January 2007 in Cebu, Philippines. See "Cebu Declaration on the Acceleration of the Establishment of an ASEAN Community by 2015", http://asean.org/?static_post=cebu-declaration-on-the-acceleration-of-the-establishment-of-an-asean-community-by-2015, accessed 24 Apr. 2017.
[101] "Asean Human Rights Body Launched", *Straits Times*, 24 Oct. 2009. For a defence of the AICHR, see "Human Rights Struggle", *Straits Times*, 23 Oct. 2009.
[102] S. Kesavapany, "Cooperation Trumps Confrontation", *Straits Times*, 27 July 2009.

whose house arrest the military junta had extended by another 18 months in August 2009,[103] was finally released on 13 November 2010. The last phases of the seven-stage roadmap thus coincided with the ratification of the ASEAN Charter in July 2008. The 2010 general election, which the NLD boycotted,[104] also coincided with the transition from the Bush to the Obama administration. New Secretary of State Clinton ordered a policy review of US relations with Myanmar stating what was known all along: that both sanctions and engagement had not worked. The new developments in Myanmar led to a policy known as pragmatic engagement, meaning that sanctions would need to coexist with various forms of engagement. It was a slow process to reorient the relationship that eventually led to Clinton's visit to Yangon in 2011 and President Obama's in November 2012; he became "the first sitting American president ever to visit Burma".[105] The Myanmar issue, which had dogged ASEAN's relations with both the United States and the European Union since Myanmar joined ASEAN in 1997, appeared to have been finally resolved.

In the context of Myanmar, one issue that needs to be highlighted is the plight of the stateless Rohingya refugees fleeing the country, claiming persecution by the Myanmar military. The issue has caused some tensions as the refugees flee into Indonesia, Thailand and Malaysia. Singapore's Prime Minister Lee Hsien Loong, in his first public speech on the Rohingya issue, noted that media reports on the "alleged ill-treatment of the Rohingya had hurt Asean's image". He warned that ASEAN would lose credibility if the organization were "unable to sort out the problem in our own region".[106]

This is where we pause to reintroduce the long-drawn-out dispute over the South China Sea islands, the subject of the next chapter.

---

[103] "Extended House Arrest of Aung San Suu Kyi Prompts Wave of Criticism", http://www.abc.net.au/worldtoday/content/2009/s2653461.htm, accessed 16 Mar. 2017.

[104] The NLD was of the view that the referendum was a farce and refused to register for the election, thus disqualifying itself as a political party. It was dissolved on orders from the junta.

[105] See Kenton Clymer, *A Delicate Relationship: The United States and Burma/Myanmar Since 1945* (Ithaca: Cornell University Press, 2015), chapter 14.

[106] "Crisis Makes Integration 'More Urgent'", and "PM Lee: Asean Must Address Rohingya Issue or Risk Losing Credibility", *Straits Times*, 2 Mar. 2009.

CHAPTER 5

2000–10: The South China Sea Dispute

"Militarily weak states like the Philippines must—of necessity—put their faith in a world order governed by international law; guided by a global code of ethics, and inspired by shared moral values."[1]

"These are incremental moves, calculated to be assertive enough to strengthen the claims, but not so strong as to provoke action by the other claimants."[2]

A Refresher on the South China Sea Dispute

Chapters 1 and 2 touched on the Chinese claim of suzerainty over the whole of the South China Sea (when it proclaimed its Territorial Waters Law) in February 1992. This led to a squabble over the legitimacy of the claim, initially with Vietnam[3] and then with the Philippines in 1994–95 because of the Chinese occupation of Mischief Reef (135 nautical miles west of Palawan), which was also claimed by the Philippines. In July 1992 the ASEAN ministers at the 25th Ministerial Meeting in Manila adopted the ASEAN Declaration on the South

[1] Jose T. Almonte, "Coordinating Asean's Position on the South China Sea Issue", speech at the ASEAN Experts on the Law of the Sea Conference, 27–28 Nov. 1997, *Towards One Southeast Asia: Collected Speeches*, Jose T. Almonte (Quezon City: Institute for Strategic and Development Studies, 2004), p. 201.

[2] Rodolfo Severino (former ASEAN secretary-general) quoted in Barry Wains, "More Claims", *Far Eastern Economic Review*, 15 Apr. 2004, p. 20.

[3] The maritime dispute between Vietnam and China goes back to before the end of the Cold War, notably over the Paracels in 1974 and Johnson Reef in 1988.

China Sea. The declaration emphasized "the necessity to resolve all sovereignty and jurisdictional issues pertaining to the South China Sea by peaceful means, without resort to force" and requested "all parties concerned to apply the principles contained in the Treaty of Amity and Cooperation in Southeast Asia as the basis for establishing a code of international conduct over the South China Sea". Lastly, it invited "all parties concerned to subscribe to this Declaration of principles".[4] Beijing expressed only lukewarm support for the declaration and went on to build structures on Mischief Reef. The Mischief Reef incident in early 1995 compelled ASEAN to adopt a united position vis-a-vis China, albeit pressured by the Philippines to do so.

ASEAN eventually issued a statement, two days before the bilateral talks between Beijing and Manila (on 18 March 1995), calling on all parties to adhere to the letter and spirit of the 1992 ASEAN Declaration on the South China Sea. China and the Philippines subsequently signed a Joint Statement on PRC-RP Consultations on the South China Sea and on Other Areas of Cooperation. In 1996 ASEAN called for a code of conduct that would ensure long-term stability in the South China Sea as well as foster understanding amongst claimant states.

Meanwhile, the squabble between Vietnam and China over the Spratlys quietened down, albeit briefly, following the establishment in July 1995 of a joint working group at the vice-ministerial level to discuss the issue. The working group met twice, in November 1995 in Hanoi and July 1996 in Beijing. The third meeting convened in April 1997 during the Kanto incident. On 7 March 1997 the Chinese sent the Kanto Oil Platform Number 3 and two pilot ships, Numbers 206 and 208, to conduct exploratory oil drilling in what was supposedly Vietnam's continental shelf. Hanoi protested and called for a halt to the drilling. The Chinese maintained that they were prospecting within the Chinese continental shelf and exclusive economic zone. This dragged on for about a month until 3 April, when it was announced that both sides would meet on 9 April 1997 in Beijing. There were no details given of the meeting of 9–10 April, except that both sides agreed that even though their differences could not be resolved immediately, that

[4] See 1992 ASEAN Declaration on South China Sea, https://cil.nus.edu.sg/rp/pdf/1992%20ASEAN%20Declaration%20on%20the%20South%20China%20Sea-pdf.pdf, accessed 21 Mar. 2017.

would not affect the friendly relations between the two countries. The Sino-Vietnamese working group met again in July 1998.

In late October 1998, Chinese ships were again spotted off Mischief Reef. Manila alleged that the Chinese were building an aircraft landing strip there. The Chinese said that they were only replacing the temporary shelters for anglers built in 1995 with permanent ones. At the Sixth ASEAN Summit in Hanoi in December 1998, the Philippines was tasked to draft the code of conduct. Beijing realized that it had to find a balance between exercising sovereignty over the reefs and islands and provoking the ASEAN countries, with which it wanted to maintain good relations. But as Barry Wain noted, "from the beginning, China didn't want a regional code of conduct ... The Chinese historically are wary of multilateral entanglements, and in this case, they prefer to deal separately with each other as problems arise, an arrangement that gives them an enormous advantage."[5] Beijing's strategy was to engage in what Andrew Scobell described as "slow-intensity conflict".[6]

Developments Leading to the Drafting of a Code of Conduct

The narrative in this chapter picks up from when the Second Mischief Reef incident occurred. Between 1995 and 2002, Hanoi adopted a "dual-track engagement" policy towards China—bilaterally and multilaterally. As Do Thanh Hai noted, Vietnam "continued to put a premium on its regular bilateral party-to-party and state-to-state dialogues with China to facilitate negotiations on outstanding territorial disputes", of which the South China Sea was only one. Both countries managed to settle the land border and maritime boundary at the Gulf of Tonkin in 1999 and 2000 respectively but failed to resolve their claims on the Paracels and Spratlys. The agreements reached regarding the land border and the demarcation of the Gulf of Tonkin sea border were not without controversy within Vietnam. There was the view or impression

[5] Barry Wain, "At Loggerheads with Beijing", *Wall Street Journal Asia*, 6–8 Oct. 2000.

[6] Andrew Scobell, "Slow-Intensity Conflict in the South China Sea", presented at the Second Annual Conference of Foreign Policy Research Institute Asia Programme on "Flashpoints in East Asia", Philadelphia, 12 May 2000.

that Hanoi had compromised too much in order to accommodate the Chinese.[7] When Vietnamese President Tran Duc Luong visited China in December 2000 (his first visit since assuming the position of president in 1997 and the second visit by a Vietnamese president since the normalization of relations in 1991), the two countries signed a series of agreements while "steering clear" of the sensitive South China Sea issue. Beijing hailed the visit as a "success" while also declaring itself the "undisputed master of the islands claimed by both countries".[8]

Malaysia, one of the six claimants to the South China Sea, on the other hand, enjoyed a very good relationship with China during this period. In 1999 both countries commemorated their 25th anniversary of diplomatic relations with the signing of an agreement to expand political, trade and transport links. They also agreed to boost defence cooperation and use peaceful means to resolve tensions over disputed waters in the South China Sea. Malaysian Prime Minister Mahathir Mohamad, on his fifth visit to China, expressed his appreciation for China's "responsible attitude during the Asia financial crisis and its adherence to not devaluing the Chinese currency". Both sides also agreed that the South China Sea issue could "only be resolved by relevant countries involved, opposing any involvement and interference by any outside force".[9] Indeed, Chinese Premier Zhu Rongji remarked that Sino-Malaysian relations were "at their best now".[10] In July 2000 Rear Admiral Huang Jiang, head of the Chinese naval fleet—comprising the *Shenzhen* destroyer and the *Nancang* support ship—made a port call at Malaysia's Port Klang. Royal Malaysian Navy Chief Vice-Admiral Datuk Sri Abu Bakar Abdul Jamal in his welcome speech pointed out that good relations and cooperation between the two navies could contribute to regional peace.[11] Chinese Defence Minister General Chi Haotian visited Malaysia in November 2000 and told his Malaysian

---

[7] Do Thanh Hai, *Vietnam and the South China Sea: Politics, Security and Legality* (London: Routledge, 2017), p. 222.

[8] "PRC Spokeswoman Restates Claim to Spratly Islands, Surrounding Waters", *Hong Kong AFP*, *FBIS-CHI*-2000-1226.

[9] "Premier Zhu Rongji, Malaysia's Mahathir Hold Talks on Bilateral Ties", *Xinhua News Agency*, 18 Aug. 1999, *BBC/SWB/FE*/3618/G/1; "Malaysia and China to Boost Ties in Defence", *Straits Times*, 3 June 1999.

[10] "China-Malaysia Ties at Their Best", *Straits Times*, 24 Nov. 1999.

[11] "Malaysian Navy Chief, Chinese Fleet Delegation Discuss Relations", *Nanyang Siang Pau*, 14 July 2000, *BBC/SWB/FE*/3893/B/3.

counterpart, Datuk Seri Najib Tun Razak, that China wanted to change the perception in some quarters that it was a "potential aggressor".[12] Critics of Malaysia's attitude on the South China Sea issue, such as Wain, pointed out that "Malaysia's shabby behavior" not only weakened ASEAN's position in the ongoing negotiations but also undermined "the group's efforts to develop a common stand on the South China Sea".[13] The Malaysians had themselves erected structures on Investigator Shoal (claimed by China, Taiwan and the Philippines).

From mid-1997 until early 2000 the Asian Financial Crisis distracted Southeast Asian governments, some even having to deal with their political survival as a result. There were also two contrasting views of China during this period. One argued that China had no real intention of coming into conflict with Southeast Asian countries, as evident from its helpful attitude during the financial crisis. The other view was that much depended on China's medium- and long-term intentions, which were still very unclear. No one would know whether a powerful China would be hegemonic or benign. In the short term, China did not have the power-projection capability to control the area—although in 2000 it successfully carried out mid-air refuelling of its fighter planes, "thus expanding its ability to project power".[14] There were, however, more immediate worries than the China threat, especially for Indonesia, Malaysia and Thailand. It is worth noting that Vietnam and the Philippines were not as affected by the financial crisis as were their fellow ASEAN members. Not surprisingly, the South China Sea issue was not an immediate priority for ASEAN given that it affected principally Vietnam and the Philippines.

The draft code of conduct was never officially made public. According to Philippine Foreign Affairs Secretary Domingo Siazon and ASEAN Secretary-General Severino, there were three essential elements in the code of conduct: All claimants should (a) settle their differences peacefully and (b) in accordance with international law and the UN Convention of the Law of the Sea (UNCLOS) and (c) maintain the status quo, which meant that currently unoccupied islands and shoals

[12] "China Wants to Set Right Image: Najib", *Straits Times*, 29 Nov. 2000.

[13] Wain, "At Loggerheads with Beijing".

[14] Mark J. Valencia, "Beijing Is Setting the Stage for Trouble in the South China Sea", *International Herald Tribune*, 3 July 2000.

should remain so and there should not be any further construction of buildings or structures. The code should also indicate the area in which it would apply.[15] Confidential ASEAN documents obtained by Kyodo News revealed that the ASEAN claimants themselves could not agree on many critical areas in the code of conduct. For example, Vietnam wanted the code to apply to the whole South China Sea, Malaysia wanted it to apply to only the Spratlys and Paracels, and China opposed the inclusion of the Paracels. Vietnam wanted to ban new occupations in all forms, but both Malaysia and the Philippines objected. The Philippines wanted only multilateral activities in the South China Sea, whereas Malaysia insisted that bilateral activities be allowed.[16]

According to the Taiwan-based analyst Chen Hurng Yu, "because each state in the region has its own perception of the South China Sea, the execution of a regional code of conduct is complicated". There were differences between the codes proposed by ASEAN and China: ASEAN wanted conflict resolution through a multilateral approach, whereas China wanted a bilateral approach. ASEAN wanted the area to cover the entire South China Sea, whereas China wanted to focus on the Spratlys. ASEAN preferred cooperation through bilateral or multilateral agreements, while China preferred joint development. ASEAN emphasized the suspension of further occupation of the islets and a freeze on construction. The Chinese draft did not mention this. ASEAN was silent on military exercises, reconnaissance or patrols. The Chinese draft clearly stated that it opposed such activities, saying that claimant countries should "refrain from conducting any military exercises directed against other countries in the Nansha Islands and their adjacent waters, and from carrying out any dangerous and close-in military reconnaissance". The Chinese code also included a ban on military patrols and seizure of fishing boats that strayed into disputed areas.[17]

Before the Mischief Reef claim could be resolved, in early 2000 the Philippines and China were embroiled in another dispute, this time

[15] *GMA-7 Radio-Television Arts*, 21 Nov. 1999, *SWB/FE/*3699/B/6.

[16] *Kyodo News Service*, 22 Nov. 1999, *BBC/SWB/FE/*3700/B/9.

[17] The above is summarized from Chen Hurng Yu, "A Solution to Conflict in the Spratlys" (Taiwan Security Research), *Taipei Times*, 23 Dec. 1999; "China's Sea Change", *Far Eastern Economic Review*, 10 Feb. 2000; and "China Wants Strict S. China Sea Code", *Straits Times*, 21 Feb. 2000.

over the ownership of Scarborough Shoal (or Huangyan Island), located 135 nautical miles from Zambales. The shoal served as a bombing range for the United States forces during the Cold War, when that country had bases in Subic, Zambales and Clark Airfield in Pampanga. The Chinese expressed deep concern about the Philippine military's expulsion of six Chinese fishing boats from waters around the island in early January and reiterated that "Huangyan Island is an integral part of Chinese territory".[18] Manila, on the other hand, insisted that Scarborough Shoal was "within the exclusive economic zone of the Philippines".[19]

In March the Philippines reported that China had deployed "spy" ships (the Chinese said that they were just fishing vessels) to the vicinity of Scarborough Shoal (off Zambales) "to monitor the movements of the Philippine military in the area". The concern was that if the Philippines failed to drive away the "encroaching Chinese vessels", that would give China "a convenient excuse to put up permanent structures in Scarborough ... exactly what they did in Mischief Reef". By taking over Scarborough Shoal, China could "make the area the reckoning point for its exclusive economic zone", which would overlap with the exclusive economic zone of the Philippines.[20] In May Philippine President Estrada visited Beijing, for the first time after becoming president in 1998, and claimed the visit was "more successful than I expected". According to him, "both sides agreed not to take any action that might complicate or escalate the situation".[21] Chinese Premier Zhu said that on the South China Sea issue, "both sides should proceed from the overall interests of safeguarding the development of the two countries' relations as well as regional peace and stability; exercise restraint; and properly handle the relevant problems through friendly consultations".[22]

---

[18] "Beijing Concerned over Fishing Boat Expulsions", *Xinhua News Agency*, 11 Jan. 2000, *BBC/SWB/FE*/3735/G/2.

[19] "Lawmaker Says China Moving to Claim Disputed Shoal", *GMA-7 Radio-Television Arts*, 21 Jan. 2000, *BBC/SWB/FE*/3745/B/5.

[20] "China Deployed Spy Ships in Spratlys, Legislator Says", *Manila Times*, 20 Mar. 2000, *BBC/SWB/FE*/3795/B/3.

[21] "Philippine President Says China Visit 'More Successful Than I Expected'", *Xinhua News Agency*, 17 May 2000, *BBC/SWB/FE*/3844/G/2.

[22] "Zhu Rongji Says He Is Full of Confidence in Prospects of Sino-Philippine Relations," *Beijing Zhongguo Xinwen She*, 17 May 2000, *FBIS-CHI*-2000-0517.

Besides Scarborough Shoal, there were reports of mostly Chinese fishing boats—as well as the occasional Vietnamese one—sighted in different parts of the South China Sea, near reefs and islands supposedly owned by the Philippines. In March 2000 senior officials from China and ASEAN met for the first time in Hua Hin to discuss the "controversial draft code of conduct aimed at easing conflict in the South China Sea".[23] The meeting agreed that disputes between nations with conflicting territorial claims in the South China Sea should be resolved on a bilateral basis. Both sides resolved to frame a common code of conduct, which would be "designed to build trust and not be legally binding".[24] In an apparent reference to the US-Philippine military exercises in January 2000, China cautioned Southeast Asian countries against engaging in joint military exercises.[25] The Chinese also had in mind the visit to Vietnam of US Secretary of Defence William Cohen (also in March), the first secretary of defence to visit the country since the Vietnam War ended in 1975. The one-day Hua Hin meeting did not go into specifics, but the Chinese left ASEAN with the impression that they did not want ASEAN members to act collectively to promote their own interests and that it was "unwise for any Asean member to strengthen its military ties with outsiders". As one analysis put it, "the last thing that China wants is an Asean with the strength to look out for its 'collective interests'".[26]

In April 2000, at the Sixth ASEAN-China Senior Officials Meeting in Kuching, both ASEAN and China supposedly agreed to "speed up" the drafting of a code of conduct. According to Thai Foreign Minister Surin, at the ARF meeting (in July 2000) ASEAN and China agreed in principle "to make a political, rather than a legal, commitment" to the code of conduct.[27] Zhu's view was that they should not rush the process to sign a code of conduct.[28] The senior officials met again on

[23] "Thailand to Host ASEAN-China Meeting on Spratlys", *The Nation*, 8 Mar. 2000, *BBC/SWB/FE*/3784/B/1.

[24] "South China Sea, 'Code of Conduct'", *Straits Times*, 16 Mar. 2000.

[25] "Beijing Warns Against Joint Military Games", *South China Morning Post*, 16 Mar. 2000.

[26] "Bully in the South China Sea", *Wall Street Journal Asia*, 17 Mar. 2000.

[27] "Malaysia's Plan for Submarine Raises Fears Among Thailand, China", *The Nation*, 1 Aug. 2000, *BBC/SWB/FE*/3909/B/6.

[28] "PRC FM Spokesman on South China Sea Issue", *Xinhua News Agency*, 13 July 2000, *FBIS-CHI*-2000-0713.

24–25 August 2000 in Dalian (northeast China). However, both sides failed to reach consensus and were thus unable to sign the code of conduct at the ASEAN Summit in November in Singapore. In May 2001 officials met for a third time, apparently for only half an hour. There was no progress. In November 2001 Philippine Foreign Secretary Lauro Baja Jr. revealed that the issue had "gone beyond the senior officials' level" and "it was up to the foreign ministers to discuss the matter on the basis of a Philippine nonpaper".[29] The working group was supposed to meet again in April 2002, but the meeting did not take place.[30]

There was a growing perception that China was taking advantage of ASEAN's preoccupation with the financial crisis to strengthen its position in the South China Sea, and the Philippines happened to be the target. Defence analysts also believed that Beijing was "capitalizing on the extremely focused and narrowly construed existing position of the United States to take actions at the margins of US policy".[31] Washington's main concern was that there be no interference with sea lanes. China was also improving its ability to back up its claims in the Spratlys with the People's Liberation Army.[32]

The United States' Attitude Towards the South China Sea Dispute

The US position regarding the South China Sea dispute was consistent from the Cold War to the post-Cold War period. In the wake of the Paracels clash in January 1974, the US State Department said that the South China Sea dispute was "for the claimants to settle among themselves".[33] In his annual report to Congress, US Secretary of Defence Harold Brown hardly mentioned the South China Sea except in the context of Soviet interests in Cam Ranh Bay and Danang, and how

[29] "Asean Summit Will Not Discuss RP Proposal", *Manila Standard*, 1 Nov. 2001.
[30] "Asean Faces Difficulty in Beijing Negotiations: Divisions Within Group Block Consensus on Code for South China Sea", *Wall Street Journal Asia*, 1 Aug. 2002.
[31] Michael McDevitt, "China and the South China Sea: A Conference Summary Report", Pacific Forum, CSIS, *PacNet* #15, 16 Apr. 1999.
[32] Ibid.
[33] "Today Hsisha, Tomorrow ...?" *Far Eastern Economic Review*, 28 Jan. 1974.

that would complicate "the task of the seventh fleet in helping to defend Japan's lines of communications".[34] This was also the case with Admiral William J. Crowe, then commander in chief of the US Pacific Command, in an interview in 1984. His concern was with the growing Soviet presence in Cam Ranh Bay, which made it possible for the Russians to interdict the sea lines of communication in the South China Sea.[35] Since 1990, the US Department of Defense (DOD) has delivered four reports to Congress on US policy towards East Asia. The first, titled "A Strategic Framework for the Asia Pacific Rim: Looking Towards the 21st Century", was in April 1990. The report, produced during the period that saw the Soviet withdrawal from Afghanistan and the collapse of Communism in Eastern Europe, paid particular emphasis to the situation in Northeast Asia, which despite the end of the Cold War was still unstable and volatile. There was hardly any mention of the South China Sea except that one of the US wartime objectives for East Asia was to maintain the security of the lines of communication throughout the Pacific.[36] In an interview in Malaysia in October 1991, Admiral Charles Larson, then commander in chief of the US Pacific Command, said the following regarding the Spratlys:

(a) The US maintained a non-committal stand as there was no interest for the US to intervene;
(b) It was a regional issue and the US had no contingency plan to go to the Spratlys in the event of a conflict;
(c) It would be up to the countries concerned to work together and regional groupings (such as ASEAN) to find a solution;
(d) The US preferred that the claimants resolve the issue through political channels rather than by military means; and
(e) If China and Vietnam became hostile in asserting their claims, the US might work with ASEAN, the Soviet Union and other

[34] "America's Attitude to the Asian Region", *Asia-Pacific Defence Reporter*, Apr. 1980, pp. 25–8.
[35] "Help Wanted in Protecting Vital Sea Lines", *Asia-Pacific Defence Reporter*, Annual Reference Edition, Dec. 1984/Jan. 1985, pp. 53–7.
[36] *A Strategic Framework for the Asian Pacific Rim: Looking Toward the 21st Century* (prepared by the Office of the US Assistant Secretary of Defense for International Security Affairs [East Asia and Pacific Region], Apr. 1990).

nations under the auspices of the United Nations to ensure that the aggressor followed accepted international behaviour.[37]

In the second DOD report, submitted to Congress in mid-1992, the Spratlys received passing mention as one of nine potential sources of East Asian and Pacific regional instability but not an imminent threat.[38] During a Worldnet dialogue with panellists from Kuala Lumpur, Manila, Jakarta and Tokyo in March 1992, the US assistant defence secretary said that although the United States still had a formidable force in Asia despite its troop withdrawal from the Philippines, Washington had no specific commitment in the Spratlys. He also dismissed regional concerns that followed China passing a law on 25 February declaring its sovereignty over the islands, saying that the move was just a reaffirmation of Beijing's long-term stance. He mentioned that ASEAN could work with China to resolve the Spratlys row.[39] US Ambassador to the Philippines Frank Wisner reiterated that the US opposed the use of force to back any claims on the Spratlys and that there were limits to what the US could do if fighting broke out over the area. Wisner added that he did not expect rivalry in the Spratlys to be the next flashpoint.[40] According to US Undersecretary of State Robert Zoellick, Washington's position on the South China Sea remained unchanged, that is, the US would not make judgements on the merits of the claims, it wanted freedom of navigation to be preserved, and it supported a peaceful resolution of disputes.[41]

While there was at least one short paragraph about the Spratlys in the DOD's 1992 report, the subsequent DOD report submitted in February 1995 hardly mentioned the Spratlys issue. The latter report noted the ongoing official and non-official discussions regarding the matter, and it reiterated the US concern that the high seas remain as an international commons. A statement issued by the State Department

---

[37] "US 'Will Not Interfere' in Spratly Conflicts", *Straits Times*, 23 Oct. 1991.

[38] *A Strategic Framework for the Asian Pacific Rim* (Department of Defense, Office of International Security Affairs, 1992).

[39] "Work with China on Spratlys Row, US Urges Asean", *Straits Times*, 28 Mar. 1992.

[40] Ibid.; "US Has to Help if Navy Is Attacked in Spratlys, Says Manglapus", *Straits Times*, 14 Mar. 1992.

[41] "Washington's Priorities", *Far Eastern Economic Review*, 13 Aug. 1992, p. 18.

on 10 May 1995 regarding the Spratlys and the South China Sea made four now-familiar points:

(a) The US opposes the use of force;
(b) The US has an abiding interest in the maintenance of peace and stability in the area;
(c) Maintaining freedom of navigation and all maritime activities consistent with international law are fundamental interests of the US; and
(d) The US takes no position on the legal merits of the competing claims.[42]

In 1995 the United States did not help the Philippines deter the Chinese occupation of Mischief Reef, although the State Department did issue a statement denouncing the threat or the use of force to assert territorial claims.[43]

The fourth DOD report in November 1998 did not mention the South China Sea at all. In a 1998 interview Admiral Archie Clemins, commander in chief of the US Pacific Fleet, said that while the US was aware that the Spratlys was a contentious area, it would like to see a peaceful resolution to the matter. He reiterated that the US would not support any one claimant over another. While some of China's actions led others to believe that it had expansionary ambitions, the US did not think so.[44] US Chief of Naval Operations Admiral Jay Johnson told reporters that the US was watching the situation in the South China Sea "very carefully". He expressed hopes that rival claims could be resolved peacefully. Finally, he reiterated the importance of keeping sea lanes open as 90 per cent of the world's commerce was moved by sea.[45] In October 1999 US Secretary of Defence William Cohen

---

[42] Ralph A. Cossa (ed.), "Security Implications of Conflict in the South China Sea: Exploring Potential Triggers of Conflict" (Honolulu: Pacific Forum CSIS Special Report, 1996), appendix G.
[43] Jason Swergold, "U.S. Military Transformation and the Rise of China: Restructuring Regional Alliances", http://hdl.handle.net/2345/496, p. 36, accessed 24 Mar. 2017.
[44] "Interview with Admiral Archie Clemins, Commander in Chief of the US Pacific Fleet", *Asian Defence and Diplomacy*, Sept. 1998, pp. 14–7.
[45] "Exercises with Asian Allies 'to Continue'", *Straits Times*, 7 Apr. 1999.

reiterated the American position that claimant states should resolve their disputes peacefully.[46]

Because of the Mischief Reef episode, Manila (under the Estrada administration) realized the "necessity of stronger ties with the United States", which led to the signing of the 1998 RP-US Visiting Forces Agreement, a "major step in the reconstruction of the US-Philippine defense relationship and, from Manila's standpoint, of reestablishing deterrence in the region".[47] The Philippines Senate ratified it at the end of May 1999. The 19,200-ton USS *Blue Ridge*, command ship of the US Seventh Fleet, visited Manila in July. The United States Senate also approved US$5 million in foreign military aid to the Philippines. A joint military exercise was held at the former US bases of Subic Bay and Clark Field and in Manila Bay in January 2000, the first joint exercise since 1997.

In January 2000 US Assistant Secretary of State for East Asian Affairs Stanley Roth noted that "while there had been no major shoot-outs, there had been ill-feeling generated by the ramming and sinking of ships and an increase in military presence ..." He was concerned about the lack of any "diplomatic process" to counter the trend. However, "on the plus side", he noted that there was nothing to suggest any effort by any of the countries in the area "to obstruct freedom of navigation".[48] That essentially was the United States' foremost concern. Beijing assiduously assured the international community, particularly the United States, that its claims would not affect the freedom and safety of navigation.

Developments Leading to the Declaration on the Conduct of Parties in the South China Sea

The Philippines got a new president in January 2001 when Gloria Macapagal Arroyo succeeded Joseph Estrada (who was impeached). Soon after, there was a tense standoff between Philippine navy ships and aircraft and Chinese fishing vessels near Scarborough Shoal. The newly appointed National Security Adviser Roilo Golez described the dispute

[46] *Philippines Broadcaster GMA-7*, 3 Oct. 1999, *BBC/SWB/FE*/3657/B/8.
[47] Swergold, "U.S. Military Transformation and the Rise of China", p. 36.
[48] "US Sees Flash Points in South China Sea", *Straits Times*, 9 Jan. 2000.

over the Spratly Islands as "the number one threat to the security of the region".[49] In an interview with the BBC, Golez said that sorting out the long-running dispute was his top security priority. He also acknowledged that taking on China would not be easy: "... it doesn't matter whether it would take decades because we know that China is very patiently, in a very creeping manner, inching into our own exclusive economic zone and they're very patient in doing it, but we have to continue protesting."[50] He thought that hitting China's "international image" might be an effective strategy.

President Arroyo, however, on more than one occasion emphasized that the Philippines' dispute with China over the Spratly Islands was "a small portion of the entire picture of China-Philippine ties, which generally remain good".[51] The tension over Scarborough Shoal eased in April 2001, when both sides agreed to take steps to avoid any further escalation of the dispute. Both sides also agreed to expand military dialogue and cooperation and study a mechanism for settling fishing disputes, amongst other measures. Willy Goa (head of the Philippine delegation to the bilateral talks) said that the Filipinos were trying their best to ease tensions in the area as well as build confidence. "It's of course tough," he added. On the Chinese side, Fu Ying stated, "We are neighbours and the differences are normal, but with a friendly people like you, I'm confident that there is nothing we cannot resolve."[52] The Chinese delegation, however, insisted that Beijing had sovereignty over the shoal.[53] Reports in April revealed that China had upgraded its communication facilities on Mischief Reef.[54]

---

[49] "Official Says Manila to Insist on Removal of Chinese Structures in Spratlys", *Quezon City GMA 7 Television*, 21 Feb. 2001, *FBIS-EAS*-20001-0221.

[50] "How Does Manila Propose to Deal with Beijing on Spratly Islands Claim?" *BBC London (English), The World Today*, 22 Feb. 2001.

[51] "President Says Spratlys Dispute Not to Hamper Ties with China", *Kyodo News Service*, Tokyo, in English, 8 Feb. 2001, *SWB/FE*/4067/B/6.

[52] "South China Sea Accord", *NAPSNet Daily Report*, 4 Apr. 2001.

[53] "Beijing Is Shifting Security Concerns from Land to Maritime Areas", *International Herald Tribune*, 12 Apr. 2001.

[54] "Philippines Military Officer: China Upgrades Spratlys' Communication Facilities", *BBC Monitoring Global Newsline — Asia-Pacific Political, Philippine Daily Inquirer* website, in English, 16 Apr. 2001.

On the eve of Arroyo's first visit to China in October 2001 since becoming president, Chinese vessels were spotted near Mischief Reef, which the Department of Foreign Affairs described as "ill-timed".[55] Bilateral talks continued after Arroyo's visit on the joint use and development of Mischief Reef, with no result. The Chinese side laid out three conditions that would allow joint development in the disputed reef "when the time is ripe": (a) when improvement of the facilities and the administrative system had been laid down in the reef; (b) when Philippines-China relations had returned to normalcy; and (c) when fishing arrangements and cooperation between the two countries had been clearly established.[56] Philippine National Security Adviser Golez, in fact, admitted, "it might be impossible to stop the Chinese troops from setting up on the islands" even though the Philippines had more forces in the area. Golez added that Manila would continue its protest and diplomatic measures through the Department of Foreign Affairs.[57]

Meanwhile, after a brief lull, tensions between Vietnam and China resurfaced in February 2001 over Hanoi's plan to establish local governments on parts of the Spratly archipelago. This led Beijing to reiterate China's "indisputable sovereignty over Nansha (Spratly) Islands and the adjacent waters" and that "any unilateral act on Nansha Islands by any other country infringes upon the territorial integrity of China and is illegal". The Vietnamese retorted, "every measure was being taken to defend Vietnamese sovereignty over the Spratlys" and that while Vietnam "strives to settle these disputes in a peaceful manner", it remained "determined to defend its sovereignty over every metre of its sea border".[58] It would be neither the first nor the last time that these words would be heard. Soon after, in April, the Vietnamese sought clarification regarding Chinese intentions to develop the Paracels into a city that could become a "political, economic and cultural hub and assume control of the islands of the Hoang Sa and Truong Sa (Spratly)

[55] "Philippine ForMin Spokesman Describes Chinese Incursion in Spratlys 'Ill-Timed'", *Manila Times*, 31 Oct. 2001, *FBIS-EAS*-2001-1031.

[56] "RP, China Officials Meet on Joint Fishing Rights", *Manila Standard*, 9 Dec. 2001.

[57] "Philippines Rules out Military Exercises with US on Spratly Islands", *BBC Monitoring*, *Philippine Star*, 8 Feb. 2002.

[58] "Vietnam Warned on Spratly Govts Plan", *Straits Times*, 14 Feb. 2001.

archipelagos". The Foreign Ministry spokesperson declared, "any activities conducted in the region without Vietnam's consent are illegal and unacceptable encroachments upon Vietnam's sovereignty".[59]

In August 2001 the United States conducted a one-day "training exercise" involving two aircraft carrier groups—led by the USS *Constellation* and USS *Carl Vinson*—which was described as "the first major drill of this scale by the US in the region for several years". Soon after, China carried out its "largest-ever integrated military exercises" around Dongshan Island (southeast of Fujian and not far from Taiwan). While these two sets of military exercises were not about the South China Sea island disputes (and had more to do with the EP-3 incident off the coast of Hainan in April), they showed the dynamics of Sino-US relations in the region. The United States saw China as "a threat to peace and sea-lane security" in the South China Sea. China, on the other hand, believed that the United States was "intent on encircling it with military alliances, bases and military-access arrangements involving Japan, South Korea, Taiwan, the Philippines, Thailand and Singapore".[60]

At the 68th Royal Malaysian Navy celebrations in 2002, Chief of Navy Admiral Abu Bakar made the following observations with regard to the South China Sea dispute, which gives a rare insight into the Malaysian perspective. First, the overlapping claims to the South China Sea islands were one of the closest threats to Malaysia's stability (the other was the "geopolitical uncertainty of its neighbours"). Second, the dispute between Vietnam and China over the Spratly Islands "had the potential of blowing up into armed conflict". Thus, the dispute needed to be "handled with discretion, for if we fail to resolve it via negotiation there could be a strong possibility of it turning into armed conflict". Third, Malaysia "should be prepared to defend" its sovereignty.[61]

Admiral Abu Bakar's reference to the Sino-Vietnamese dispute is noteworthy. As the *Dow Jones Asian Equities Report* noted, the dispute over the Spratlys "has been particularly bitter" between China and

---

[59] *Voice of Vietnam text website*, Hanoi, in Vietnamese, 17 Apr. 2001, *BBC Monitoring Global Newsline—Asia-Pacific Political.*

[60] Mark J. Valencia, "South China Sea Beijing's Buffer", *Washington Times*, 24 Aug. 2001.

[61] "Claims to Islands a Threat: Malaysia's Navy Chief", *Straits Times*, 27 Apr. 2002.

Vietnam and dated back to 1974.[62] In May 2001 China conducted a large-scale military exercise in the South China Sea from Hainan Island and on Woody Island (which the Vietnamese also claimed). Analysts believed that China was building up its forces there for power projection. In June 2002 China conducted a military exercise southwest of Hainan Island, which the Vietnamese claimed was in "some sectors situated in the maritime zone and Vietnam's continental shelf". In both cases, the Chinese simply ignored the Vietnamese protests.[63]

Despite "the increasing spirit of cooperation" between China and the ASEAN countries (as described in chapter 4), there remained a "great deal of nervousness" amongst the Southeast Asian states about China's growing economic and political power, particularly in relation to the South China Sea dispute. At a closed-door session of the Shangri-La Dialogue in Singapore, the Chinese delegation was asked whether the South China Sea was considered part of the motherland. The Chinese delegates "brushed aside the question as ridiculous, using a tone and manner that left the audience momentarily silent".[64]

The Southeast Asian countries were aware that China would not budge on territorial claims on the South China Sea, "as has been the case in every dispute involving what it considers to be its territory".[65] As such, the ASEAN countries were anxious to get China committed to a code of conduct. In July 2002, at a media briefing ahead of the 35th ASEAN Ministerial Meeting in Brunei (26 July–2 August 2002), Malaysian Foreign Minister Syed Hamid Albar said that Kuala Lumpur would propose the signing of a declaration to solve the South China Sea's code of conduct impasse in the upcoming ASEAN Ministerial Meeting. It would be, according to him, "an ideal step to take if the meeting was still unable to reach an agreement over the geographical scope concerning the disputed areas, which had been discussed so many times". The difficulty was not so much about navigation but the scope

---

[62] Xu Yihe, "China Energy Watch: Spratlys Dispute Blocks Exploration", *Dow Jones Asian Equities Report*, 6 May 2002.

[63] "Beijing Readies China Sea Exercises", *Washington Times*, 17 May 2001; "China Dismisses Vietnam Protest Against Naval Drill as 'Groundless'", *Beijing*, 11 June 2002 (AFP).

[64] "Sea of Troubles Reflects Unease over China's Role", *South China Morning Post*, 9 June 2002.

[65] Ibid.

of the disputed area. Malaysia's preference was to limit the area to the disputed area, which was the Spratlys, but some other member states had different views (particularly Vietnam, which wanted the Paracels named in the code whereas China did not). Thus the need to "find a way out" and "if we cannot arrive at a consensus, then we must be seen to be doing something that contributes to the easing of tension if any, to contribute to the peace and stability in our region". The declaration (which everyone could sign and "declare our position"), Syed Hamid Albar explained, "would at least enable a peaceful use of the areas for all parties involved in overlapping claims to the islands, as long as it was not for military purposes".[66]

ASEAN senior officials endorsed the proposal for a Declaration on the Code of Conduct on the South China Sea in July 2002. Following that, the ASEAN foreign ministers approved it and presented it to Chinese Foreign Minister Tang Jiaxuan for discussion when they met on 1 August during the 35th ASEAN Ministerial Meetings and other related meetings held in Bandar Seri Begawan. Tang reportedly remarked that it did not matter whether the paper under consideration was called a code, a declaration or a resolution—as long as it was acceptable to Beijing.[67] The optimists viewed the compromised formula as a significant breakthrough of a long-standing deadlock, which would pave the way for a possible code of conduct with Beijing in the future. Critics saw it as highlighting "the disarray in Asean ranks", which would only leave ASEAN divided and unable to continue negotiations with Beijing.[68]

While Beijing mulled over ASEAN's proposal, there were reports that Vietnam and the Philippines briefly tussled over the disputed Parola and Pugad Islands. Mischief Reef, occupied by the Chinese since 1995, bore "the look of a future military installation", according to the Pentagon.[69] It is worth mentioning that in October 2002, the US Navy announced that three *Los Angeles*-class attack submarines would

---

[66] "Malaysia Toying with Idea of Declaration to Solve Disputed Areas", *Bernama*, Kuala Lumpur, 23 July 2002.

[67] "Chinese Foreign Minister Takes Wait-and-See Attitude on Spratlys Document", *Associated Press Newswires*, 29 July 2002.

[68] "Asean Paves the Way for a South China Sea Code", *Straits Times*, 27 July 2002; "Asean Faces Difficulty in Beijing Negotiations".

[69] "Philippine Plane Fired upon over Spratlys", *Straits Times*, 5 Sept. 2002; "Don't Neglect the Spratlys", *Far Eastern Economic Review*, 26 Sept. 2002.

be stationed in Guam. The first, the USS *City of Corpus Christi*, arrived in late October—"the first time a nuclear-powered attack submarine has had a home port on the Pacific island". The other two submarines were expected to arrive before the end of 2002.[70]

ASEAN and China finally signed the non-binding ten-point Declaration on the Conduct of Parties in the South China Sea (DOC, for short) in Phnom Penh on 4 November 2002. One Southeast Asian official was quoted to have said, "a political declaration is not as good as a code" but "it's all that is possible at the moment".[71] Analysts were generally of the view that "as an interim accord, the declaration is a step in the right direction, though certainly not a landmark agreement as stated in some media reports". The breakthrough agreement was unlikely to have much impact on tensions in the South China Sea. Finally, it remained "uncertain" whether the parties would ever succeed in signing a legally binding code of conduct.[72] After the signing of the DOC in November 2002, there were a few years—until 2008—of relative calm in the South China Sea.

The DOC fell short of ASEAN's objective of having a legally binding code of conduct. It would take another decade before all parties could agree on how to implement the guidelines of the DOC. However, the general view was that from about 1995 until 2008–09, the South China Sea dispute—while important especially to Vietnam and the Philippines—was not a high-priority security issue to other countries. Do Thanh Hai noted that both Hanoi and Manila, while dissatisfied with the DOC, also had no interest in seeing a collapse of the negotiations. They viewed the DOC as a "confidence building measure" and a "stepping-stone towards the COC".[73] The code of conduct remained a work in progress.

---

[70] "New Submarine Deployment Sends Message", *South China Morning Post*, 14 Oct. 2002.

[71] "Taking Charge", *Far Eastern Economic Review*, 14 Nov. 2002. For the full text of the Declaration, see https://cil.nus.edu.sg/rp/pdf/2002%20Declaration%20on%20the%20Conduct%20of%20Parties%20in%20the%20South%20China%20Sea-pdf.pdf, accessed 18 Apr. 2017.

[72] Barry Wain, "Taking Charge", *Far Eastern Economic Review*, 14 Nov. 2002; Ralf Emmers, "ASEAN, China and the South China Sea: An Opportunity Missed", *IDSS Commentaries*, 19 Nov. 2002.

[73] Hai, *Vietnam and the South China Sea*, p. 223.

With regard to the Sino-Vietnamese dispute over the Spratlys, between 2002 and 2004 the South China Sea was "relatively tranquil with few incidents that sparked tensions". Most of the complaints and protests (from China, Taiwan and the Philippines) had to do with Vietnam introducing tourism activities in the disputed islands. Mark J. Valencia noted that Vietnam's announcement in August 2004 that it was constructing an airport on Truong Sa as well as starting commercial flights as part of its tourism effort was "the first significant sign that the 'code of conduct' was not holding". Vietnam's move was "undoubtedly an attempt" to "enhance its legal claim by demonstrating 'effectivities'".[74] From 2005, however, "disputes over fishing became heated with increased number of incidents and greater severity". In early 2007 Hanoi adopted "an ambitious maritime strategic plan to develop a marine-based economy with special emphasis on hydrocarbon exploitation, the fishing industry, shipbuilding and fishing", which conflicted with Chinese interests in disputed areas. Beijing began to apply pressure on foreign oil firms against taking up Vietnamese projects in the disputed waters.[75] Over two consecutive weekends in December 2007, there were street protests against the Chinese occupation of the Spratly and Paracel Islands in Hanoi and Ho Chi Minh City, which ended only when the government called an end to the anti-China protests on 20 December. Although the protests ended in Vietnam, Vietnamese in the United States, France and Canada held anti-China protests on the 23–24 December weekend. On 9 January 2008, it was reported that hundreds of police had ringed Chinese diplomatic missions where students had planned renewed anti-China protests.[76] As one political observer noted, the South China Sea issue is "so emotional" for the Vietnamese that "it unites virtually all of them under an anti-China nationalist banner, even those in exile who usually abhor Vietnam's ruling Communist Party".[77]

[74] Mark J. Valencia, "China's Push for Offshore Oil: A Chance for Joint Deal", *Straits Times*, 29 Sept. 2004.

[75] The above is from Hai, *Vietnam and the South China Sea*, pp. 223–4, chapter 5. This is the most recent and detailed study of the South China Sea dispute from the Vietnamese perspective. "Vietnam, China Clash Again over Spratlys", *Straits Times*, 19 July 2007.

[76] "Vietnam Deploys Police to Pre-empt Anti-Chinese Protests", *AFP*, 9 Jan. 2008.

[77] "Vietnam Enlists Allies to Stave off China's Reach", *New York Times*, 5 Feb. 2010.

Sino-Philippine relations during the Arroyo administration from January 2001 to June 2010 had been described as a "golden age of partnership".[78] This description was particularly true during Arroyo's second term in office from 2005. Arroyo had, in her first term, managed to keep a balance between the United States and China. Part of the US-Philippine 2004 "Balikatan" (Shoulder-to-Shoulder) military exercises (February to early March 2004) were conducted on Palawan, bordering the Spratly archipelago. In one of her weekly radio programmes, Arroyo revealed that the US military had been training Philippine soldiers to defend the Spratlys against China but that she had since asked that training be focused on fighting the Abu Sayyaf extremist group.[79] Much to the annoyance of the Americans, in July 2004 Manila withdrew its 51 soldiers and police officers from Iraq a month earlier than scheduled because of domestic pressure over the capture of a Filipino contract worker in Iraq by an Islamic terrorist group. Arroyo had "aggressively" positioned herself as "Asia's leading proponent of the 'war on terrorism'". Apparently, Manila's decision caught Washington off guard and furthered the perception that the "international coalition" led by the United States was breaking apart.[80]

Arroyo wanted to attract foreign aid and investment from China. She therefore encouraged bilateral political and economic exchanges, and took measures to ease tensions between both countries on the South China Sea issue. In September 2004 (during Arroyo's second visit to China since becoming president in 2001), both countries agreed to a Joint Maritime Seismic Undertaking (JMSU) covering disputed areas in the Spratlys. It subsequently evolved into a tripartite JMSU involving the Philippine National Oil Company-Exploration Corp., China National Offshore Oil Corp. and PetroVietnam. Vietnam initially protested against the bilateral agreement because it covered areas that Vietnam also claimed, but it decided to join when invited, albeit

[78] See Renato Cruz De Castro, "China, the Philippines, and US influence in Asia", *Asian Outlook* 2 (July 2017) (Washington, DC: American Enterprise Institute for Public Policy Research).

[79] "War Games with US Targeted China: Arroyo", *Straits Times*, 5 Apr. 2004.

[80] "Philippines Government to Withdraw Troops from Iraq", 16 July 2004, https://www.wsws.org/en/articles/2004/07/phil-j16.html, accessed 20 Apr. 2017. For a brief insider account, see Almonte (as told to Vitug), *Endless Journey*, p. 322.

reluctantly, by both Manila and Beijing. As Aileen S.P. Baviera noted, "By agreeing to cooperate with China, the Arroyo government broke from previous Philippine policy emphasizing multilateral solutions to the disputes in the framework of ASEAN and international law. It appeared to be accommodating China's preference for a bilateral approach and its desire for joint development."[81] Baviera's observation would apply to Vietnam too.

President Arroyo's September 2004 visit to China was, in the words of Philippine Foreign Affairs Secretary Alberto G. Romulo, "the highest point" of Philippines-China diplomatic relations, established in 1975.[82] In 2005, which marked the 30th anniversary of the establishment of diplomatic relations between the two countries, Chinese President Hu Jintao visited Manila. The joint statement issued at the end of the visit stated, "They both believed that Sino-Philippine relations have entered the golden period of partnership" and "both countries are determined to establish the strategic and cooperative relations that aim at the [*sic*] peace and development". Amongst the many areas of cooperation, both sides also agreed to "continue to be committed to safeguarding the peace and stability in South China Sea region".[83] The JMSU, signed in 2006 and touted as the future model of cooperation in the South China Sea, was not renewed due to Filipino domestic politics. The JMSU was, in the words of Philippine Executive Secretary Eduardo Ermita, "meant to enhance cooperation and is a test of our will to resolve our disputes in a cooperative activity instead of through the force of arms".[84] The improved Sino-Philippine relations crafted by the Arroyo administration were also showing signs of fraying because of accusations of corruption related to the economic deals signed between the two countries.

From 2008, a debate started in Manila between the Senate and the House of Representatives regarding how to delineate the country's

---

[81] See Evelyn Goh (ed.), *Rising China's Influence in Developing Asia* (Oxford: Oxford University Press, 2016), p. 110, chapter 5.

[82] "Manila, Beijing Will Discuss Oil Survey Plan in Spratlys with Other Claimants", *Manila Business World*, 7 Sept. 2004.

[83] For the full text of the joint statement issued on 28 April 2005, see http://www.fmprc.gov.cn/nanhai/eng/zcfg_1/t193958.htm, accessed 19 Apr. 2017.

[84] "Palace Official Says Lapsed Spratly Oil Deal Not to Affect Philippines' Security", *Philstar*, 2 Jan. 2009.

baselines. A law defining the archipelagic baselines of the country is a fundamental requirement for submission to the UN under UNCLOS. Under UNCLOS, archipelagic nations like the Philippines were required to have a definitive law on their baselines by May 2009. The consequence of not meeting the deadline would be that extended continental shelf areas, which the Philippines wanted to claim, would be considered part of the International Seabed Area (Common Heritage of Mankind) or be awarded to a neighbour state that filed and was able to prove its claim over that area. Failure to do so could thus prejudice the Philippines' existing claims over the Kalayaan Island Group in the Spratlys as well as Scarborough Shoal. The Arroyo administration, according to the opposition, was dragging its feet over this issue. As Senate Minority Leader Aquilino Pimental Jr. said, "passing bills defining the national territory would not mean the Philippines would no longer settle disputes peacefully".[85] The Senate sought to treat the contested island groups as a regime of islands, which it argued was consistent with UNCLOS and a more realistic approach, whereas the House of Representatives chose to enclose the Kalayaan Island Group and Scarborough Shoal as part of Philippine territory. The latter approach would be, according to Senator Miriam Defensor-Santiago (chairperson, Foreign Relations Committee), a "potential diplomatic disaster".[86] Beijing, meanwhile, continued to reiterate its "indisputable sovereignty" over Scarborough Shoal and the Spratly Islands, reminding the countries involved to abide by the DOC and "not take actions that might complicate or expand disputes".[87] In the end the House version won the day, and in March 2009 President Arroyo signed a law defining Philippine territory, which included some Spratly Islands and Scarborough Shoal. It immediately sparked protests from China and Vietnam. The Arroyo administration tried to calm the situation by explaining, "the law was passed not to reiterate its claims over the Spratlys and Scarborough shoal but to

[85] "Senators to Push for Immediate Debate on Bill Redefining Philippine Baselines", *Philstar*, 28 Apr. 2008.

[86] "House Version of Baselines Bill 'on War Path': Enrile", *GMA News.TV*, 4 Feb. 2009.

[87] "PRC FM Spokesman: China Reiterates Sovereignty over 'Huangyan Island', 'Spratlys'", *Xinhua*, 3 Feb. 2009.

define the baseline used to determine its extended continental shelf".[88] A high-level Chinese delegation scheduled to visit the Philippines in March was cancelled.

Also in March, Malaysian Prime Minister Abdullah Badawi visited Swallow Reef and Ardasier Reef to buttress Malaysian claims. There was also a skirmish between two US navy ships and Chinese vessels, about 120 kilometres south of China's Hainan Island. China subsequently dispatched its largest fishing vessel (a converted warship), *Yuzheng 311*, to the disputed South China Sea. Chinese diplomats insisted that the move did not violate the DOC. One Filipino senator, however, described it as "gunboat diplomacy".[89] On 6 May 2009 Malaysia and Vietnam lodged a joint submission with the UN Commission on the Limits of the Continental Shelf, which predictably provoked Chinese protests that the claims infringed on China's indisputable sovereignty in the South China Sea.[90]

On 7 May China submitted a diplomatic note to the United Nations that included a map showing the Nine-Dash Line, supposedly showing the extent of China's claim in the South China Sea. This led to diplomatic protests by the Philippines, Vietnam, Malaysia and Indonesia. After some years on the back burner, the South China Sea dispute began to dominate the headlines again in 2009. There was a growing sense that China was becoming more aggressive in enforcing its claims in the dispute. In March 2010, Beijing for the first time told Washington that the South China Sea was part of its "core interests" and concerned China's sovereignty and territorial integrity. Analysts interpreted this to mean that the South China Sea was "on par with Taiwan and Tibet".[91]

In April 2010 the Chinese navy conducted a long-range deployment exercise that lasted almost three weeks. The flotilla from China's North Sea Fleet sailed from Qingdao into the Spratly archipelago and anchored

[88] "RP Enacts Law Claiming Disputed Islands", *Philstar*, 11 Mar. 2009.

[89] "Tensions Growing in South China Sea", *Straits Times*, 18 Mar. 2009; "China Boosts Presence in South China Sea", *Straits Times*, 20 Mar. 2009.

[90] Sam Bateman and Clive Schofield, "Outer Shelf Claims in the South China Sea: New Dimension to Old Disputes", *RSIS Commentaries*, 1 July 2009.

[91] "South China Sea Part of Core Interests: Beijing", *Straits Times*, 6 July 2010.

off Fiery Cross Reef. The Chinese had taken Fiery Cross Reef from the Vietnamese in 1988 and made it a Chinese base with an early warning station. Chinese combat aircraft had also been conducting aerial exercises in the disputed South China Sea area. China's fisheries enforcement agency started regular patrols to protect Chinese fishing boats in the disputed waters. The general view was that as long as ASEAN could not agree on a unified strategy, China would continue its assertiveness, and "other interested powers, such as the US, Japan and India" would also "find it harder to constrain China".[92] Veteran Vietnam-watcher Carlyle Thayer reported that Vietnamese officials were "internationalizing" the South China Sea issue in "a quiet way, not a direct way ... They want to solve it peacefully, but let the international community raise the issue." Hanoi was pushing hard behind the scenes to involve more foreign players in negotiations in a multilateral setting,[93] but so far without much success. Kurt Campbell (US assistant secretary of state for East Asian and Pacific affairs) remarked on 26 April 2010, "no other country in Southeast Asia wanted an improved relationship with the US more than its old enemy, Vietnam".[94] At the same time, the South China Sea dispute compelled Vietnam to embark on its force modernization programme.[95]

[92] "Chinese Exercises a Show of Assertiveness", *Straits Times*, 3 May 2010.
[93] "Vietnam Enlists Allies to Stave off China's Reach", *New York Times*, 5 Feb. 2010.
[94] "Beijing Delivers New Threats over Its Hegemony over the South China Sea", *Asia Sentinel*, 30 Apr. 2010.
[95] See, for example, "Vietnam Bolstering Spratlys Firepower", *Straits Times*, 20 May 2010. It was reported that Vietnam was buying six submarines from Russia.

CHAPTER 6

2010–12: Southeast Asia Between US and China

"The size of China makes it impossible for the rest of Asia, including Japan and India, to match it in weight and capacity in about 20 to 30 years. So we need America to strike the balance."[1]

"Don't leave us, but don't make us choose."[2]

Between Washington and Beijing

Our narrative picks up from the start of the second decade of the millennium, which marked the confluence of a number of events and developments that would have a significant impact on the international politics of the region from 2010 onwards. On 1 January 2010 the China-ASEAN Free Trade Area (CAFTA), first proposed in November 2000, finally came into effect, "establishing the world's fourth largest free trade area". The Global Financial Crisis that began in 2008, causing the United States and Europe to sink into recession, also established the importance of China to the world economy. As one analyst noted, "growth rates of close to 10% mean that the moment China overtakes the US is getting closer all the time, and the communists in the east now feel bold enough to tell the capitalists in the west how to run their

---

[1] Lee Kuan Yew quoted in Peh, "Can US Squeeze into the 'Chinasean' Bed?"

[2] Quoted in Henry Kissinger, "The Future of US-Chinese Relations", *Foreign Affairs*, Mar./Apr. 2012.

economies".[3] The prediction was that China would overtake Japan as the world's second-largest economy in 2010.[4]

While proximity to China brought economic benefits to Southeast Asia, there were also concerns of a rising China—not just in the military-security realm. As Peh Shing Huei noted, "even Cafta is ruffling some Asean feathers. Indonesia, Malaysia, Thailand and the Philippines have all expressed reservations about the agreement, fearing that tariff cuts on Chinese products would leave their domestic products defenceless ..."[5] At the same time, Beijing continued to assure the ASEAN states of China's "steadfast support for Asean centrality", a role that ASEAN was always fearful of losing. In the words of Chinese Premier Wen Jiabao, "East Asian cooperation will enjoy sound development only if Asean countries continue to play its leading role."[6]

Chien-peng Chung hit the nail on the head when he described Southeast Asia as "as a site of strategic contestation since 2010" and said, "the sovereignty dispute over the South China Sea outcrops seems to be the main issue deciding the orientation of ASEAN member states toward seeking American attention".[7] In Southeast Asia, the arrival of a new president in the Philippines—Benigno Aquino III, who succeeded Glorio Arroyo in June 2010—saw a recalibration of Manila's relations with Washington and Beijing and changed the tempo of the simmering South China Sea dispute. The combination of the United States' "pivot" (see below) and a new Filipino president inevitably leads the narrative back to the South China Sea dispute. In fact, as described in chapter 5, the warm relations between China and the Philippines, which Arroyo had been cultivating since she assumed office in 2001, gradually cooled in the last years of her presidency. She was under a lot of pressure because of corruption charges.[8] China was also becoming increasingly assertive with its claims in the South China Sea from 2009. Indeed,

[3] "Global Financial Crisis: Five Key Stages 2007–2011", *The Guardian*, 7 Aug. 2011.
[4] Ivan Png, "Watch India: It May Outgrow China", *Straits Times*, 23 Feb. 2010.
[5] Peh, "Can US Squeeze into the 'Chinasean' Bed?"
[6] "Wen Drives His Way into Asean Hearts", *Straits Times*, 7 May 2011.
[7] David W.F. Huang (ed.), *Asia Pacific Countries and the US Rebalancing Strategy* (New York: Palgrave Macmillan, 2016), p. 141.
[8] For a brief account of Arroyo's presidency, see Almonte (as told to Vitug), *Endless Journey*, pp. 318–28.

Admiral Robert Willard (head of the US Pacific Command) told the Senate Armed Services Committee that 2010 "was quite a landmark in terms of confrontations" between China and its neighbours over the South China Sea claims.[9]

Whereas Arroyo pursued a balance between China and the United States (some would argue she moved closer to Beijing), Aquino III clearly chose to strengthen bilateral relations with the United States.[10] In short, with the change of leadership in the Philippines, the Sino-Philippine equation quickly changed from a strategic partnership to China being a potential threat to the Philippines' national security. At the same time, the United States, which had been adopting a hands-off approach since the 1990s, started to view developments in the South China Sea as "undermining its strategic and commercial interests" from 2008.[11]

Recall that Vietnam had been attempting to internationalize the issue in the hope of checking Chinese assertiveness. In its capacity as the rotating chair of ASEAN in 2010, Vietnam raised the issue of the South China Sea dispute at the 17th ASEAN Regional Forum Meeting in Hanoi in July. That led the United States to declare that while it remained neutral with regard to the respective claims, it had an interest in preserving free shipping in the area and would facilitate multilateral talks on the issue. Hillary Clinton's declaration at the ARF that it was "a leading diplomatic priority" (which was seen as a small victory for the Vietnamese) immediately provoked a negative response from China, which in March had reportedly told Washington that the South China Sea was part of China's "core interest".[12] Furthermore, Beijing had consistently opposed multilateral talks, preferring to resolve disputes on a bilateral basis.[13] Chinese Foreign Minister Yang Jiechi warned the

---

[9] "Manila to Push Ahead with Oil-Gas Exploration in South China Sea", *Straits Times*, 1 Mar. 2012.

[10] "Aquino in US for Talks on Strategic Partnership", *Straits Times*, 8 June 2012.

[11] Ian Storey, "Power Play in S. China Sea Stirs up Tensions", *Straits Times*, 27 July 2010.

[12] Beijing neither confirmed nor denied the report that China had told American officials that the South China Sea sovereignty claim was its "core interest".

[13] "Offering to Aid Talks, U.S. Challenges China on Disputed Islands", *New York Times*, 23 July 2010. See also Robert M. Gates, *Duty: Memoirs of a Secretary at War* (New York: Alfred A. Knopf, 2014), pp. 413–20.

United States not to internationalize the issue, saying that "would only make matters worse and more difficult to solve". Yang added, "Asean was not an appropriate forum to resolve the issue".[14] Ahead of the Second US-ASEAN Summit, Indonesian Foreign Minister Natalegawa reportedly expressed disagreement with the Chinese position saying that while ASEAN was aware of China's position, "at the same time, the issues on the South China Sea need resolution".[15] Jose Almonte recalled that barely two months after Aquino III became president in June 2010, he met Admiral Willard in his hotel suite at the Makati Shangri-La. The admiral was in Manila for a review of the Mutual Defense Treaty. They discussed the South China Sea issue and China. Willard told Almonte that he "was personally instructed by President Obama to help the Philippine government" and that "it was in the interest of America that the government of Aquino succeed".[16] In June 2011 Hillary Clinton said that Washington was committed to the defence of the Philippines and to providing it with "affordable weaponry" as well as boosting its "intelligence capabilities", but she stopped short of stating specifically whether the US would assist the Philippines in the event of a Chinese attack on the disputed Spratly islands.[17]

Both Vietnam and the Philippines appeared to be trying to encourage the United States to be more involved in the South China Sea dispute as a countervailing force against China. However, while concerned about China, not all Southeast Asian countries were completely comfortable with the United States' new-found activism in the South China Sea dispute, partly because they feared a deterioration of Sino-US relations would force them to take sides, and partly because they still doubted America's commitment in the region.[18]

China, sensing the changing atmospherics and to pre-empt a revival of the "China threat" idea, started talks with the ASEAN states on strengthening the accord with the aim of preventing disputes in the South China Sea. China had initially wanted to focus on the

---

[14] "Beijing Slams US Remarks on South China Sea", *Straits Times*, 26 July 2010.

[15] "Indonesia Rejects China's Stand on US", *Today*, 23 Sept. 2010.

[16] Almonte (as told to Vitug), *Endless Journey*, pp. 329–30.

[17] "US Will Help in Philippine Defence", *Straits Times*, 25 June 2011; "Manila Gets US Intelligence Pledge", *Straits Times*, 26 June 2011.

[18] Barry Wain, "Asean Caught in a Tight Spot", *Straits Times*, 16 Sept. 2010.

implementation of the DOC and preferred to leave the Code of Conduct (COC) on the back burner. ASEAN, on the other hand, never gave up on its objective of a signed, legally binding COC. As Philippine Foreign Secretary Romulo said, the DOC was "only an intermediate step towards the establishment of a regional code of conduct for the parties with interests in the South China Sea".[19] The "eventual attainment" or "adoption" of a COC was also reaffirmed in Article 10 of the DOC. Addressing the issue of the COC, Indonesian Foreign Minister Natalegawa said that nine years had passed since ASEAN and China agreed to develop a COC "and the time has come for talks to produce results ... There has been plenty of time for the guidelines to be considered ... If we allow the situation ... to remain dormant and inactive, it can create unnecessary complications."[20] According to Natalegawa in January 2011, the ASEAN foreign ministers agreed that there must be a greater sense of urgency in finalizing the COC. One only needed to scan through the news reports in 2011–12 to notice the high level of acrimony over the South China Sea dispute, particularly between China and the Philippines, and China and Vietnam. The ASEAN-China Joint Working Group on the Implementation of the DOC finally reached agreement on the guidelines for the implementation of the DOC in July 2011, seven years after the working group had been formed in December 2004.

The "Pivot"

Meanwhile, the new policies of the Obama administration (which began in January 2009) were beginning to have an impact on the region. The Obama administration's principal interest was China. As Clinton told Campbell (assistant secretary of state for East Asian and Pacific affairs from 2009 to 2013) in December 2008, "China is the big story, no doubt. But for us to be successful, we're going to have to work with others more effectively. We've to embed our China policy in a larger framework."[21] This is where Southeast Asia/ASEAN fits into American

[19] "Philippines Urges ASEAN, China to Agree to Ensure Peace in South China Sea Report", *Philippine Daily Inquirer*, 11 Dec. 2005.
[20] "'Urgent Need' for China, Asean Code of Conduct", *Straits Times*, 18 Jan. 2011.
[21] Campbell, *The Pivot*, p. xxi.

strategy. As mentioned in chapter 4, Secretary of State Clinton's declaration after signing the TAC in July 2009 that "the United States is back" was a clear indication that Washington intended to challenge China's rising influence in Southeast Asia. The Southeast Asian states, while pleased to hear that, were unsure whether the distractions in the Middle East and Afghanistan, compounded by an economic recession, would only lead to a case of "a willing heart but tiring flesh for the Americans".[22] Washington's renewed interest in the South China Sea in 2010 was described earlier in this chapter.

The last quarter of 2011 was a significant period with respect to US-Southeast Asian relations. The November 2011 issue of *Foreign Policy* carried an article dated 11 October 2011 by Secretary of State Clinton titled "America's Pacific Century". The secretary of state used the article to announce a shift in the direction of American foreign policy from Iraq and Afghanistan to Asia-Pacific, which she described as "the key driver of global politics". It was in this article that the now infamous term "pivot" was introduced, which started a debate on the appropriateness of Clinton's choice of the word. Whether "pivot" or "rebalancing" would have been the better choice of word is not important. The message was clear: an admission that since the Cold War ended, US policy in Asia had been "adrift".[23]

According to Clinton, "as the war in Iraq winds down and America begins to withdraw its forces from Afghanistan, the United States stands at a pivot point ... The future of politics will be decided in Asia, not Afghanistan and Iraq, and the United States will be right at the center of the action." She acknowledged that "this kind of pivot is not easy" but the United States had "paved the way for it over the last two-and-a-half years, and we are committed to seeing it through the most important diplomatic efforts of our time".[24] Soon after the publication of the "pivot" article, the United States (sceptical of EAS when it had

---

[22] Peh, "Can US Squeeze into the 'Chinasean' Bed?"

[23] Campbell, *The Pivot*, p. 144.

[24] Hillary Clinton, "America's Pacific Century", http://foreignpolicy.com/2011/10/11/americas-pacific-century/, accessed 3 May 2017. See also "Secretary Clinton's Op-Ed: 'America's Pacific Century'", http://www.cfr.org/asia-and-pacific/secretary-clintons-op-ed-americas-pacific-century/p30265, accessed 3 May 2017; speech by US President Barack Obama to the Australian Parliament (excerpt), 17 Nov. 2011, "Asia-Pacific Presence a Top US Priority", *Straits Times*, 19 Nov. 2011.

been formed in 2005) and Russia finally became members of the EAS in November 2011. The decision to join the EAS, as Ann Marie Murphy (National Asia Research Fellow and Southeast Asia expert) explained, was "part of a broader strategy to pivot American foreign policy away from the Middle East toward the dynamic Asia-Pacific region. The United States wants to help build the regional architecture through which future challenges will be addressed."[25] Clinton's historic though low-key visit to Myanmar in November/December 2011, the first visit to that country by a US secretary of state since February 1955—when the secretary of state during the Eisenhower administration, John Foster Dulles, visited Rangoon—was indicative of the new turn in US foreign policy towards the region.[26] It also served as the precursor to President Barack Obama's visit to Yangon a year later, in November 2012.

At the ASEAN Summit in Bali in November 2011, Clinton pushed for an expansion of the Trans-Pacific Partnership (TPP). President Obama did the same at the 19th APEC Summit in Honolulu in the same month. The TPP was first proposed by Singapore, Chile and New Zealand in 2002 in response to the APEC Business Advisory Council recommendation to APEC leaders to work towards a Free Trade Area of the Asia-Pacific (FTAAP). It was an open-ended partnership, which meant it was open to any interested APEC economy willing and able to comply with the standards set by the TPP. Brunei subsequently joined. The United States joined the negotiations in 2008. In 2011 four more countries—Australia, Peru, Vietnam and Malaysia—were engaged in negotiations to join the partnership. At the APEC meeting in November 2011, Japan, Canada and Mexico also expressed interest. Canada and Mexico joined in the negotiations in 2012, and Japan did so in 2015. It was when the United States joined the negotiations that the TPP attracted the interest of other economies. The TPP has been described as a "central pillar of the Obama administration's 'rebalance' policy in the Asia Pacific region".[27] Washington saw the TPP as a way to

---

[25] "U.S Joins East Asia Summit: Implications for Regional Cooperation—An Interview with Ann Marie Murphy", http://www.nbr.org/research/activity.aspx?id=183, accessed 3 May 2017.

[26] See Kenton Clymer, *A Delicate Relationship: The United States and Burma/Myanmar Since 1945* (Ithaca: Cornell University Press, 2015), pp. 303–20.

[27] Matthew P. Goodman, "Yes, TPP is About Who Writes the Rules", Pacific Forum, CSIS, *PacNet* #66, 6 Sept. 2016.

expand its presence in the region. In Clinton's words, "Foreign policy is economic policy, and by strengthening the diplomacy and presence abroad, we can strengthen our economies back home and vice versa ... The United States recognizes that we are making a pivot towards the Asia-Pacific region where we intend to be a diplomatic, economic and strategic force in the 21st century." Analysts were of the view that the American interest in the region was a "two-pronged attempt to boost a flagging US economy while maintaining a balance to China's giant—and growing—economic presence".[28] The TPP was supposedly the "gold standard" of trade agreements. At the same time it was more than just a trade agreement, as recognized by Clinton. China did not join the TPP as it was unable to fulfil the requirements. Left out of the TPP, Beijing was, however, keen to push forward the FTAAP, which Chinese Foreign Minister Wang Yi said would be "a new step forward in regional economic integration" given that "the realization of the FTAAP is a longstanding consensus and vision of Apec economic leaders".[29]

But we are running ahead of our narrative. At the 44th ASEAN Economic Ministers Meeting in 2012, the ASEAN countries, China, Japan, South Korea, India, Australia and New Zealand agreed to begin talks on establishing a free trade area spanning Asia. Known as the Regional Comprehensive Economic Partnership (RCEP), it was hailed by ASEAN's secretary-general as "a big achievement".[30] Not surprisingly, political observers quickly concluded that the RCEP, in which China would be the dominant economic power, was a competitor to the TPP, the top trade priority of the Obama administration. Kavi Chongkittavorn, however, pointed out that while ASEAN understood that the maintenance of economic growth required linkages to "broader economic communities", it was concerned that the TPP could eventually "dilute the leadership role of Asean". The idea of an ASEAN-led RCEP was thus "a precautionary measure", which could, it was hoped, "mitigate possible implications from the fast-moving TPP".[31] The politically correct

---

[28] "US Seeks Support for Trans-Pacific Trade Pact", *Straits Times*, 19 Nov. 2011.

[29] "China Eyes Apec Free Trade Zone", *Straits Times*, 30 Oct. 2014.

[30] "16 Countries Take First Step to an Asian Free Trade Area", *Straits Times*, 1 Sept. 2012.

[31] Kavi Chongkittavorn, "The Way Ahead for Asean", *Straits Times*, 3 Jan. 2014.

response to this, according to US Trade Representative Ron Kirk, was, "we see them as complementary, not necessarily competition".[32]

It may be useful at this point to present an alternative narrative about the pivot. In her article titled "The Pivot Before the Pivot", published in *International Security*,[33] Nina Silove argued that the United States' "reorientation toward Asia" began from the mid-2000s and "the Obama administration's pivot to Asia was both a belated labeling as well as an extension of that little-recognized reorientation strategy". The aim of the Bush administration had, in fact, been no different from the Obama administration's. The primary "strategic challenge" of the Asia strategy was "China's rise". According to Silove, the Bush administration deliberately kept the strategy "muted" to avoid antagonizing China. Instead of constructing multilateral alliances, what the United States did was increase "the military capabilities of allies and partners and building greater multilateral interoperability among them". The article describes the two approaches that were adopted—"external" and "internal" balancing, primarily military and diplomatic in nature. There was no trade or FTA strategy during this period because the Congressional trade committees were "extremely sensitive" about "using FTAs for 'foreign policy' reasons", according to US Trade Representative Zoellick. It was only after the United States joined the TPP negotiations in February 2008 that an economic dimension was included in the reorientation. In sum, neither the Bush nor the Obama administration was aiming to slow China's growth; both "sought to increase the combined power of the United States and its allies and partners to match China's rise and thereby preserve the relative power in the region". Rizal Sukma noted that Obama's Southeast Asia policy did not constitute "a significant departure" from his predecessor's: "in fact, a degree of continuation is quite apparent." The one striking difference, however, was that while US Southeast Asia policy under Bush was "primarily framed within a US-led war on terror", Obama "took a more comprehensive approach in defining US relationships with the region". It was

[32] "16 Countries Take First Step to an Asian Free Trade Area".

[33] Nina Silove, "The Pivot Before the Pivot: U.S. Strategy to Preserve the Power Balance in Asia", *International Security* 40, 4 (Spring 2016): 45–88. The author had access to the personal archive of Secretary of Defence Donald Rumsfeld.

the same goal but with different approaches, and "for Southeast Asian nations, that matters".[34]

The 45th ASEAN Ministerial Meeting

After agreeing on the guidelines for the implementation of the DOC in July 2011, ASEAN and China met in January 2012 to discuss how to implement the guidelines. Altogether, depending on whether one starts counting from the time the South China Sea issue entered the consciousness of ASEAN in 1992, or the official endorsement of a regional COC in 1996, it took almost 16 years to reach agreement on the implementation of the DOC. After that, ASEAN quickly established a special working group to start drafting the COC. Meanwhile, in April 2012, China and the Philippines were engaged in another spat over the disputed Scarborough Shoal. It started on 10 April, when the Philippines accused Chinese anglers of poaching in the vicinity of the shoal, which Manila claimed was Philippines territory. As mentioned in chapter 5, in early 2000 China and the Philippines disagreed over the ownership of the shoal. During Philippine President Estrada's visit to Beijing in May 2000, both sides agreed not to escalate the situation. Amidst the 2012 standoff, American and Filipino troops launched a two-week naval exercise beginning on 16 April in the South China Sea area. To the Chinese, the naval drills "reflected a mentality that will lead the South China Sea issue down a fork in the road towards military confrontation and resolution through armed force". Through "this kind of meddling and intervention", the US "would only stir up the entire South China Sea situation towards increasing chaos, and this will inevitably have a massive impact on regional peace and stability".[35] According to Peking University professor Jia Qingguo, the Chinese believed the Americans were instigating or encouraging Manila "to create a problem for China in the South China Sea".[36] It was obvious that Manila was counting on US support against China.

---

[34] Rizal Sukma, "US Policy Towards Southeast Asia: A New Paradigm?" paper presented at the 24th Asia-Pacific Roundtable, Kuala Lumpur, 7–9 June 2010.

[35] "China's Military Warns of Confrontation over Seas", *Today*, 23 Apr. 2012.

[36] "Slew of Chinese Agencies Complicates S. China Sea Issue", *Straits Times*, 24 Apr. 2012.

During his visit to Washington, DC in June 2012, Philippine President Aquino revealed that Manila and Beijing were "engaged in bilateral dialogue to find a mutually beneficial way to break the impasse", but he also issued a veiled warning to Beijing to think twice about pushing Manila around on the issue.[37] Manila wanted to send a strong signal that it had a powerful ally. However, as Acharya pointed out, it was "not one that will give Manila a blank cheque to do whatever it wants", only that Washington was "willing to support the country and help it boost its own defence". In July Aquino reportedly said that he was considering asking the United States to deploy spy planes over the South China Sea to help monitor the disputed waters, as the Philippines did not have aircraft with those capabilities.[38] It is, however, evident that none of the sides—China, the Philippines or the United States—wanted the dispute to escalate into armed conflict. China could have easily taken over Scarborough Shoal from the Philippines using its naval, air and amphibious capabilities but chose not to.[39] When they met in Washington, DC, both Aquino and Obama emphasized that the United States and the Philippines were committed to a diplomatic solution to the South China Sea dispute.[40]

Sino-Vietnamese relations were also difficult at this time, although after the 11th National Congress of the Communist Party of Vietnam in January 2011, the Vietnamese leadership made efforts to improve relations with China and manage the South China Sea dispute.[41] However, in May 2012 two Chinese maritime surveillance ships cut the exploration cable of the Vietnamese survey ship *Binh Minh 02* in the disputed waters between the Vietnamese coast and Hainan. In June China's announcement that it would elevate the administrative status of the Spratly and Paracel Islands from county to prefectural level under the control of the newly established Sansha City once again brought the dispute to the fore. Both Manila and Hanoi protested against the Chinese decision to establish Sansha City. The Chinese, however,

---

[37] "Aquino in US for Talks on Strategic Partnership", *Straits Times*, 8 June 2012; "Aquino Urges US Backing in Spat with China", *Straits Times*, 9 June 2012.

[38] "Aquino May Ask US to Deploy Spy Planes", *Straits Times*, 3 July 2012.

[39] "Nine Dragons Stir up S. China Sea", *Straits Times*, 25 June 2012.

[40] "US, Philippines Stress Diplomacy", *Straits Times*, 10 June 2012.

[41] Hai, *Vietnam and the South China Sea*, pp. 187–91.

claimed that Sansha's creation was a response to Vietnam's passing of a maritime law in June declaring sovereignty and jurisdiction over the Paracels and Spratlys.

At the 45th ASEAN Ministerial Meeting (AMM) in July 2012, the member states finally agreed on a set of "ASEAN's Proposed Elements of a Regional Code of Conduct in the South China Sea Between ASEAN and the People's Republic of China" (also known as the Zero Draft of the COC). However, most would remember the July 2012 meeting in Phnom Penh as the ministerial meeting (after the formation of ASEAN in 1967) that ended without the adoption of a joint communique. It was because of the inability, or some would say unwillingness, of the chair, Cambodia, "to find a consensus on how to depict the recent intensification of disputes in the South China Sea between the Philippines and Vietnam, on the one hand, and China, on the other, in the joint communique".[42] The Philippines had insisted on the inclusion of a reference to the recent confrontation over Scarborough Shoal, while Vietnam wanted a statement on respect for the Exclusive Economic Zones included in the communique. Cambodia refused to accede.[43]

The failure to issue a joint communique over one paragraph led to "immediate public recriminations".[44] Some diplomats wondered whether

[42] Tommy Koh, "Asean up to Tackling Sixth Challenge", *Straits Times*, 1 Sept. 2012. According to Carlyle Thayer, the record indicated that the failure was the result of Cambodia's handling of its role as ASEAN chair. Foreign Minister Hor Namhong was not conciliatory and rejected repeated attempts at compromise. See Carlyle A. Thayer, "ASEAN's Code of Conduct in the South China Sea: A Litmus Test for Community-Building", *Asia-Pacific Journal* 10, 34, 4 (Aug. 2012): 1–22. For the Cambodian perspective by Sin Serey (Cambodia's ambassador to Singapore), see "Cambodia Acted in Asean's Best Interests: Ambassador", *Straits Times*, 9 Aug. 2012; "Cambodia Rebuts Criticism of Role in Asean", *Straits Times*, 17 Aug. 2012.
[43] For an account of this episode, see Mark Valencia, "Is ASEAN Becoming a Big-Power Battleground?" *Straits Times*, 24 July 2012. The most detailed account of what occurred during the 45th ASEAN Ministerial Meeting is in Thayer, "ASEAN's Code of Conduct in the South China Sea", pp. 1–22. Australian Foreign Minister Bob Carr also provided interesting and useful snippets of this episode in his memoir; see Bob Carr, *Diary of a Foreign Minister* (Sydney: NewSouth, 2014), pp. 110–1, 116, 128. Indonesian Foreign Minister Natalegawa (2009–14) provides a first-person account in his memoir, *Does ASEAN Matter? A View from Within* (Singapore: Institute of Southeast Asian Studies, 2018), pp. 127–30.
[44] Thayer, "ASEAN's Code of Conduct in the South China Sea", p. 14.

Cambodia was "irretrievably in the pocket of China".[45] Manila definitely thought so. Almonte recalled:

> When Aquino publicly disagreed with Prime Minister Hun Sen during an Asean meeting in Phnom Penh, disputing the Cambodian leader's claim that ASEAN had reached a consensus not to internationalize the competing claims to the South China Sea, that, to me, was very important. Aquino was criticized for breaking protocol. But he had to match the wiliness of Hun Sen, who was using protocol to do what he wanted because China had given his country millions of dollars in soft loans and grants.[46]

Indonesian Foreign Minister Natalegawa told reporters it was 'totally unsatisfactory ... that Asean is unable to come up with simple paragraphs that say what we have been saying all this time".[47] He immediately embarked on a salvage exercise and managed to broker a six-point statement on the South China Sea, issued on 20 July 2012 in Phnom Penh, which essentially reiterated previous statements. As Valencia noted, "there was nothing new in the declaration".[48] In a 1 September 2012 article, Singapore's consummate diplomat Tommy Koh wrote, "I am confident that when our leaders meet in Phnom Penh in November, they will restore Asean's credibility by forging a consensus on the South China Sea."[49] In the event, nothing substantial emerged at the November summit except that ASEAN narrowly avoided a repeat of the July episode. A joint statement marking the tenth anniversary of the Declaration on the Conduct of Parties in the South China Sea was issued on 19 November 2012. The joint statement recalled the "decade of enhancing mutual confidence and trust" and looked towards "a future of peace, friendship and cooperation".[50] No one expected a quick

---

[45] "Divided We Stagger", *The Economist*, 18 Aug. 2012.
[46] Almonte (as told to Vitug), *Endless Journey*, p. 330.
[47] "Row Overshadows Summit", *Straits Times*, 16 July 2012.
[48] Valencia, "Is ASEAN Becoming a Big-Power Battleground?"
[49] Koh, "Asean up to Tackling Sixth Challenge".
[50] "Joint Statement of the 15th ASEAN-China Summit on the 10th Anniversary of the Declaration on the Conduct of Parties in the South China Sea: Enhancing Peace, Friendship and Cooperation", Phnom Penh, 19 Nov. 2010, http://www.asean.org/wp-content/uploads/images/2012/news/documents/Joint%20Statement%20of%20the%2015th%20ASEAN-China%20Summit%20on%20the%2010th%20Anniversary%20of%20the%20Declaration%20on%20the%20Conduct%20of%20Parties%20in%20the%20South%20China%20Sea.pdf, accessed 15 May 2017.

resolution to the South China Sea territorial dispute, but everyone, in the words of Surin, "understood that they could not afford to let the disputes hold back lucrative trade agreements".[51] There was also the hope that the leadership transition in China might lead to some positive changes. There were reports that within the Chinese leadership there were different views on how assertive and reactive their South China Sea policy should be.[52] (Xi Jinping was appointed head of the Chinese Communist Party and chairman of the Central Military Commission in November 2012 and became president of China in March 2013.) However, the reality was that on the ground, all parties in the dispute continued to take steps to shore up or defend their claims. According to official Australian sources, Canberra was told that in response to "China's truculence on the South China Sea", the State Department "has set aside the caution it showed in Phnom Penh and now concludes some anti-Chinese action is required". A cable from Honolulu (headquarters of the US Pacific Fleet) stated that the United States had been "too understated" on Scarborough Shoal.[53]

ASEAN States' Relations with US and China

The failure of the ASEAN states to act in unison, particularly at the 45th AMM, raised the important question of ASEAN's unity and credibility—whether it could achieve its goal of creating a security community and, even more seriously, whether it would be able to sustain its position as the absolute core of the regional security architecture. One essential requirement would be the ability to play the role of an honest broker in the unfolding rivalry between the United States and China. This is thus the appropriate point to take a step back and briefly review the different relationships and ties of the Southeast Asian states with both the United States and China until this time, beginning with Cambodia, which had been rightly or wrongly much maligned after the July 2012 fiasco. It is worth noting that both Cambodia and Laos, perhaps more than any other Southeast Asian state, had—and continue

[51] "Towards Two Giant Free Trade Pacts", *Straits Times*, 21 Nov. 2012.

[52] See Carr, *Diary of a Foreign Minister*, pp. 32–3.

[53] Ibid., p. 128. Carr gives a gist of the contents of the cables sent from Washington to Canberra in July/August 2012.

to have—a special need for China. For Phnom Penh and Vientiane, China serves as a countervailing force against their much larger and historically aggrandizing neighbours, such as Thailand (and Vietnam).

After the 1993 elections, which initially saw the formation of an uneasy coalition government led by Sihanouk's son Norodom Ranariddh and Hun Sen, Cambodia took some years to develop a coherent foreign policy. After the breakdown of that coalition in 1997, Cambodia has been led by Hun Sen, whom Sihanouk once described as a more astute politician (and an image of himself) than his son Ranariddh. Between 1993 and 1997, China did not have a preference as to who led Cambodia. China had been unwavering in its support of Sihanouk and by extension his FUNCINPEC Party (led by Ranariddh), while it viewed Hun Sen as a Vietnam protégé. However, after 1997 Hun Sen began taking proactive steps to endear himself to China. The most prominent example was when he cut links with Taiwan and paid a visit to Beijing to pay his respects. He also accepted China's help in building the National Assembly building after the 1998 elections, which he won with a simple majority and thereafter became the sole prime minister. Like Sihanouk, Hun Sen continued to maintain good relations with Beijing (despite its previous support of the Khmer Rouge). The Chinese apparently also realized that between Hun Sen and Ranariddh, they preferred dealing with the former. China quickly became Cambodia's top aid donor and foreign investor. Cambodia's close relationship with China is well known. Lee Kuan Yew reportedly commented that within hours, everything that was discussed in ASEAN meetings was known in Beijing, given China's close ties with Cambodia (and Laos as well). What was perhaps unexpected was Phnom Penh's failure, in its capacity as ASEAN chair of the 45th AMM, to produce a joint communique—for the first time in the association's history. In the aftermath of the meeting, Sino-Cambodian relations became the subject of intense scrutiny. Soon after the AMM kerfuffle, it was reported that China had pledged more than US$500 million in soft loans and grants to Cambodia, which looked like a reward to Phnom Penh for putting China's interests on the issue of the South China Sea dispute ahead of ASEAN's.

Although diplomatic relations between the US and Cambodia were established after the UN-sponsored election in 1993, relations were cool as a consequence of Hun Sen's seizure of power in 1997 and his subsequent poor human rights record. Relations improved only from around 2006–07, when US officials began to take cognizance of the increasingly close ties between Phnom Penh and Beijing. In early 2007 Washington lifted a decade-old ban on direct aid to Cambodia, which observers viewed as a harbinger of better US-Cambodia relations. In 2010 US Secretary of State Clinton used the occasion of her visit to Phnom Penh to urge Cambodians to diversify their international relationships and not be overdependent on China; by that time the Chinese had already established a significant presence in the country.

In the case of Laos, the successful settlement of the Sino-Laos frontier demarcation in 1992 saw the development of a thriving cross-border trade. China began actively competing with Vietnam for Laos' political allegiance. In 2010 China supplanted Thailand as the largest foreign investor in Laos. According to Dominique Van der Borght of Oxfam Belgium, Chinese projects in Laos were on a massive scale and led to concerns in Vientiane that China, Vietnam and Thailand were competing to use Laos as an "extension of their territory".[54] Although Laos never broke off diplomatic relations with the US, the relationship was plagued by the legacies of the Vietnam War. Vientiane suspected that the CIA continued to be in league with the Hmong leader to undermine the government. Laos did not gain Normal Trade Relations status with the United States until 2004, a prerequisite under US law for any bilateral trade agreement. The US arrest of Vang Pao (a former Hmong general who fought on the US side in the Vietnam War) in 2007 apparently gave the relationship a fillip. Vang Pao's death in 2011 finally closed this chapter, even if not fully, in US-Lao relations. Clinton visited Vientiane in July 2012, the first secretary of state to do so in almost five decades. This was seen as part of Washington's effort to counter the growing Chinese influence in the region. It was reported that during her four-hour visit, Clinton discussed environmental concerns about dam projects on the Mekong River and other investment opportunities.[55] Laos-watchers felt that Beijing was "rapidly expanding its political and economic influence" in the landlocked and mountainous

[54] "Laos Swamped by Foreign Investment", 18 May 2011, https://khampoua.wordpress.com/tag/laotians/page/2/, accessed 18 May 2017.

[55] "US Secretary of State Hillary Clinton Makes Historic Visit to Laos", https://www.independent.co.uk/news/world/asia/us-secretary-of-state-hillary-clinton-makes-historic-visit-to-laos-7936239.html, accessed 16 Aug. 2018.

country, which had "long served as a geographical buffer between China and the rest of mainland Southeast Asia".[56] Vientiane, in contrast to Phnom Penh, tried to be "even handed" in its relations with China. Whether or not it will succeed is an open question.[57]

Soon after the normalization of relations in 1991, both Vietnam and China moved to resolve their outstanding bilateral issues, of which there were four. It took nearly ten years before the two countries agreed on the demarcation of their land borders and the Tonkin Gulf in 1999 and 2000 respectively, thus settling two of the four issues. The remaining two—the sovereignty dispute over the Paracel and Spratly Islands—persist until today. It is unlikely that Vietnam will be able to regain sovereignty of the Paracels as they are effectively under Chinese control. As for the Spratly dispute, the involvement of other claimants makes it more than a simple bilateral problem. Vietnam normalized relations with the US in 1995 (just before its admission into ASEAN) but was given Normal Trade Relations status only in 2001. As in the case of Laos, the legacies of the Vietnam War, notably the POW/MIA and Agent Orange issues, impeded the development of better bilateral relations. The conservative elements in the Vietnamese leadership remained suspicious of the United States and preferred to accommodate China to the extent possible. Since President Clinton visited Vietnam in 2000, the first US president to do so, relations have been improving despite the occasional hiccups over trade and human rights issues. In 2012 it was common knowledge that because of the South China Sea dispute, Hanoi was quietly encouraging the United States to be a countervailing force against China. Assistant Secretary of State for East Asian and Pacific Affairs Campbell pointed out that close ties with Vietnam was an "important component of the Pivot" and that "although US-Vietnam relations have come far in recent decades and are arguably at a high point", there was still much potential for improvement. He advised that Washington "should forgo public shaming in favor of dialogue, private counsel, and support for Vietnamese reforms".[58] All

---

[56] Bertil Lintner, "Little Laos Risks Losing It All to China", *Asia Times*, 13 May 2018.

[57] Edgar Pang, "'Same-Same but Different': Laos and Cambodia's Political Embrace of China", *ISEAS Perspective*, 5 Sept. 2017.

[58] Campbell, *The Pivot*, pp. 261–2.

said, with regard to US-Vietnam relations, particularly in the military dimension, the Chinese had drawn a "red line" across Vietnam, and most analysts did not think Washington would cross it. Campbell hinted as much in March 2012 during a meeting with Bob Carr, Australia's minister of foreign affairs from 2012 to 2013.[59] Notably, Campbell, in his book, had little policy recommendation with regard to Cambodia and Laos.[60]

In summary, the three Indochinese states—Cambodia, Laos and Vietnam—having emerged from the Cold War as the three poorest countries in the region all saw economic benefits from improving relations with China. The Chinese economy was developing at a rapid pace and showed potential of becoming a global economic power in the future. For the two smaller Indochinese countries—Cambodia and Laos—China also served their interests as a bulwark against Thai or Vietnamese hegemony, particularly since historically China had never physically invaded Cambodia or Laos. Beijing, too, was keen to improve relations with its immediate neighbours strategically located along its southern border, which some writers have dubbed as "China's backyard". China's good neighbourliness in Indochina stemmed from its desire for a peaceful and stable external environment to allow it to concentrate on its own economic development. Beijing was aware that relations with the Indochinese countries, if not properly managed, could disrupt or contain its aspiration of being a global power.

It was not that the Indochinese states did not want to have better relations with the United States. However, the main impediments to enhancing Indochina-US relations were the baggage of the Indochina War and America's focus on human rights and corruption in those countries, particularly in the 1990s and early 2000s. Until very recently, US relations with the Indochinese states were very much driven by Washington's broader interest in and engagement with ASEAN. For example, the US normalized relations with Vietnam on 11 July 1995, just before Vietnam became a full-fledged ASEAN member the same month, but bilateral relations were slow to develop. After years of debate, Laos was eventually granted normal trade status in 2004, the year Vientiane assumed the rotating ASEAN chair. It took even longer

[59] Carr, *Diary of a Foreign Minister*, p. 67.

[60] See Campbell, *The Pivot*, chapter 6.

in the case of Cambodia, as mentioned above. When Obama visited Cambodia in 2012, he raised the issue of human rights in his private meetings. The meetings were described as "tense".[61] In the case of Myanmar, the thaw in US-Myanmar relations was only just beginning in 2012, and it was too early to tell its future trajectory. Secretary of State Clinton's visit to Yangon in late 2011 was the first by a US secretary of state in over half a century. Derek Mitchell, appointed US ambassador to Myanmar in 2012, was the first person to hold this position in two decades. Obama was the first sitting American president to visit Myanmar (as well as Cambodia), which he did in November 2012. It was reported that "tens of thousands of ecstatic Burmese" greeted him.[62] On the Myanmar side, the leadership indicated that they wanted to recalibrate their relations vis-à-vis the US and China. The military junta in a secret study concluded that having China as a diplomatic ally and economic patron "threatened the country's independence" and that improving relations with the US would be a recommended course of action.[63] Ambassador Mitchell noted in December 2013 that US-Myanmar relations had become "very constructive, essentially 180 degrees from what it was perhaps two and a half years ago".[64]

Turning to the original ASEAN member states—which have had close relations with the United States since the Cold War years—Singapore, according to Campbell, is "perhaps the most defining example of a country that has stretched the definition of *partner* by providing uncommon capacity and support to the United States". At the same time, Singapore, because it maintained positive relations with China,

---

[61] "The Importance of Obama's Asian Pivot", *Times of India*, 24 Nov. 2012. Washington's condemnation of the Hun Sen-led Cambodian People's Party government's dissolution of the opposition Cambodia National Rescue Party ahead of the July 2018 general election only worsened Cambodia-US relations and pushed Phnom Penh even closer to Beijing.

[62] Ibid.

[63] Ibid.

[64] Clymer, *A Delicate Relationship*, p. 319. When Aung San Suu Kyi's National League for Democracy formed the government in 2016, there was hope for further improvement in US-Myanmar relations. However, the Rohingya crisis, amongst other issues, slowed the process. In light of the Rohingya crisis, in December 2017 Washington reintroduced selected sanctions.

[65] Campbell, *The Pivot*, pp. 220–4.

also acted as "a regional diplomatic fulcrum".[65] Next is the Philippines. Because of its complicated history with the United States, "there remain complex attitudes toward the United States that are a mixture of respect and nationalistic wariness". Like Vietnam, the Philippines was involved in a long-running dispute with China over the South China Sea claims. Campbell described Philippine-US relations in 2013–14 as "better than any point" since the Cold War ended.[66] Relations with Thailand, "America's oldest treaty partner in Asia", became complicated and challenging because of the Thai military coup on 22 May 2014. In fact, relations started to strain after the 2006 military coup. As Campbell noted, "frustration with US response to these events has reawakened some of the antecedents of Thai strategic culture, leading its military junta to turn closer to China for support as a way of balancing Thailand's external relations".[67] As mentioned earlier, Indonesia-US relations took a dive after the 1997 Asian Financial Crisis, and particularly after the East Timor episode. Relations began to improve, very gradually during the Bush administration and faster under Obama. In 2010 both countries signed the US-Indonesia Comprehensive Partnership, and defence relations revived.[68] CIA Director David Petraeus told Australian Foreign Minister Carr that Indonesia was not on "the top-ten foreign-policy issues of concern to the administration", but given the "pivot", Washington needed to focus on the country. Clinton said that the American side had "worked hard" on Indonesia and it had taken three meetings "to create some trust". Campbell credited Indonesian President Yudhoyono's leadership and role in ASEAN for reviving Indonesia-US relations. He revealed that Washington had decided to treat Indonesia as "a global player and that was central to the US engagement". However, it would require a serious effort over several administrations to deepen the relationship. This conversation took place in April 2012 in the last year of Obama's first term as president. President Yudhoyono's term would expire in 2014. The prevailing view was that his successor would not be as internationalist as he had been.[69] Relations with Malaysia, "at times plagued by domestic anti-Americanism as well as

[66] Ibid., pp. 224–7.
[67] Ibid., pp. 227–30.
[68] Ibid., pp. 260–1.
[69] Carr, *Diary of a Foreign Minister*, pp. 31, 35, 40–1.

disagreements over the Cold War and the Asian financial crisis", also improved under the premiership of Abdullah Ahmad Badawi (2003–09) and Najib Razak. The South China Sea dispute had "pushed Malaysia to pursue deep but quiet strategic relations" with the United States.[70] Brunei and the United States, too, had "close strategic ties". Campbell believed that the relationship had not achieved its full potential.[71] The general feeling of these Southeast Asian states towards the United States may be summed up with the following two quotes: "We want the US ... but just over the horizon ... under the radar" and "Don't leave us, but don't make us choose."[72] This sentiment echoes the sentiment in 1966. Then, the Thai foreign minister (who in 1967 would be one of the founding leaders at the inauguration of ASEAN) told US Secretary of State Dean Rusk that while the ASEAN states hoped to have the "discreet blessing of the United States", Washington should not "bestow the kiss of death by too close an embrace".[73] The Indonesians, too, expressed a similar view to the Americans in 1968.[74]

Sino-US Rivalry in Southeast Asia

There was clearly growing US-China competition in the region beginning in the Obama administration. It was a sensitive issue for the Southeast Asian governments, which preferred not to choose one or the other and maintain ASEAN's centrality. The Southeast Asian governments would have had many internal discussions on how they should

---

[70] There is more than meets the eye in Malaysia-US relations, as revealed in a secret document exposed in July 2018. See "Malaysia's Najib Sought CIA Support Before Election Defeat", 20 July 2018, http://www.atimes.com/article/malaysias-najib-sought-cia-support-before-election-defeat/, accessed 20 Aug. 2018; "Najib Mum on Alleged Letter Seeking US Backing", *Straits Times*, 27 July 2018.

[71] Campbell, *The Pivot*, pp. 262–3.

[72] Quoted in Carr, *Diary of a Foreign Minister*, p. 10.

[73] SEATO Council Meeting, Canberra, 27–29 June 1966; ANZUS Ministerial Meeting, Canberra, 30 June–1 July 1966, in *Foreign Relations of the United States (FRUS), 1964–1968*, Vol. 27, *Mainland Southeast Asia; Regional Affairs* (Washington, DC: United States Government Printing Office, 2000).

[74] Airgram from the Embassy in Indonesia to the Department of States, Djakarta, 21 Feb. 1968, in *Foreign Relations of the United States, 1964–1968*, Vol. 26, *Indonesia, Malaysia-Singapore, Philippines* (Washington, DC: United States Government Printing Office, 2001).

position themselves between these two powers. It was Hugh White, an Australian academic,[75] who kindled the debate within academic/policy circles, especially from 2012, and brought the dilemma into public discourse. White was no ordinary academic. From 1995 to 2000 he was the deputy secretary for strategy and intelligence in the Australian Department of Defence. Australia was (and still is) one of the United States' closest allies in the region. In fact, in 2010 White published a 74-page article titled "Power Shift: Australia's Future Between Washington and Beijing",[76] which essentially argued that the current situation was untenable as a rising China would not accept American dominance in the region. Therefore, as a close ally of the United States, Australia should persuade Washington to concede its primacy or its goal of primacy in the region and instead work towards a power-sharing arrangement with China for the sake of the region's long-term stability and to forestall another Cold War. White proposed a "concert of Asia", not unlike that of 19th-century Europe. White's analysis and proposal provoked a vigorous debate, particularly within Australia as his article was about Australia's "future between Washington and Beijing". It was his second publication, in 2012, *The China Choice: Why America Should Share Power*,[77] that attracted some attention in Southeast Asia and provoked a rebuttal from the Singaporean diplomat Tommy Koh.[78] The book reiterated White's 2010 arguments. The idea of a "concert" is reminiscent of a similar proposal made by Kevin Rudd, which was discussed in chapter 4. As Remy Davison noted, "no leaders in Asia or North America treated Rudd's initiative with any seriousness. Nevertheless, Rudd's views have found some resonance in White's book ..."[79] Koh essentially argued that White's central argument that various ASEAN-led institutions such as the EAS should be replaced by a

[75] For his bio-data, see "Hugh White (Strategist)", https://en.wikipedia.org/wiki/Hugh_White_(strategist), accessed 26 May 2017.

[76] Hugh White, "Power Shift: Australia's Future Between Washington and China", *Quarterly Essay* 39 (2010): 1–74.

[77] Hugh White, *The China Choice: Why America Should Share Power* (Oxford: Oxford University Press, 2012).

[78] Tommy Koh was Singapore's ambassador to the United States from 1984 to 1990.

[79] See Remy Davison, "The China Choice: Why America Needs to Share Power", 31 Aug. 2012, http://theconversation.com/the-china-choice-why-america-needs-to-share-power-9196, accessed 26 May 2017.

"concert of Asia" (comprising the US, China, Japan and India) was flawed. White's proposal would have made ASEAN or ASEAN-led institutions irrelevant in the new regional order, except for perhaps Indonesia, which, according to White, had the "potential to become a genuine Asian great power eventually—but not before mid-century".[80] Koh defended ASEAN's centrality: "The inclusion of Asean and other small and middle powers changes the atmospherics of the group. As a trusted facilitator, Asean is often able to forge a consensus and reconcile the competing interests of the various parties. This is a role which the major powers cannot play, individually or collectively."[81]

By way of ending this discussion, it is of interest to quote Carr. In his memoir, Carr recalled the book launch of *The China Choice* by former Australian Prime Minister Paul Keating on 14 August 2012 in Canberra. Keating spoke about giving China "strategic space", but it was not clear what that meant and involved. Would Japan and South Korea need to end their alliances with the United States, or should Vietnam accept Chinese dominance? Carr wrote, "The pro-China lobby are over-egging the pudding. They want to make us fidgety and defensive about our China policy. Make us anxious. That's not the way to respond. In this phase of the relationship, with them making us uncomfortable, a bit of benign neglect is needed, not letting the Chinese think we care too much ..."[82] White continues to peddle his proposal to this day.[83]

[80] White, *The China Choice*, p. 144. White believed that at some point in the future Indonesia could join the concert of four.

[81] Tommy Koh, "A Reply to Hugh White: Who Will Lead Asia", *Straits Times*, 29 Sept. 2012. Koh was actually rebutting not the book but an article by Hugh White, "Time for a Small Meeting of Big Powers", *Straits Times*, 19 Sept. 2012. The article is a distillation of the main thesis of the book.

[82] Carr, *Diary of a Foreign Minister*, pp. 139–40.

[83] See, for example, Hugh White, "China's Power and the Future of Australia", CIW 2017 Annual Lecture, 11 Apr. 2017, http://ciw.anu.edu.au/lectures_seminars/2017.php, accessed 26 May 2017; "Shangri-La Dialogue Should Address Asia's New Strategic Order", *Straits Times*, 23 May 2017.

CHAPTER 7

2013–15: The South China Sea Dispute Moves Centre Stage

> *"... But is the US rebalance sustainable? This is the question that most concerns Asian countries that want America fully engaged in the region to help keep the peace and discourage China from using force or intimidation to achieve its objective."*[1]

> *"It is becoming more difficult to reach consensus, and the sense of prioritization has gone down. There are different countries with different issues, more sources of conflict ..."*[2]

Japan and India

Chapter 6 described how the Southeast Asian countries managed to keep the long-simmering South China Sea dispute from escalating, although by 2012 barely so. Before 2012 many other developments took precedence over the South China Sea issue, even though the latter was never very far in the background. From 2013 it became increasingly difficult not to focus on the maritime dispute in any discussion of the international politics of the region and the unity of ASEAN. New rules (which the Chinese clarified were not new) that permitted Chinese police to board vessels deemed to have broken Chinese law raised concerns that Chinese police could board ships anywhere in the disputed

[1] Michael Richardson, "The Mechanics of US Engagement in Asia", *Straits Times*, 25 Mar. 2013.

[2] Bridget Welsh quoted in "S'pore Calls for Review to Make ASEAN More Effective", *Today*, 12 Apr. 2013.

seas. Beijing eventually (some would insist belatedly) clarified that the law was confined to only a "narrow coastal zone off Hainan Island". This happened not long after China issued a new passport in November 2012, which showed the outline of a map of the country that included Taiwan and the disputed territories in the South China Sea. It was further reported that China had transferred two destroyers and nine other retired navy vessels to its maritime surveillance fleet, which many expected would be even further strengthened in the future.[3] Reacting to Chinese deployment of a patrol ship to guard the territory it claimed in the South China Sea, Philippine Foreign Secretary Albert del Rosario lamented that Manila had been asking China to specify the limits of the territory that it would guard, but "they're not answering". There was the fear that the inability of the ASEAN states to agree on how to manage the dispute with one voice, such as what happened at the 45th ASEAN Ministerial Meeting in July 2012, could frustrate efforts to achieve an ASEAN-centred regional order. It would provide the opportunity for "increasingly assertive big powers like China" to drive "a wedge in the group's unity".[4] Le Luong Minh succeeded Surin as ASEAN's secretary-general in January 2013. In his speech at the handover ceremony he said, "Asean should speed up efforts towards an early start of negotiations with China, with a view to achieving an early conclusion on a Code of Conduct on the South China Sea."[5]

Concern over China's growing military and economic power brought the Southeast Asian states and Japan (which had its own share of disputes with China in the East China Sea) closer. Shinzo Abe became prime minister of Japan for the second time in December 2012. Abe was perceived to be an "ultra-nationalist" out to revise the history of Japan's role in World War II. Nevertheless, Southeast Asian states "welcomed signs of its re-emerging military presence".[6] Del Rosario said that Manila supported "a stronger Japanese military as a counterweight to China's territorial provocation". Japan and the Philippines, in particular, moved closer together because of a common concern as described

[3] "Beijing Clarifies Maritime Search Rules", *Straits Times*, 1 Jan. 2013; "China 'Adds Destroyers to Marine Surveillance'", *Straits Times*, 1 Jan. 2013.
[4] "Keeping the Peace a Priority for New Asean Chief", *Straits Times*, 10 Jan. 2013.
[5] Ibid.
[6] "Japan to Review Statements on Wartime History", *Straits Times*, 30 Jan. 2013.

by Japanese Defence Minister Itsunori Onodera. According to Onodera, Japan "faced a similar situation in the East China Sea ... The Japan side is very concerned that this kind of situation in the South China Sea could affect the situation in the East China Sea."[7] Manila wanted to build a deterrent naval force. Tokyo was willing to help and promised concessionary loans to build ten coast guard patrol boats.[8]

Singapore, too, expressed its desire for Japan to exert "stronger and robust leadership in the region". Southeast Asian states generally hoped to benefit from a Japanese economic recovery if Abe's latest efforts to resuscitate the Japanese economy succeeded. Japan joined the Trans-Pacific Partnership in March 2013.[9] Abe's first overseas visit after assuming office was to Vietnam, Thailand and Indonesia. Before Abe's trip, Finance Minister Taro Aso had visited Myanmar and Foreign Minister Fumio Kishida had visited the Philippines, Singapore, Brunei and Australia, "with an emphasis on regional strategic ties". According to Lee Kuan Yew, "it has become the norm in South-east Asia for China to take the lead and Japan to tag along. Since Japan is unable to recover its economy, it has no choice but to allow China to take the initiative."[10] As Ian Storey noted, "In the last decade or more, Japan largely reacted to Chinese initiatives ... the Abe government is trying ... to reinforce and rebuild its relationships in Southeast Asia."[11]

While the Southeast Asian states welcomed Japan's reinvigorated interest in the region and shared Abe's principle on the use of law to resolve maritime disputes, they did not want to give the impression that Japan and ASEAN were trying to contain China. Relations between Tokyo and Beijing had deteriorated since September 2012, when Japan nationalized some islands in the disputed East China Sea. Indonesian President Yudhoyono's response when asked by an *Asahi Shimbun* journalist during Abe's visit to Jakarta is worth citing here:

[7] "The Philippines and Japan 'Closer' in Defence", *Straits Times*, 28 June 2013.

[8] "Japan Helps Manila Build Patrol Boats", *Straits Times*, 28 July 2013.

[9] "Japan Joins an Uncertain Club", *Straits Times*, 4 Mar. 2013; "Japan Joins Pacific Trade Talks at Last", *Straits Times*, 16 Mar. 2013.

[10] Lee Kuan Yew quoted in Pavin Chachavalpongpun, "Japan Vies with China for Asean's Favour", *Straits Times*, 10 Apr. 2014.

[11] See "Tokyo Seeks Closer Ties with ASEAN", *Today*, 15 Jan. 2013.

> We want to see our region as one that is stable, safe and peaceful. For that reason, if there is a problem whether in the South China Sea or the East Sea, the solution must be a solution that is peaceful, not one that entails might or military force without thinking, and with reference to international law ...[12]

As Simon Tay warned, "ASEAN must not be dragged into an anti-China coalition with Japan. Instead, the group must more calmly manage differences and rebuild trust with Beijing as a basis to negotiate a Code of Conduct. The nuances of Japanese rhetoric must, therefore, be watched."[13] Tay remarked, "Everyone is pivoting to Asia—even Asians." Not everyone thought the pivot to Asia initiated by the Obama administration, now in its third year, was a good idea. The pivot was also being increasingly called into question as the United States underwent drastic defence budget cuts due to social and domestic pressures. Robert Ross, for example, described it as "unnecessary", "counter-productive" and based on the wrong premise of China's assertiveness. In his analysis, Chinese assertiveness was "largely domestic-driven". According to this argument, China had to appease the hardline nationalists "who wanted to project the image of a tough China to the world" in order to detract the population from issues such as unemployment and inequality. As such, the right China policy, in Ross' view, would be "to assuage, not exploit, Beijing's anxieties, while protecting US interests in the region".[14] Singapore think-tankers apparently shared this view. Besides Japan, the Southeast Asian states also looked to India. At the Fifth India-ASEAN Dialogue[15] in February 2013, the Southeast Asian participants encouraged India to engage deeper with the region based on the

---

[12] "Japan Has Role to Play in Ensuring Law of Sea: Abe", *Straits Times*, 19 Jan. 2013. For a concise history of Indonesia and the South China Sea issue, see Shafiah F. Muhibat, "Nationalism, Sovereignty and Foreign Policy: Indonesia and the Disputes over the South China Sea", in *Indonesia in the New World: Globalisation, Nationalism and Sovereignty*, ed. Arianto A. Panturu, Mari Pangestu and M. Chatib Basri (Singapore: Institute of Southeast Asian Studies, 2018), chapter 4.

[13] "View with Caution: Abe's Pivot to South-east Asia", *Today*, 21 Jan. 2013.

[14] Quoted in William Choong, "US Should Focus on Easing China's Anxieties", *Straits Times*, 14 Jan. 2013.

[15] For details of the India-ASEAN Dialogue, see "Delhi Dialogue V", 30 Dec. 2012, http://www.mea.gov.in/in-focus-article.htm?21125/Delhi+Dialogue+V#.WWQUmiTYj7Y.email, accessed 11 July 2014.

"strategic partnership" that the two sides had agreed to in December 2012, "across a broad range of areas, from people-to-people exchange to trade to security". Whereas the diplomats who attended were much more careful with their words,[16] the others were clear that China was the principal concern. As Goh Sui Noi reported:

> ... it was left to the academics on the second day to name the elephant —or dragon—in the room, China, and its growing assertiveness that has got its smaller, weaker neighbours worried. These states are concerned that, with the United States' ability to sustain its pivot uncertain, there is a need to draw in other powers to hedge against China's assertive tendencies.[17]

The term used for drawing in the other powers to hedge against China was "soft balancing", which meant that unlike the US—whose presence in the region had a "strong military element"—the Southeast Asian states wanted India "to add its heft to the region through its participation in the region's security structure and deepening its economic and other ties". Soft balancing, however, could include "a strategic defence dialogue with Japan" or "joint naval exercises with Asean countries".[18] The "China factor" also brought Vietnam and India closer together. While India was either not able or not ready to help Vietnam in the South China Sea dispute, India's navy chief, D.K. Joshi, had said that the Indian Navy would respond if India's interests were involved. In the meantime, both countries had been increasing their engagement on other fronts, particularly trade.[19] India adopted its "Look East" policy in 1991 and became a dialogue partner of ASEAN in 1995, which was followed by the convening of annual bilateral summits from 2002. The relationship was elevated to a strategic partnership in 2012. However, the prevailing view was that so far "there has been a lot of talk but little

---

[16] See "Keynote Address by H.E. Mr. Le Luong Minh, Secretary-General of ASEAN at the Inaugural Session, Delhi Dialogue V, 19 February 2013, New Delhi", http://asean.org/?static_post=keynote-address-by-he-mrle-luong-minh-secretary-general-of-asean-at-the-inaugural-session-delhi-dialogue-v-19-february-2013-new-delhi-2-2, accessed 11 July 2017.

[17] "Asean Eyes India as 'Soft Balancer'", *Straits Times,* 11 Mar. 2013.

[18] Ibid.

[19] "Vietnam Courts India as Likely Protector in Sea Spat", *Straits Times,* 18 Jan. 2013.

concrete action in bilateral cooperation".[20] The growing ties between the US and India, once described by former US Secretary of Defence Leon Panetta as the potential "linchpin" of American military strategy in Asia-Pacific, was also viewed by the Southeast Asian states as a plus factor. Thomas Donilon (national security adviser in the Obama administration) said that President Obama considered US relations with India to be "one of the defining partnerships of the 21st century".[21] Like everyone else, New Delhi found it necessary to declare, in the words of External Affairs Minister Salman Khurshid, that it did not subscribe to "any thesis of containment of any power" or balance of power.[22] India, however, had ambitions beyond ASEAN and East Asia (which was what New Delhi's Look East policy was usually understood to mean). According to Khurshid, "We are actually looking at the Indo-Pacific now."[23] The term "Indo-Pacific" was first introduced by Indian and Australian analysts "as an update of the traditional term, Asia-Pacific, which conceptually separated the Indian Ocean region from the Pacific Ocean area". As Sreeram Chaulia further explained, "viewing the vast littoral stretch from the eastern coast of Africa ... to Australia as one shared space with common challenges is a radically different perspective from the conventional compartmentalized notion of South Asia, South-east Asia, North-east Asia and Australia as separate entities". In addition, it gave India, which was not a member of APEC, "a vantage point to position itself as a hub".[24] It is worth noting that both India and Japan have a history of territorial issues with China. In August 2013 India launched its first locally built aircraft carrier, INS *Vikrant*, which was expected to be operational by 2018 (the date has been pushed to 2020). It was reported that India hoped to induct the 44,570-tonne refitted Russian aircraft carrier INS *Vikramaditya* in 2014 (which it did) and was designing another carrier, INS *Vishal*, which would be 25,000 tonnes bigger than the 40,000-tonne *Vikrant* (INS *Vishal* is expected to enter service in the 2030s). Only the US, Russia,

[20] "Asean Eyes India as 'Soft Balancer'".
[21] "Revisiting That Pivot to Asia", *Today*, 13 Mar. 2013.
[22] Quoted in "Asean Eyes India as 'Soft Balancer'"; "Watershed Moment for Indian Navy", *Straits Times*, 10 Aug. 2013.
[23] "India Eyes Stronger Ties with S-E Asia", *Straits Times*, 5 July 2013.
[24] "Out of APEC, India Eyes Indo-Pacific Influence", *Today*, 13 Nov. 2014.

Britain and France had been able to build aircraft carriers of this size so far.[25] (In January 2016 China confirmed that it was building its first indigenous 50,000-tonne aircraft carrier.[26])

Avoiding the "Thucydides's Trap"

There was a real concern that the rising power, China, would clash with the ruling power, the United States, what Graham Allison termed the "Thucydides's trap",[27] although both Chinese President Xi Jinping and US President Obama had said that the Thucydides's trap thesis was not inevitable. But as Gideon Rachman noted:

> [T]he US has little problem with giving China a greater voice in global institutions ... The real difficulty is over the apparent Chinese desire to carve out a "sphere of influence" in its immediate neighbourhood. To the Chinese, nothing could be more natural. After all, the US assumes it will remain the dominant power in the Western hemisphere. Why can't a rising China aspire to the same role in East Asia? Yet, with East Asia set to become the core of the global economy, the US is unwilling to concede the dominant region role to China.[28]

Ashley Tellis argued, "the loss of primacy to China would fundamentally undermine the national security interests of the United States in the most comprehensive sense imaginable". Washington, as Valencia noted, "has not been able to unify ASEAN against China, stem China's assertiveness or even enhance stability in the South China Sea".[29]

---

[25] "Watershed Moment for Indian Navy".

[26] "China Now Building Its Own Aircraft Carrier", *Straits Times*, 1 Jan. 2016. China's sole aircraft carrier at this time was the 60,000-tonne *Liaoning*, which it had bought from Ukraine in 1998 and commissioned in late 2012.

[27] Graham Allison, "Thucydides's Trap Has Been Sprung in the Pacific", *Financial Times*, 22 Aug. 2012. The book on this theme was published in 2017: Graham Allison, *Destined for War: Can America and China Escape Thucydides's Trap?* (Boston: Houghton Mifflin Harcourt, 2017). See also Mark J. Valencia, "Are US-China Relations Beyond the Tipping Point?" *Straits Times*, 6 Aug. 2014.

[28] "Obama, Xi Must Halt Rise of Risky Rivalry", *Straits Times*, 5 June 2013.

[29] Ashley Tellis quoted in Valencia, "Are US-China Relations Beyond the Tipping Point?"

ASEAN repeatedly said that it did not want a situation where it had to choose sides.[30] It also continued to promote its centrality in the region. As Indonesian Foreign Minister Natalegawa said, there was a "deficit of trust among countries". Jakarta thus proposed the idea of a new region-wide treaty that would help build trust across the countries in Asia-Pacific and bind them to resolve problems in a peaceful manner even as conflicts flared up alarmingly from time to time. Such an "Indo-Pacific wide" treaty (Indo-Pacific Wide Treaty of Friendship and Cooperation), he suggested, could be modelled on ASEAN's Treaty of Amity and Cooperation.[31] Jakarta continued to push its proposal for a "treaty in the Indo-Pacific region in which signatories would renounce the use of force and commit to settling disputes peacefully" into 2014.[32] In his memoir, Natalegawa explained, "the complex dynamics in the wider region could benefit from the trust-building impact of the commitment of the non-use of force ... Such was the rationale that motivated me to push for an EAS treaty of Friendship and Cooperation."[33] However, as Chinyong Liow pointed out, while the Indonesian message "of how security is a common good ... is a timely reminder of their collective interest in regional stability ... to get from that to the establishment of an institution in the form of a treaty requires a great leap".[34] Furthermore, Joko Widodo, the new Indonesian president who succeeded Yudhoyono in October 2014, was not expected to have the "bandwidth, resources or energy to expend on the level of international diplomacy" that his predecessors had, given the myriad domestic challenges. This was a view shared by many Indonesia-watchers.[35] Indeed, in his memoir Bob Carr recalled that in 2012, in discussions of the future of Indonesian leadership after Yudhoyono

---

[30] Former US Assistant Secretary of State for East Asian and Pacific Affairs Kurt Campbell quoted at an Indonesian conference at the Center for Strategic and International Studies (CSIS), Washington, DC, May 2013. See "Asia-Pacific 'Needs Region-wide Treaty to Preserve Peace'", *Straits Times*, 18 May 2013.

[31] "Asia-Pacific 'Needs Region-wide Treaty to Preserve Peace'". See Natalegawa, *Does ASEAN Matter?* pp. 106–7.

[32] "Jakarta Pushing for Indo-Pacific Peace Treaty", *Straits Times*, 8 Jan. 2014.

[33] Natalegawa, *Does ASEAN Matter?* pp. 106–7.

[34] "What to Make of Indonesia's Indo-Pacific Treaty", *Straits Times*, 16 Oct. 2014.

[35] Ibid.

stepped down in 2014, the consensus was that his successor "would not be anywhere near as internationalist as he has been".[36] Natalegawa himself ended his tenure as foreign minister in October 2014.

The idea of "strategic trust"[37] was the dominant theme of the 12th Shangri-La Dialogue (31 May–2 June 2013), organized by the London-based Institute of International and Strategic Studies and held annually in Singapore.[38] Meanwhile, Moscow and Beijing were not sitting idly by. Russia also proposed its own framework for strengthening security and cooperation in the Asia-Pacific region, which was presented for discussion at the EAS Foreign Ministers Meeting in July 2013. The Russian proposal had the backing of China. As Kavi Chongkittavorn noted, "what had drawn China and Russia together is their common desire to counter what they perceive to be US hegemony. They also want to ensure that the US revitalization of security alliances and the new rebalancing strategies would not in any way weaken their presence and influence in Asia."[39] Russia pulling closer to China would, analysts believed, present "a profound challenge to the United States and Europe" given the estrangement between them over Ukraine.[40] The United States had increased its allocation for foreign military financing and training programmes to "US$900 million", which was 50 per cent more than four years ago.[41] It was reported that a number of military deals were signed with Kuala Lumpur, Jakarta and Manila during US Secretary of Defence Chuck Hagel's visit to those countries in August en route to the ASEAN Defence Ministers Meeting in Bandar Seri Begawan. At the same time, the Pentagon was also undergoing spending cuts. US officials repeatedly assured their allies in the region

[36] Carr, *Diary of a Foreign Minister*, p. 31.

[37] This term was apparently first used by Chinese Vice President Xi Jinping in a short speech when he visited Washington in February 2012, https://geopolicraticus.wordpress.com/2012/02/16/what-is-strategic-trust/, accessed 16 Aug. 2018. Vietnam's Prime Minister Nguyen Tan Dung also employed this term in his keynote speech at the 2013 Shangri-La Dialogue quoting a Vietnamese saying, "If trust is lost, all is lost", https://thediplomat.com/2014/07/strategic-trust-an-oil-rig-and-vietnams-dilemma/, accessed 16 Aug. 2018. See also Natalegawa, *Does ASEAN Matter?* chapter 2.

[38] "From Shangri-La to Sunnylands", *Straits Times*, 8 June 2013.

[39] "China, Russia Respond to US Pivot to Asia", *Straits Times*, 17 July 2013.

[40] "Russia's Alliance with China Presents a Challenge to US", *Today*, 10 Nov. 2014.

[41] "S-E Asia Military Programmes Get More US Funds", *Straits Times*, 26 Aug. 2013.

that it would not affect them. As Hagel said, "[The Asian rebalance] is a priority. You always adjust your resources to match your priorities."[42] However, doubts remained. Back in Washington, the US government's partial shutdown because of disagreement over the budget and government funding, which caused President Obama to miss both the EAS and the APEC summit as well as his planned visit to Malaysia and the Philippines, did not raise confidence. As Christopher Hill (former assistant secretary of state for East Asian and Pacific affairs) wrote, "... his decision (missing APEC), while correct, had the effect of reviving an increasingly common refrain in the East Asian region: What happened to the 'pivot'?"[43]

Developments in the Spratlys

Meanwhile, in January 2013 Manila informed the Chinese government through its ambassador to the Philippines, Ma Keqing, that the Philippine government was bringing its dispute over the South China Sea territories to an international tribunal. According to del Rosario, this move was because the Philippines had "exhausted almost all political and diplomatic avenues for a peaceful negotiated settlement of its maritime disputes with China". Manila hoped that by going to an arbitration tribunal in accordance with the 1982 UNCLOS, it would bring the dispute "to a durable solution". "We are all for improving our economic relations with China but it should not be at the expense of surrendering our national sovereignty," the foreign secretary said.[44] According to President Benigno Aquino, two recent Scarborough Shoal incidents—Chinese harassment of two Philippine fishing boats in the disputed area—led Manila to turn to UN arbitration. Manila could not allow China to claim "effective control over Bajo de Masinloc" as that could encourage Beijing to take over Reed Bank,[45] which Manila

[42] "Back in Asia, Hagel Pursues Pivot in US Policy", *Today*, 3 Oct. 2013.
[43] Christopher R. Hill, "Pivot away from Pivot: The Obama Anti-doctrine", *Today*, 28 Oct. 2013.
[44] "Manila to Take South China Sea Fight to UN Tribunal", *Today*, 23 Jan. 2013.
[45] "Philippine Boats 'Harassed by China'", *Straits Times*, 27 Jan. 2013. Bajo de Masinloc is the Filipino name for Scarborough Shoal, which the Chinese refer to as Huangyan Island.

said was within the country's 200-nautical-mile exclusive economic zone. Analysts believe that the Second Thomas Shoal region, "a strategic gateway to Reed Bank", which was supposedly rich in oil and natural gas, could be a new flashpoint. The Philippines had deliberately run aground its navy transport ship BRP *Sierra* at Second Thomas Shoal in 1999 to mark its territory.[46] As predicted, China sent ships to Second Thomas Shoal (which the Chinese called Ren'ai) in June. Almonte, in his memoir, recalled Manila's decision:

> Aquino stood up against China when he decided to take the dispute to a court of law, the International Tribunal for the Law of the Sea. I have always believed that the authoritative power of world opinion can temper China, if not stop it, from aggressively asserting its claim. The administration of President Aquino has, so far, done all that could possibly be done, in the short term, to defend our nation's interests in the South China Sea. But this is not enough. Our nation's long-term security hangs in the balance.[47]

In his dissection of Manila's 21-page note verbale and statement of claim, William Choong noted that Manila did not ask the tribunal to decide which country had sovereignty over specifically named islands. Instead, Manila simply asked the tribunal to decide on the legality of China's "nine-dash or nine-dotted line claim". Choong believed that Manila had "essentially dealt a clever hand" as "China might have to clarify the extent and basis for its nine-dotted line claim".[48] Thayer was of the view that even if China chose not to participate, "a decision by the tribunal in Manila's favour would put it on higher legal and moral ground". Storey believed that China was faced with a "lose-lose situation"—not participating would leave it "open to criticism that it does not adhere to international legal norms". However, if it participated, it would have "a very difficult task of justifying the legality of the nine-dash line".[49]

---

[46] "Wrecked Philippine Ship Could Be Next Flashpoint", *Straits Times*, 30 May 2013. Second Thomas Reef is also known as Ayungin Reef in Tagalog.

[47] Almonte (as told to Vitug), *Endless Journey*, pp. 330–1.

[48] "Manila Deals a Clever Hand with Knock-on Effects on Asean", *Straits Times*, 28 Jan. 2013.

[49] Ibid.

Beijing, not surprisingly, responded negatively to the move, insisting that getting a United Nations tribunal involved would only complicate the issue, which, in the view of the Chinese, was best resolved bilaterally.[50] In fact, in 2006 Beijing informed the UN that it did not accept any international court or arbitration in maritime-related disputes as it was "a question of Chinese sovereignty and not international law of the sea".[51] Rightly or wrongly, Beijing also suspected collusion between Manila and Washington. Visiting Manila (as the leader of a six-member US congressional delegation tour of Asia), US Representative Ed Royce (chairman, House Foreign Affairs Committee) reiterated that Washington would not take sides in the territorial dispute but backed "an internationally accepted diplomatic solution". He added that it was best for China to participate in the process so that "we can move forward under international law".[52] Royce was only one example of many American officials who spoke in support of Manila's legal move. Others included Admiral Samuel Locklear (head of the US Pacific Command, Hawaii) and James Clapper (director of national intelligence). Gary Li (head, Marine and Aviation Forecasting at Exclusive Analysis) spoke for many who wondered how Manila's unilateral initiation of the arbitration tribunal, which had no power of enforcement, would be helpful. Li predicted, "This move from the Philippines ... is likely to achieve little apart from highlighting its dispute on the international stage but alienating China even more."[53] It is, however, worth noting that Manila's move was not exceptional. Singapore and Malaysia had referred their dispute over the island of Pedra Branca to the International Court of Justice. The difference was that this was a decision agreed to by both sides, and both accepted the court's judgement. Apparently Manila had not consulted or given advance notice to its fellow ASEAN members before making its announcement. The other ASEAN member states were very careful in their response, although they mostly agreed with Manila's legal move and would certainly have liked to know the Chinese justification for the Nine-Dash Line. On 12 March 2014 Jakarta, which for the last two decades had positioned itself as a neutral

[50] "Beijing Rejects Manila's UN Mediation Effort", *Today*, 20 Feb. 2013.

[51] "Getting Past Jurisdictional Hurdle Won't Be Easy", *Straits Times*, 28 Jan. 2013.

[52] "China Urged to Face Philippines at UN Tribunal", *Today*, 30 Jan. 2013.

[53] "Manila's UN Request Complicates Issue: China", *Today*, 24 Jan. 2013.

mediator or "honest broker" in the South China Sea dispute, announced that the Nine-Dash Line overlapped Indonesia's Riau province and the Natuna Island chain. Indonesian President Joko Widodo in March 2015 said that China's Nine-Dash Line had no basis in international law. In November 2015 Jakarta complained that Beijing had still not responded to Indonesia's call to clarify its claims.[54] (Beijing and Jakarta would be involved in a fishing spat near the Natuna Islands in March 2016.[55]) Veteran Singapore diplomat Tommy Koh urged China to "send a clear signal that its rise will be a peaceful one by reconsidering its current objection to submitting territorial disputes to international courts".[56] When asked, most said that it was a "Filipino decision", a "national decision", Manila's "legitimate right", and that all parties should pursue peaceful means to resolve the dispute. ASEAN would continue with its agenda of pushing for a code of conduct with even more urgency. Indonesian Vice-President Jusuf Kalla summed it up well: "Better to go to court than to war, but even better to go to the table than to court."[57]

The Vietnamese response to the Philippines' legal move is worth going into some detail. Besides the Philippines, Vietnam had had the most altercations with China over the South China Sea claims over the years. Amongst the Southeast Asian countries, Vietnam also had the most experience in dealing with China (and we can assume the best knowledge of China) given the long history of Sino-Vietnamese relations. According to Philippine Congressman Walden Bello in a 12 January 2014 article published after his recent visit to Hanoi (on the invitation of Madame Nguyen Thi Binh to give a series of lectures on foreign policy and economic issues), the Vietnamese believed that the Chinese leadership had not anticipated Manila's move and was "really

[54] Ann Marie Murphy, "The End of Strategic Ambiguity: Indonesia Formally Announces Its Dispute with China in the South China Sea", *PacNet* #26, 1 Apr. 2014; "Jakarta Seeks Clarification from Beijing on Claims in South China Sea", *Today*, 8 Apr. 2014; "Jokowi Rejects Key Beijing Claim to South China Sea", *Straits Times*, 24 Mar. 2015; "Clarify South China Sea Claims, China Told", *Straits Times*, 13 Nov. 2015.

[55] "Fishing Spat Won't Hurt Beijing Ties, Says Jakarta", *Straits Times*, 24 Mar. 2016.

[56] "China Urged to Go to Court for Territorial Disputes", *Straits Times*, 12 Apr. 2014.

[57] "Cool Responses to Push for Arbitration by Manila", *Straits Times*, 24 Jan. 2013. Jusuf Kalla made that remark at a press briefing held by the Bangkok-based Asian Peace and Reconciliation Council (established in September 2012).

embarrassed by it". It put China on the defensive and prompted Beijing to agree to begin discussions on the code of conduct. The Philippines' move, however, made Manila the "number one target" of Beijing, "replacing Vietnam". "They're now isolating you, while relations between Vietnam and China are getting back to normal"; however, "we still feel the chill ... In terms of China's least favoured countries in Asean, we're number nine for the moment and you're number 10. In the long run, however, Vietnam is Beijing's main strategic problem," the Vietnamese told Bello. They also told him that the government fully supported Manila's legal move "at an informal level" but could not "fully publicly support it". One retired Vietnamese ambassador described the Philippine move as "heroic". Bello's analysis was that Hanoi did not want to enrage China at a time when Sino-Vietnamese relations were showing signs of improvement. Another reason was that the judgement might have negative implications for Vietnam. One expert on Chinese diplomacy told Bello that China was upset because Beijing already had five battlefields to contend with—political, diplomatic, mass media, security and military—and now there was a legal one. The Chinese were least prepared for a legal battle "where experts in international law will be calling the shots".[58]

After refusing to participate in the arbitration proceedings, China did two things. On the one hand, it sent a naval force, which included four Chinese warships, on an eight-day training tour of the South China Sea. In late March the naval force was reported to be near James Shoal, 1,800 kilometres from the Chinese mainland and 80 kilometres off the Malaysian coast. James Shoal (known to the Chinese as Zengmu Reef), according to a Xinhua report of April 2012, was the "southernmost point of China's territory". Malaysia had been quietly boosting its naval defence, for example building a new naval base in Bintutu (Sarawak). Bintutu is approximately 80 nautical miles from James Shoal, which was claimed by both Malaysia and China.[59] Kuala Lumpur, however, wanted to avoid a public spat with Beijing. The Malaysian navy chief denied a report that Chinese navy ships had trespassed into Malaysian

[58] The above paragraph is distilled/summarized from Walden Bello, "Converging Interests: Hanoi and Manila Confront Leviathan", *Philippine Daily Inquirer*, 12 Jan. 2014.

[59] "KL's Boost for Naval Defence 'a Strategic Shift'", *Straits Times*, 28 Oct. 2013. James Shoal is entirely submerged underwater.

waters.[60] Analysts were of the view that this was a deliberate show of force on the part of the Chinese, and a demonstration of their capabilities.[61] In May China dispatched "one of its largest-recorded fishing fleets in the South China Sea" on a 40-day trip.[62] On the other hand, Beijing proposed a special meeting of ASEAN's and China's foreign ministers to "hasten progress on a Code of Conduct". At the 45th ASEAN Meeting in July 2012, the member states had agreed on a set of "ASEAN's proposed Elements of a Regional Code of Conduct in the South China Sea between ASEAN and the People's Republic of China" (Zero Draft of the COC). The new Chinese foreign minister, Wang Yi, stressed that ASEAN and China "should not let recent territorial spats undermine the trust underpinning mutual relations". China's Foreign Ministry spokesperson Hua Chunying reiterated that the consensus of China and ASEAN was that "the South China Sea problem is not a problem between China and Asean".[63] In May 2013 Wang agreed to soon start talks with ASEAN on the legally binding COC, as well as set up an Eminent Persons Group to complement the government-to-government talks.[64] In July it was announced that ASEAN and China would meet to discuss the COC in September 2013 "within the framework of the sixth senior officials' meeting and the ninth joint working group on the implementation of the DOC".[65] Wang also pledged to upgrade the CAFTA that took effect in 2010 and "push forward" the Regional Comprehensive Economic Partnership (RCEP).[66] China launched what was described as a "charm offensive" on the tenth anniversary of the formalization of the China-ASEAN strategic partnership on 29 August 2013, to bring the relationship

---

[60] "Malaysia's Navy Chief Denies Chinese Incursion", *Straits Times*, 30 Jan. 2014.

[61] "China's Navy Flexes Muscles in South China Sea", *Straits Times*, 28 Mar. 2013; "Getting Past Jurisdictional Hurdle Won't Be Easy".

[62] "China Sends Big Fishing Fleet to Disputed Spratlys", *Straits Times*, 8 May 2013.

[63] "Territorial Spats 'Must Not Harm Asean-China Trust'", *Straits Times*, 19 Apr. 2013.

[64] "China to Start Code of Conduct Talks with Asean Soon", *Straits Times*, 3 May 2013.

[65] "Asean, China to Start Talks on Maritime Code of Conduct", *Straits Times*, 1 July 2013.

[66] The RCEP was conceived at the ASEAN Summit in Phnom Penh in 2012. It includes ASEAN 10, Australia, China, India, Japan, South Korea and New Zealand.

from a "golden decade" to a "diamond decade". Analysts believed it was an attempt to both counter US influence as well as isolate the Philippines. Whereas the US had focused on the military side, such as improving military cooperation and joint exercises (as proposed by US Secretary of Defence Hagel during the Second ADMM-Plus Meeting in August), Beijing offered a "slew of 'sweeteners' for Asean in the form of billion-dollar development projects". As Yang Razali Kassim noted, "the implicit message was that China has sufficiently deep pockets to back up its 'diamond decade' plan with Asean at a time when the US is not really in the best of political and economic health".[67] For example, while holding firm to its claims in the South China Sea, Beijing offered ASEAN countries US$20 billion in preferential and special loans to develop infrastructure. This was "an attractive proposition for a region struggling to fund the roads, ports and railways needed for growth".[68]

While there was general consensus that China was a world power and some believed it would replace the United States as the dominant power in Asia-Pacific, a 2013 survey conducted by China's *Global Times* showed that a significant proportion of respondents, particularly China's neighbours, were distrustful towards and had a negative view of the country.[69] Not surprisingly, Chinese President Xi's call for Asia's matters to be handled by Asians, Asia's problems to be resolved by Asians, and Asia's security to be protected by Asians did not gain much traction. At least one academic likened it to the "East Asian Co-prosperity Sphere" of the 1930s and 1940s.[70] At the same time, although US Secretary of State John Kerry made more trips to Asia after he assumed the post compared to his predecessor, Washington was still unable to allay concerns over US policy drift, given its budget uncertainties. Kerry, it was reported, was "finding it hard to convince sceptics in Asia that quantity has translated into quality". Analysts also noted that Kerry was "still trying to find the right balance of

[67] "China's Overture to Cement Ties with Asean", *Straits Times*, 12 Oct. 2013.

[68] "China Offers 'Friendship Treaty' with ASEAN", *Today*, 14 Nov. 2014.

[69] "Neighbours Deem China 'Belligerent': Poll", *Straits Times*, 11 Dec. 2013.

[70] "Leave Asia to Asians, Says China", *Straits Times*, 22 May 2014; "Don't Bet on China's 'Asia for Asians Only' Vision Yet", *Straits Times*, 30 May 2014; Minxin Pei, "Why China Should Drop Its Slogan of 'Asia for Asians", *Straits Times*, 5 Dec. 2014.

assertiveness and diplomacy".[71] For example, ASEAN wanted the US to be involved in the region but did not want Washington to "occupy centre stage". Kavi Chongkittavorn noted that it was "an open secret that Asean prefers to see the US playing a discreet or low-profile role in the maritime disputes".[72]

Another survey of thought leaders from 11 Asian countries, this time conducted by the Washington-based Center for Strategic and International Studies (24 March–22 April 2014), showed that the region welcomed China's economic growth but also clearly wanted continued US leadership.[73] A Pew Research survey on global perception of the United States and China (conducted in July 2014) showed the Asia-Pacific region (which included Southeast Asia) to be "a jumble of mixed strategic interests". China was rated favourably, but the region was also very worried about military conflict with China. The US was looked upon positively, particularly in light of China's assertiveness. While China was the top economic partner, the United States was the preferred security partner. Malaysia, Thailand and Indonesia had the most favourable view of China compared, not surprisingly, to the Philippines and Vietnam. Indonesian respondents named the US as both their top ally and their top threat. On the one hand, the respondents were happy for the US to be a counterbalance to China. On the other hand, they continued to believe that the US was anti-Muslim.[74]

US Secretary of State Kerry had expressed support for a "substantive code of conduct" for the South China Sea. He also supported the ASEAN goal of establishing an economic community by the end of 2015 and promised to help ASEAN states build capacity against cyber threats. Kerry reiterated that US-ASEAN ties were of the "highest importance".[75] It was reported that both Manila and Washington were discussing expanding military cooperation and that both sides hoped to conclude agreements before Aquino's term as president ended in June 2016.[76] The United States had been increasing its military assistance

[71] "Frequent-Flier Kerry Yet to Win over Sceptics", *Straits Times*, 20 Feb. 2014.

[72] "Asean's Show of Unity", *Straits Times*, 19 Aug. 2014.

[73] "World Wants 'China's Money, US Leadership'", *Straits Times*, 2 June 2014.

[74] "Assertive China a 'Boon to US Image'", *Straits Times*, 18 July 2014.

[75] "Kerry Backs 'Substantive Code of Conduct' for South China Sea" and "US-Asean Ties of 'Highest Importance'", *Today*, 2 July 2013.

[76] "Manila, Washington Widen Talks on Military Deal", *Today*, 17 July 2013.

to the Philippines, besides helping the Filipinos build up their naval deterrence. It was further revealed that American spy planes had been providing "crucial intelligence" on Chinese military activities in the South China Sea.[77] Manila also planned to move major navy and air force units to Subic Bay, closer to disputed areas in the South China Sea (which the Philippine government called the West Philippine Sea). Analysts believed that the move would also benefit the United States and other allies.[78] It was no secret that the Aquino administration was keen to host more US troops as a counter to China. There was thus an alignment of interests: "The Philippines desire to bolster its external defence and security has dovetailed with US intention to pivot away from years of military engagement in the Middle East."[79] It was not just the Philippines. It was reported that the United States would also help modernize Indonesia's military. US Ambassador to Indonesia Robert Blake remarked, "We have excellent security cooperation between our two countries."[80] Beijing, concerned about possible collusion between the US, Australia and Japan, warned all three countries against using their alliances as pretexts for intervention in the territorial disputes in the South China Sea (and the East China Sea).[81] Political observers noted that Japanese Prime Minister Shinzo Abe appeared to be trying to create a bloc of like-minded countries to restrain what, in his view, was an increasingly belligerent China.

Meanwhile, President Aquino vowed that the Philippines would not back down from any challenge to its sovereignty and would continue with the arbitration with or without the Chinese. Foreign Secretary del Rosario said that the Philippines was taking a two-pronged approach: arbitration under international law (a United Nations arbitration tribunal had since convened in The Hague to consider the merits of the Filipino complaint) and the pursuit of a COC between ASEAN and China.[82] On 30 March Manila submitted a 4,000-page document

---

[77] "US Increases Military Aid to the Philippines", *Straits Times*, 1 Aug. 2013.

[78] "Manila Plans to Reposition Troops to Counter China", *Straits Times*, 29 July 2013.

[79] "Manila Wants to Host More US Troops", *Straits Times*, 10 Aug. 2013.

[80] "US to Help Modernize Indonesia's Military", *Straits Times*, 25 Feb. 2014.

[81] See "Partners & Friends: Japan, Australia Elevate Ties with New Defence and Trade Deals", *Straits Times*, 9 July 2014.

[82] "Philippines Slams Military Build-up at Sea", *Straits Times*, 1 July 2013.

to an arbitration tribunal in The Hague. Secretary of State Kerry gave tacit support to the arbitration case when he told leaders at the EAS in October 2013 that all claimants "can engage in arbitration and other means of peaceful negotiation". His remark riled the Chinese, who warned Washington to "stop stirring up waves".[83] As for the second prong, while the ASEAN leaders were hoping for a firm commitment from China to start negotiations, they were not optimistic of an early breakthrough because of "Beijing's lack of enthusiasm". The two-day September meeting in Suzhou showed that the Chinese, while willing to begin consultations, were in no rush to conclude an agreement with ASEAN.[84] China's declaration of an Air Defence Identification Zone over the East China Sea in November 2013 created new worries for the ASEAN states that Beijing might do the same in the South China Sea. Indonesian Foreign Minister Natalegawa revealed that Jakarta had "firmly told China we will not accept a similar zone if it is adopted in the South China Sea ... And the signal we have received thus far is, China does not plan to adopt a similar zone in the South China Sea."[85] However, Beijing remained insistent that it had the right to do so.[86] Two months later, in January 2014, it passed another law that required foreign fishing vessels to obtain approval before entering its waters in the South China Sea. Some analysts, however, argued that Beijing was unlikely to enforce this stringently, citing the November 2011 law that gave its police the right to board foreign ships, which had apparently not been strictly enforced. Nevertheless, it was still worrisome to neighbouring states.[87] In March 2014 China announced its biggest rise in

[83] "China Hits out at US for Giving Tacit Backing to Philippines in Sea Dispute", *Today*, 12 Oct. 2013.

[84] "South China Sea Issue Seen Dogging Asean-Beijing Meet", *Straits Times*, 29 Aug. 2013; "S. China Sea Row: 'Gradual' Talks on Code of Conduct", *Straits Times*, 17 Sept. 2013.

[85] "Jakarta Against an Air Zone in S. China Sea", *Straits Times*, 20 Feb. 2014.

[86] "China Reserves Right to Create Air Zone over South China Sea", *Japan Times*, 9 May 2015; "China Urged Not to Set up Air Zone over South China Sea", *Straits Times*, 11 May 2015.

[87] "China May Not Strictly Enforce Latest Fishing Curbs", *Straits Times*, 11 Jan. 2011; "Uproar over China's New Fishing Law in S. China Sea", *Straits Times*, 11 Jan. 2014; Mark J. Valencia, "Why All the Fuss About 'New' Hainan Fishing Law", *Straits Times*, 17 Jan. 2014.

military spending since 2011. Regardless of how Beijing justified it to its neighbours, the rise in military spending indicated that China was "not about to back away from its growing assertiveness in Asia".[88] Furthermore, it was a known fact that China was developing three carrier battle groups, the first of which was expected to be ready in 2017.

In contrast, the region continued to receive mixed signals from Washington, where the Pentagon had to defend its defence budget in Congress. Washington's problems were more than just budget pressure. The Obama administration also had to avoid plunging the United States into another period of "large military commitments and heavy casualties".[89] Katrina McFarland, assistant secretary of defence acquisition, reportedly told a conference, "Right now, the pivot is being looked at again, because candidly it can't happen." Her comment was subsequently rescinded, and she issued a new statement reiterating Secretary of Defence Hagel's assurance that "the rebalance to Asia can and will continue".[90] In April 2014 the US for the first time hosted a meeting between ASEAN and US heads of defence in Hawaii. Analysts were of the view that while nothing substantial was expected to emerge from the three-day meeting, it nevertheless demonstrated US engagement in the region.[91] The same month, President Obama made an eight-day trip to four Asian countries: Japan, South Korea, Malaysia and the Philippines. The objective was to reaffirm the United States' pivot and commitment to the region. The visit to Malaysia is historically significant as it was the first visit by a US president since President Lyndon Johnson visited the country in 1966, at the height of the Vietnam War. The US and the Philippines signed an "enhanced defence cooperation agreement" shortly before Obama's two-day visit. The ten-year defence agreement would boost American military presence in the

---

[88] "Big Rise in Chinese Defence Budget Stirs Disquiet Among Neighbours", *Today*, 6 Mar. 2014.

[89] "Obama Faces Budget Pressure in Pledge to Help Global Hot Spots", *Straits Times*, 5 Sept. 2014.

[90] "US Restates Pivot Commitment After 'No Go' Remarks", *Straits Times*, 9 Mar. 2014.

[91] "Meeting with Asean 'Shows Commitment of US to the Region'", *Straits Times*, 2 Apr. 2014.

Philippines as well as give the US military access to some Philippine bases. Even though this was Obama's fifth visit to Asia since becoming president in January 2009, "the trip was bogged down by the prevailing 'American weakness' narrative'".[92] Despite Obama's frequent reaffirmations of the pivot, many Asian leaders questioned whether he and his successor would be able to carry through the plan to shift US presence to the Pacific over the next six years.[93] Jonathan Eyal provided perhaps the most credible and positive spin when he described the US pivot as "still a work in progress".[94]

The United States' relations with one of its oldest Southeast Asian allies, Thailand, however, were seriously tested when the Thai military carried out its 19th coup in 82 years on 22 May 2014. The coup ousted the government led by Yingluck Shinawatra (sister of former Prime Minister Thaksin Shinawatra, who was ousted in 2006), often perceived to be a proxy for Thaksin. Washington was critical of the coup and suspended some military aid as well as cancelled a number of military exercises and visits. In response, the junta turned to China, which had expressed "understanding" for the "political situation in Thailand". A delegation of Thai military commanders visited China for talks on regional security and joint training in June. The junta claimed that it had Chinese support[95] but at the same time tried "to correct an impression that its long alliance with the United States is frosting over and it is veering closer to China".[96] US State Department officials told a Congressional committee in Washington that it was "impossible for our relationship with Thailand to go on with 'business as usual'". China's ambassador to Thailand, Ning Fukui, on the other hand, told the junta's deputy chief that Beijing understood the coup and praised the junta for restoring business confidence.[97] Most analysts, however,

[92] "Obama's Asia Trip Lacks Trade Breakthrough", *Straits Times*, 30 Apr. 2014.

[93] See, for example, "Obama Reaffirms 'Pivot' to Asia-Pacific", *Sunday Times*, 16 Nov. 2014.

[94] Jonathan Eyal, "US' Asia Pivot Still a Work in Progress", *Straits Times*, 28 Apr. 2014.

[95] "Thai Army Delegation Visits China for Regional Talks", *Today*, 12 June 2014; "Thailand, China in Military Alliance", *Straits Times*, 7 Feb. 2015.

[96] "Thai Junta Says Alliance with US Is Still Intact", *Straits Times*, 30 June 2014.

[97] Ibid.

did not think Washington would alienate Thailand to the extent that it pushed Bangkok into Chinese arms. In February 2015 Bangkok and Beijing agreed to boost military ties over the next five years, including increased intelligence sharing, fighting transnational crime, and increasing joint military exercises.[98] As Panitan Wattanayagorn remarked, "Thailand does listen to the US ... In the end the nervousness is not so much in Bangkok as in Washington—that Thailand may be moving closer to China and other powers like Japan, Russia and India."[99] In December 2015 China and Thailand inked an agreement to build a 900km railway line from the Thai-Laos border to Bangkok.[100] The same month, Bangkok and Washington resumed the Thai-US Strategic Dialogue after a three-year hiatus. However, as US Assistant Secretary of State for East Asian and Pacific Affairs Daniel Russel pointed out, US law did not allow Washington to resume full military ties with Bangkok "until democracy returns to Thailand".[101]

Meanwhile, the improvement in Sino-Vietnamese relations in the last year or so did not last. On 2 May 2014 the Chinese deployed a giant oil rig (Haiyang Shiyou 981) in disputed waters near the Paracel Islands. Vietnam protested and sent its own vessels to disrupt the rig's operations. China in turn sent its ships to protect the rig, which eventually led to a clash on 7 May that resulted in some injuries and damage on the Vietnamese side. There were also anti-Chinese protests in Vietnam (tolerated, if not sanctioned, by the government). With limited options against China, Hanoi embarked on a public relations exercise to win support for its position. Sam Bateman observed that the Vietnamese appeared "to be winning the public relations battle with much global commentary supporting its claim that the rig is illegal and painting the situation as yet another example of China's assertiveness". Bateman, however, also opined that a closer look at the episode would

---

[98] "Thailand, China in Military Alliance".

[99] Panitan Wattanayagorn quoted in "Why Thais Are Prickly over Diplomat's Criticism", *Straits Times*, 3 Feb. 2015. See also "Thailand Seeks Closer Relations with Russia as US Ties Cool", *Straits Times*, 21 Feb. 2016; "From Russia to Thailand, with Love", *Straits Times*, 7 Apr. 2016.

[100] "China Inks Deal to Build 900km Thai Railway Line", *Straits Times*, 5 Dec. 2015.

[101] "Thailand, US Resume High-Level Talks", *Straits Times*, 17 Dec. 2015.

suggest that China might be "within its rights with the rig".[102] Regardless of whether the Chinese deployment was within its rights, China now found itself in confrontation with both the Philippines and Vietnam. ASEAN, whose leaders were attending the 24th leaders retreat at Naypyidaw, could only urge all parties involved in the disputes to "exercise self-restraint and refrain from action that could further escalate tensions". Singapore's Prime Minister Lee Hsien Loong said that the recent flare-ups in the South China Sea were a "wake-up call". The group, he said, "needed to adopt a common position on issues affecting all member states". He further underscored "the need for urgent progress" on the proposed COC.[103] ASEAN hoped to shield its relationship with China from the South China Sea dispute by emphasizing that the relationship was "multifaceted" and should not be dominated by one issue.[104]

The meeting between Chinese State Councillor Yang Jiechi (who ranked higher than the Chinese foreign minister) and Vietnamese Foreign Minister Phan Binh Minh in June was reported to be "unpleasant". Hanoi then turned to Washington as well as New Delhi, essentially to show the Chinese that Vietnam could cultivate strategic relationships unfavourable to Beijing. The United States subsequently (for the first time) partially lifted a long-time ban on lethal arms sales to Vietnam and allowed for a transfer of maritime-security related armaments. India agreed to sell patrol boats to the Vietnamese.[105] However, even as Deputy Prime Minister Pham Binh Minh visited the United States in September and Prime Minister Nguyen Tan Dung visited India in October, contact with Beijing was never broken. In August Standing

---

[102] See Sam Bateman, "New Tensions in the South China Sea: Whose Sovereignty over Paracels?" *RSIS Commentaries*, 14 May 2014. For a counter-response, see Huy Duong and Tuan Pham, "Sovereignty over Paracels: Article Lets off Beijing Lightly", *RSIS Commentaries*, 26 May 2014. The commentary argues that Bateman presented "an unbalanced perspective of the relative merits of Vietnam's and China's cases".

[103] "ASEAN Urges Self-restraint in Disputes with China" and "Need for Urgency on Code of Conduct in South China Sea: PM", *Today*, 12 May 2014.

[104] "Territorial Disputes 'Must Not Dominate China-Asean Agenda", *Straits Times*, 13 June 2014.

[105] "US Set to Lift Arms Embargo on Vietnam", *Straits Times*, 25 Sept. 2014; "India to Sell Patrol Boats to Vietnam", *Straits Times*, 29 Oct. 2014.

Secretary of the Vietnamese Communist Party Le Hong Anh visited China as a special envoy. In October Vietnamese Defence Minister Phung Quang Thanh paid a quiet visit to Beijing, where he met his Chinese counterpart and both sides agreed to gradually resume military ties.[106] The same month, State Councillor Yang visited Hanoi again; this visit was more successful than his June one. Both sides agreed to use their border dispute mechanism to seek a lasting solution to the South China Sea dispute. This was followed by a December visit by Yu Zhengsheng (head of the advisory body to the Chinese Parliament and the fourth-highest ranking official in the Chinese Communist Party). Both sides agreed to eschew megaphone diplomacy in their bid to resolve their territorial dispute in the South China Sea.[107] According to Do Thanh Hai, neither the Hainan authority nor any single department could have initiated it. Hai was of the view that "such a large-scale and well-coordinated operation" must have had direction from Beijing.[108] Hai was correct. We now know (from an editorial put out by the Central Party School) that President Xi "personally steered a series of measures to expand [China's] strategic advantage and safeguard the national interests".[109] Those familiar with the history of Sino-Vietnamese relations would find the responses from both sides following a familiar pattern: Hanoi cried foul, and the Chinese stood firm before removing the rig one month ahead of schedule in July, ostensibly because it had completed its work. However, in October China completed a runway for military aircraft on the disputed Woody Island (Yongxing Island or Phu Lam Island to the Vietnamese). This was a significant development as it enhanced "Chinese ability to exercise its sovereignty claims over the South China Sea".[110]

---

106 "Defense Minister's China Visit Fosters Ties", *VNA*, 18 Oct. 2014.

107 "China, Vietnam Agree to Seek Lasting Solution to Sea Dispute", *Straits Times*, 28 Oct. 2014; "China, Vietnam Turn to Dialogue", *Straits Times*, 28 Dec. 2014.

108 Hai, *Vietnam and the South China Sea*, p. 202.

109 "Xi Personally Behind Island-Building in the South China Sea", *South China Morning Post*, 28 July 2017.

110 "Beijing Finishes Runway on Disputed South China Sea Isle", *Today*, 9 Oct. 2014; "Upgraded Airstrip Set to Ignite China-Vietnam Row", *Straits Times*, 11 Oct. 2014.

Perhaps more serious than the above would be China's land reclamation activities. As President Aquino noted, China's reclaimed land in the disputed waters if used militarily could be a game changer in the future settlement of the dispute.[111] In May 2014 Manila released photographs showing Chinese land reclamation on Johnson South Reef (Mabini Reef), claimed by both the Philippines and Vietnam, with the intention of building an airstrip. Apparently the land reclamation had been ongoing for a few months already and would continue into 2015.[112] Land reclamation on any of the disputed land would be a violation of the Declaration on the Conduct of Parties in the South China Sea, which both China and the ASEAN member states had signed in 2002. Beijing's standard response was that the reef was part of Chinese territory. In June Manila claimed that China was beginning to carry out land reclamation at Gaven[113] and Cuarteron Reefs. China apparently already had permanent reef fortresses, supply platforms and harbours at Johnson South, Gaven and Cuarteron Reefs. It had also built structures at Fiery Cross (Yongshu Reef), Mischief and Subi Reefs.[114] According to a *South China Morning Post* report, China's intention was to expand its installations at Fiery Cross Reef, its biggest in the Spratlys and designated in 2011 as its "main command headquarters", into a "fully formed artificial island, complete with airstrip and sea port". The transformation of Fiery Cross Reef would make it "twice as large as the United States' military base in Diego Garcia".[115] Much international attention was focused on Fiery Cross Reef, but as Rear Admiral Alexander Lopez (commander of the Philippine military's Western Command) said, "we don't know what they plan in Mischief... They have long been doing that (dredging), only that it was Fiery Cross

[111] "Manila Pushes Arbitration in China Sea Row", *Today*, 23 Oct. 2014.

[112] "Philippines Releases Photos Showing China 'Reclamation'", *Straits Times*, 16 May 2014; "Land Reclamation by Beijing a Threat: Manila", *Straits Times*, 23 Jan. 2015.

[113] "China Creating Huge Structure on Spratlys", *Straits Times*, 13 Mar. 2015.

[114] "Chinese 'Land Reclamation' Ships at Reefs: Aquino", *Straits Times*, 6 June 2014; "New Photos to Show China's Work in Spratlys", *Straits Times*, 20 Apr. 2015; "China Building Runway on Subi Reef", *Straits Times*, 28 July 2015.

[115] "Beijing Reclaiming Land at Fourth Spratly Reef: Manila", *Straits Times*, 8 June 2014; "Manila Protest Against New Beijing Moves in Spratlys", *Straits Times*, 15 June 2014; "China 'Could Build Airstrip' on Spratly Reef", *Straits Times*, 23 Nov. 2014; "Spratly Reef Project Justifiable: PLA General", *Straits Times*, 25 Nov. 2014.

Reef that got a lot of attention as that was on a bigger scale."[116] In early 2016 Beijing carried out test flights from Fiery Cross Reef, prompting protests from both Vietnam and the Philippines. Manila further proposed joint naval patrols with the United States.[117] Also in early 2016, it was reported that the Chinese had installed a surface-to-air missile system on Woody Island, the largest island in the Paracels controlled by China and which Vietnam also claimed.

Aerial photographs in June 2014 showed that China was reclaiming land off a fourth reef known as Eldad Reef as well as McKennan Reef. Whenever confronted with such accusations, Beijing either denied that it was building or reclaiming land, or maintained that the territory belonged to China and, as such, it could build whatever it wanted.[118] However, it was not just China. According to Rommel Banlaoi (head of the Philippine Institution for Peace, Violence and Terrorism Research), Vietnam was carrying out more reclamation activities than China.[119] Major-General Luo Yuan of the People's Liberation Army also highlighted that the Philippines, Vietnam and Malaysia had built military facilities on their islands.[120] However, those paled in comparison to China. A March 2015 report noted that the reclamation works on at least six reefs, increasing land mass fivefold, had "become possibly the most visible sign" of China's "more muscular form of diplomacy".[121] ASEAN, despite its concern and Manila's urging for stronger action,

---

[116] "Beijing Defends Ship's Actions Against Manila in South China Sea", *Today*, 6 Feb. 2015.

[117] "US 'Open' to Patrols with Philippines as S. China Sea Tensions Keep Rising", *Today*, 4 Feb. 2016.

[118] "Beijing Reclaiming Land at Fourth Spratly Reef: Manila"; "Manila Protest Against New Beijing Moves in Spratlys"; "Beijing Defends Reclamation Work in South China Sea", *Today*, 9 Mar. 2015.

[119] "Philippines Seeks Pause in S. China Sea Development Activities", https://www.voanews.com/a/philippines-seeks-pause-in-development-activities-in-disputed-south-china-sea/1970945.html, accessed 2 Aug. 2017.

[120] "Spratly Reef Project Justifiable: PLA General", *Straits Times*, 25 Nov. 2014; "China Turns Tables on Rivals", *Straits Times*, 30 Apr. 2015; "Philippines Building on Disputed Isles: China", *Straits Times*, 6 May 2015; "Images Show Vietnam Reclaiming Land in South China Sea", http://www.reuters.com/article/us-southchinasea-vietnam-idUSKBN0NT04820150508, accessed 4 Aug. 2017; "Vietnam 'Did Major Work in Disputed S. China Sea", *Straits Times*, 9 May 2015.

[121] "Beijing Defends Reclamation Work In South China Sea".

was unable to reach a consensus on how to respond to China's reclamation works in the South China Sea. The regional grouping continued to hold on to the hope that the COC, when it eventually happened, would sort things out.[122] The closest ASEAN came to addressing the issue was the insertion of a paragraph in the Chairman's Statement of the 26th ASEAN Summit in Kuala Lumpur that read: "We share the serious concerns expressed by some leaders on land reclamation being undertaken …, which eroded trust and confidence, and may undermine peace, security and stability in the South China Sea." The statement also said that ASEAN had instructed its foreign ministers "to urgently address this matter constructively, including under various ASEAN frameworks such as ASEAN-China relations as well as the principle of peaceful coexistence".[123] Beijing was very unhappy with the inclusion of the two paragraphs, which according to Kyoto News were not in the original draft.[124] One significant consequence of China's land reclamation and construction activities was that it led the Pentagon to consider having ships and planes increase patrols in the disputed waters. In October 2015 Washington said that it would conduct "freedom of navigation" patrols in the disputed waters.[125] The USS *Lassen*, a guided-missile destroyer (based in Yokosuka, Japan), subsequently sailed

---

[122] "No ASEAN Consensus on Chinese Reclamation", *Today*, 28 Apr. 2015; "Manila Urges Stronger Action on China", *Straits Times*, 29 Jan. 2015.

[123] "Beijing Hits out at ASEAN over South China Sea", *Today*, 29 Apr. 2015; Tang Siew Mun explained why this statement was notable. See "Asean's Strongest Rebuke to China on Reclamation", *Straits Times*, 1 May 2015. This was very much an exception as ASEAN did not issue another such statement at the end of the 48th ASEAN Foreign Ministers Meeting in August 2015. The communique (issued a day late) noted the concerns but did not call for a halt to reclamation and other activities. Chinese Foreign Minister Wang apparently assured the ASEAN states that China had completed all its reclamation works (this was subsequently shown to be untrue). See "ASEAN Again Split on South China Sea Reclamation Issue", *Today*, 7 Aug. 2015; "Asean Scrambles to Put out Joint Statement on Sea Row", *Straits Times*, 7 Aug. 2015. At the ADMM Plus Meeting in November 2015, no joint statement was issued as the disagreements over the reference to the South China Sea dispute could not be reconciled.

[124] "Beijing Hits out at ASEAN over South China Sea".

[125] The commonly used term is FONOP (freedom of navigation operation). "3 Sino-US Scenarios in South China Sea Dispute", *Straits Times*, 19 May 2015; "US Tells Asian Allies That It Will Patrol Near S. China Sea Islands", *Today*, 14 Oct. 2015.

within 12 nautical miles of Subi Reef, marking what Richard Javad Heydarian described as the point when the "US was *directly* drawn into the South China Sea disputes [emphasis added]".[126] Beijing described this highly publicized event as a "deliberate provocation" and accused the United States of attempting to militarize the South China Sea.[127] (A second guided-missile destroyer, the USS *Curtis Wilbur*, sailed within 12 nautical miles of Triton Island in the Paracels in January 2016. This was followed by a third, the USS *William P. Lawrence*, which sailed within 22 kilometres of Fiery Cross Reef in May.[128] It was reported in early September 2017 that the US Pacific Command had, "for the first time, developed a schedule for naval patrols in the South China Sea". If this were true, it would, according to the *Wall Street Journal*, "mark a more regular approach to FONOP in the South China Sea".[129] Meanwhile, 15 December 2014, the deadline for China to respond to Manila's arguments submitted to the Permanent Court of Arbitration at The Hague, came and went. Beijing ignored the deadline. The case would thus proceed without China, and a ruling was expected in late 2015 or early 2016.

Trans-Pacific Partnership, One Belt One Road

By mid-June 2015, the Trans-Pacific Partnership (TPP) free trade deal looked like it would not materialize any time soon when Congress voted against giving President Obama the fast-track authority to get the US-led free trade agreement approved. The TPP was the "central pillar of the Obama administration's 'rebalance' policy in the Asia Pacific region".[130] Japan finally joined in 2013. While the vote did not yet mark the death knell of the TPP, analysts were of the view that there were few options for a breakthrough, given the size of the Democrat

---

[126] "US Directly Drawn into South China Sea Disputes", *Straits Times*, 30 Oct. 2015.

[127] "China Slams US for 'Deliberate Provocation' in South China Sea", *Today*, 28 Oct. 2015.

[128] "US Navy Ship Sails Near Disputed Island", *Straits Times*, 31 Jan. 2016; "China Fumes as US Warship Sails by Disputed Reef", *Straits Times*, 11 May 2016.

[129] "US Sets Schedule for S. China Sea Patrols for the First Time: Report", *Straits Times*, 3 Sept. 2017.

[130] Matthew P. Goodman, "Yes, TPP Is About Who Writes the Rules", Pacific Forum, CSIS, *PacNet* #66, 6 Sept. 2016.

opposition. Furthermore, time was running out as Congress headed into the campaign season. President Obama's term of office officially ended on 20 January 2017, but much of 2016 would be focused on the campaign. On 5 October 2015 the TPP negotiations finally ended. Soon after, president-aspirant Hillary Clinton, who in her capacity as secretary of state had promoted the TPP, announced that she no longer supported it.[131] Singapore's Foreign Minister K. Shanmugam starkly laid out the consequence of not approving the TPP—Singapore was one of its strongest and most vocal supporters in the region—"Strategically what is your engagement with Asia, what is your leverage of engagement with the fastest-growing region in the world? The only game in town is the TPP." The TPP was critical "more because of its implications on America's strategy towards Asia than any economic considerations". In short, it was not simply about economics. Economics was, in fact, only a "small part of the equation".[132]

Obama made a final effort to further shore up US-Southeast Asia relations when he hosted the US-ASEAN Sunnylands Special Summit in February 2016—the first summit between the US and ASEAN held in the United States. In a short statement issued at the end of two days of relatively informal talks, everyone reiterated their "firm adherence to a rules-based regional and international order" and "a shared commitment to peaceful resolution of disputes, including full respect for legal and diplomatic processes, without resorting to threat or use of force".[133] The United States was entering into the heat of the presidential election season. It was thus hard to disagree with the view that "it was late-term exercise in symbolism over substance, lacking any clear affirmation of future U.S. commitment to Washington's Asian rebalance policy".[134]

In contrast, China appeared to have shown more vision. President Xi had two ideas to increase Chinese influence in the region. One was the China-led Asian Infrastructure Investment Bank, which in 2015 had more than 57 members, including Australia, Germany and Britain.

---

[131] "Clinton Splits Again with White House, This Time over TPP", *Straits Times*, 9 Oct. 2015.

[132] "TPP Deal 'Less About Economics, More About US Strategy in Asia'", *Straits Times*, 18 June 2015.

[133] "Rules-Based Regional Order Backed by US, ASEAN", *Today*, 18 Feb. 2016.

[134] Malcolm Cook, "Manila Takes US Pivot Well Beyond Sunnylands", *Nikkei Asian Review*, 17 Feb. 2016.

In December 2015 the Philippines, despite its ongoing dispute with China over the South China Sea islands, also joined.[135] The other was the "One Belt One Road" (OBOR). This is a good place to introduce the "Silk Road Economic Belt" and the "21st Century Maritime Silk Road" that could connect China with Southeast Asia, Africa and Europe. The twin initiatives were proposed by Xi in late 2013. The key word here is "initiatives". They were not a clearly laid-out plan or strategy, at least not at the beginning. President Xi first proposed "jointly building an 'economic belt along the Silk Road'" on 7 September 2013 in a speech at Nazarbayev University, Kazakhstan. On 3 October the same year, he spoke about "strengthening maritime cooperation with ASEAN countries, and making full use of the China-ASEAN Maritime Cooperation Fund to develop maritime cooperation partnership" in a speech at the Indonesian Parliament. The initiatives, which emerged from the two speeches, did not attract much attention then, and as Li Mingjiang noted, the responses of neighbouring countries were "ambivalent". However, after late 2013 OBOR became a "priority in China's foreign-policy drive".[136] In March 2015 Beijing finally published a guiding document on the OBOR initiative, and on 28 March 2015 State Councillor Yang Jiechi elaborated on the "21st Century Maritime Silk Road" at the Boao Forum for Asia annual conference.[137] OBOR is discussed further in chapter 8. It is useful to end here by comparing the TPP—its future resting on a knife edge—with the visionary OBOR. According to Shanmugam:

> If you (United States) are out of the region, not playing a useful role, your only lever to shape the architecture, to influence events is the Seventh Fleet and that's not the lever you want to use, or you can't use it at every instance. Trade is the strategy and you're either in or you're out ... The world doesn't wait, not even for the United States.[138]

---

135 "AIIB Gains from Inclusive Stance", *Straits Times*, 3 Apr. 2015; "Manila to Join China-Led AIIB", *Straits Times*, 21 Dec. 2015.

136 "World Not Excited About China's Belt and Road Plan", *Today*, 18 Mar. 2015.

137 Bal Kishan Sharma and Nivedita Das Kundu (eds), *China's One Belt One Road: Initiative, Challenges and Prospects* (New Delhi: Vij Books, 2016), p. 15.

138 "Shanmugam: US Risks Irrelevance in Asia", *Straits Times*, 17 June 2015. The OBOR is now more commonly referred to as the Belt and Road Initiative (BRI). In recent years its activities have come under increasing scrutiny by participating countries.

CHAPTER 8

2016–17: At the Crossroads of History

"Seismic 2016 ... The Year Asia's Power Balance Shifted"[1]

"... the old is dying and the new cannot be born."[2]

An "ASEAN Community"

Southeast Asia entered the year 2016 ostensibly as a single "ASEAN community". Most analysts, however, agreed that the region was still far from what it proclaimed to be. Muthiah Alagappa spoke for many when he wrote that ASEAN was "unlikely to become a single community any time soon. ASEAN integration and community building should remain long-term aspirations for decades to come."[3] Politicians did not disagree but preferred to focus on the positive side, noting that it was a historic juncture in ASEAN's development and, in the words of Barry Desker, "a demonstration of its institutional maturity". Amidst the celebration, there was the acknowledgement that it was "by no means the end point"—if there is one at all. Rather, it was a "journey", beginning

---

[1] Headline in the *Straits Times*, 31 Dec. 2016.

[2] Antonio Gramsci, *Selections of the Prison Note-books of Antonio Gramsci*, transl. Quentin Hoare and Geoffrey Nowell Smith (London: Lawrence & Wishart, 1971), p. 556.

[3] Muthiah Alagappa, "Community Building: ASEAN's Milestone?" *RSIS Commentary*, 24 Mar. 2015; Endy M. Bayuni, "At 50, Asean Is a Neighbourhood, Not Yet Community", *Straits Times*, 29 July 2017; Barry Desker, "Is ASEAN a Community?" *RSIS Commentary*, 2 Aug. 2017.

with the establishment of the AEC, which would contribute significantly to the region's competitiveness and growth, to be followed by the two other pillars—the Political-Security Community and the Socio-Cultural Community.[4] The AEC itself is also "hampered", its development hindered by ageing populations, weak institutions, rising nationalistic arguments and protectionist policies within ASEAN.[5] In short, the ASEAN Community should be seen as a work in progress. At the same time, there is an urgent need for greater integration in order to insulate and keep ASEAN above the growing US-China fray. The issue and subsequent retraction of a joint statement after the ASEAN-China Special Foreign Ministers Meeting in Kunming in June 2016, whose cause remains murky, pointed to a lack of unity within ASEAN, particularly over the South China Sea issue, as well as the huge pressure exerted by China.[6] While ASEAN-China relations are indeed multifaceted, and Chinese Foreign Minister Wang urged his ASEAN counterparts not to view the South China Sea dispute as "the sum of China-ASEAN ties",[7] the reality is that Beijing does link the South China Sea to the broad range of ASEAN-China interactions, such as the RCEP, OBOR and AIIB.

The year, however, has a greater significance. On looking back, the reorientation of the international politics of Southeast Asia can be traced back to 2016, although it is still too early to tell whether the change (which is still ongoing) will be short-lived or more long-lasting. The first major development, which had implications for the international politics of the region, was the electoral victory of Rodrigo Duterte in May 2016; he was inaugurated the 16th president of the Philippines

[4] "Asean Community Set to Be Formed in 'Historic Milestone'", *Straits Times*, 31 Dec. 2015.

[5] Keynote speech by former ASEAN Secretary-General Ong Keng Yong, Selangor International Business Summit 2017 and Selangor-Asean Business Conference, 11 Sept. 2017, http://www.theedgemarkets.com/article/asean-economic-integration-progress-hampered, accessed 14 Sept. 2017.

[6] This episode was reported in most regional newspapers. Perhaps the most revealing account, based on Vietnamese sources, is Carlyle Thayer, "The ASEAN-China Special Meeting Mystery: Bureaucratic Snafu or Chinese Heavy-Handedness?" *The Diplomat*, 17 June 2016. See also the postscript "Revealed: The Truth Behind ASEAN's Retracted Kunming Statement", *The Diplomat*, 19 June 2016.

[7] "Asean Stresses 'Serious' S. China Sea Concerns", *Straits Times*, 15 June 2016.

on 30 June. Duterte is a controversial leader because of many of his policies and actions, both domestic and foreign. The latter concern us here. As Gregory Poling observed, Duterte appeared to be "deeply skeptical of the value of the US alliance because he doesn't believe the US will really back the Philippines against China if push comes to shove". The new president also went on record, as the *Global Times* (considered the occasional mouthpiece of the Chinese Communist Party) noted, to say that he "opposes the idea of going to war with China, wants direct negotiation with Beijing about the South China Sea, and doesn't believe in solving the conflict through an international tribunal".[8] With the election of Duterte (apart from the fact that Obama was in his lame-duck year as president), the two-day US-ASEAN Special Summit held in Sunnylands in early 2016 (chapter 7) would be relegated to a mere footnote in the annals of US-Southeast Asian relations. Duterte had reportedly called Obama "son of a whore" in response to the US president's criticism of his anti-crime campaign and extrajudicial killings. A scheduled meeting between the two presidents on the sidelines of the 28th and 29th ASEAN Summit in Laos in September 2016 was cancelled. Duterte also did not attend the US-ASEAN dialogue, signalling his intention "to lessen his nation's dependence" on the United States.[9] He is on record as having said that he was "not a fan of the Americans" and that in the Philippines' relations with the world, Manila would pursue "an independent foreign policy".[10]

ASEAN States and China

The second major development was the much-anticipated 12 July 2016 ruling by the arbitral tribunal that China had no legal basis or historic claim to the Nine-Dash Line, and that no country could claim any "historic rights" in the sea. The ruling also stated that none of the features in the Spratlys could generate a continental shelf and Exclusive

[8] "Questions over Duterte's Foreign Policy", *Today*, 12 May 2016.

[9] "Philippines Not Cutting Ties with Its Allies: Duterte", *Straits Times*, 14 Sept. 2016.

[10] "Duterte Says He Is 'Not a Fan' of the US", *Straits Times*, 11 Sept. 2016; "Manila Right to Diversify Alliances, Says Russian Envoy", *Straits Times*, 5 Jan. 2017; "Russia Navy Visits Philippines as Part of Duterte's Pivot away from US", *Today*, 21 Apr. 2017.

Economic Zone.[11] The ruling was "far more comprehensive and decisive than many legal experts had predicted".[12] Beijing's rejection of the ruling was, of course, to be expected. The Southeast Asian response to the ruling is worth noting: ASEAN was unable to issue a joint statement because of a lack of consensus. Indeed, in April 2016 it was reported that Brunei, Cambodia and Laos had reached a four-point consensus with China on the South China Sea issue in which all four countries opposed any attempt to "unilaterally impose an agenda on other countries". Singapore's diplomats Bilahari Kausikan and Ong Keng Yong accused Beijing of splitting ASEAN.[13] Cambodia, even before the ruling was announced, made clear that it would not participate in expressing any common position with regard to the Sino-Philippine dispute. Individual countries such as Laos, Indonesia and Thailand also did not make any public statement about the ruling but chose to reiterate the general aspiration of resolving the dispute peacefully, based on previous ASEAN-China agreements as well as ASEAN norms. Countries that responded to the ruling, such as Singapore and Myanmar, did so "with extreme care not to touch any sensitive Chinese nerves".[14] At the commemorative summit in September 2016 marking 25 years of Sino-ASEAN dialogue relations, no ASEAN leader even suggested that China should comply with the ruling. The joint communique also made no mention of it.[15] Indeed, although the Philippines had won a "landmark legal victory", in the words of

[11] For details, see Clive Schofield, "A Landmark Decision in the South China Sea: The Scope and Implications of the Arbitral Tribunal's Award", *Contemporary Southeast Asia* 38, 3 (Dec. 2016).

[12] See "Roundtable: The Arbitral Tribunal's Ruling on the South China Sea", *Contemporary Southeast Asia* 38, 3 (Dec. 2016).

[13] "South China Sea Consensus 'Shows up Asean Faultlines'", *Straits Times*, 25 Apr. 2016; "China's Pact with Cambodia, Laos and Interference in ASEAN's Domestic Affairs: Former Sec-Gen", http://www.channelnewsasia.com/news/asiapacific/china-s-pact-with-cambodia-laos-an-interference-in-asean-s-domes-8095812, accessed 14 Aug. 2017; "China Responds to S'pore Diplomats' Remarks", *Straits Times*, 28 Apr. 2016; "China's Actions Lent Themselves to Misunderstanding: Bilahari", *Today*, 29 Apr. 2016.

[14] Termsak Chalermpalanupap, "No ASEAN Consensus on the South China Sea", *The Diplomat*, 21 July 2016.

[15] "Tribunal Ruling on S. China Sea Is Binding, Stresses Obama", *Straits Times*, 9 Sept. 2016.

Heydarian, "not only has China managed to tame the response of the international community, but Asean itself also has missed a historic opportunity to reassert any semblance of relevance in the South China Sea".[16] Most significantly and surprisingly, Manila, which under Benigno Aquino had initiated the arbitral tribunal in 2013, now under Duterte decided to put aside the arbitral tribunal's ruling and agreed to resolve the South China Sea dispute with China through bilateral negotiations. In return, Beijing pledged US$24 billion in loans and investments and lifted the 2012 ban on Filipino anglers in the Scarborough Shoal area. Manila hoped for more Chinese financial assistance to fund various infrastructure projects, such as the railway line connecting Manila to Legazpi City in Albay province in the southern part of Luzon. As Philippine Finance Secretary Carlos Dominguez said, "the generous assistance offered by China to the Philippines is among the concrete results of the president's foreign policy re-balancing".[17]

The non-confrontational approach adopted by the Southeast Asian states after the tribunal ruling brought about some positive results in the form of an agreement reached with China on the use of a hotline during maritime emergencies, the application of the Code of Unplanned Encounters at Sea, and—perhaps most importantly—an agreement to complete a draft framework for the COC by mid-2017. In April 2017 ASEAN held its 30th Summit in Manila under the chairmanship of the Philippines. While the South China Sea issue was mentioned in the Chairman's Statement, it merely reiterated the call for a "peaceful resolution" to the dispute and did not mention the arbitral tribunal's ruling. The Chairman's Statement was also silent on the issue of Chinese land reclamation and island building in the South China Sea. According to the Asia Maritime Transparency Initiative, satellite pictures showed that China was still building in the South China Sea, particularly in the Paracels.[18] The general view was that the ASEAN countries adopted a "softer stance" in view of the agreement to draft a framework for negotiating the COC.[19] The United States, Japan and Australia had tried

[16] Richard Javad Heydarian, "Asean Fails to Rise to the Occasion", *Straits Times*, 28 July 2016.

[17] "Manila Seeks Billions in Loans from China", *Straits Times*, 28 Jan. 2017.

[18] "China Still Building in S. China Sea", *Straits Times*, 12 Aug. 2017.

[19] For the full text of the Chairman's Statement, see http://asean.org/chairmans-statement-30th-asean-summit/, accessed 31 Aug. 2017.

to persuade ASEAN to issue a stronger response. The straight-talking Duterte said before the summit that it was pointless discussing Beijing's contentious activities in the South China Sea as no one dared to pressure China anyway.[20] As a quid pro quo, Beijing apparently dropped its insistence on a "non-legally binding" COC. (ASEAN's preference had always been for a "legally binding" COC.) At the 6 August meeting, the ASEAN-China Joint Working Group on the Implementation of the Declaration of the Conduct of Parties agreed on a framework for the COC. In September representatives from ASEAN and China met to begin discussions of the "working approach" that could lead to negotiations of the COC.[21] It had taken 15 years since the signing of the Declaration of Conduct in the South China Sea in 2002 to reach this stage. In August 2017 Beijing also assured Manila that it would not build new features or occupy more territories in the South China Sea.[22] The reality is that over the years, China had already taken over a number of the disputed islands and features, of which at least three were capable of accommodating fighter jets.[23] Despite all the assurances, satellite evidence showed that Beijing had been "moving ahead steadily" and undeterred with its land reclamation and construction in the South China Sea.[24]

As for the Philippines' relations with its old ally the United States, as well as China, even if one discounts some of Duterte's more extravagant statements such as his country's "separation from the United States" or "there are three of us against the world—China, Philippines and Russia", it is true that the trajectory of Sino-Philippine relations was the inverse of US-Philippine ties. As the former soared (from the depths during the Aquino III administration), the latter plummeted

---

[20] "Pointless Discussing Beijing's South China Sea Activities at Asean Meet: Duterte", *Today*, 28 Apr. 2017. For a more diplomatic perspective, see "Vivian: Asean Focused on Code of Conduct in S. China Sea", *Straits Times*, 6 May 2017.

[21] "Work Starts on Code of Conduct for S. China Sea", *Straits Times*, 2 Sept. 2017.

[22] "Beijing Vows Not to Occupy New Territory in S. China Sea: Manila", *Straits Times*, 16 Aug. 2017.

[23] Ibid.; "Justice Carpio Bares Invasion of PH Islet", 20 Aug. 2017, *Inquirer.Net*, https://globalnation.inquirer.net/159857/antonio-carpio-maritime-dispute-south-china-sea-west-philippine-sea-sandy-cay-pag-asa-island, accessed 12 Apr. 2019.

[24] "Beijing Moving Ahead Steadily with S. China Sea Construction", *Straits Times*, 27 Dec. 2017.

(from the peak before June 2016). As Heydarian pointed out, "this is where a lot of countries were caught off guard. Duterte could actually make a huge impact, not only on Philippines foreign policy, but also the broader regional geopolitical dynamics".[25] China's Foreign Minister Wang described relations between China and the Philippines as having "entered a golden period of fast development".[26] Duterte's radical shift towards Beijing led many analysts to question its impact on ASEAN centrality.[27]

The Philippines is not the only ASEAN country that has moved closer to China in recent years. It stands out because of its traditional ties with the United States during the Cold War years and President Duterte's proclamations. Manila is also the outlier amongst the original five ASEAN member countries in this regard, although one should not exaggerate Manila's swing to China. A 2017 survey by the Pew Research Center showed that Filipinos still favoured the United States over China, but the gap was narrowing.[28] As noted in earlier chapters, of all the ASEAN countries, Cambodia has by far the closest ties with China and the poorest relations with the United States. Beijing has been strengthening its economic as well as defence ties with Cambodia. In February 2016 both countries carried out a joint exercise for training in rescue operations. The Tianjin Union Development Group, a Chinese company with connections to the People's Liberation Army, signed an agreement with the Phnom Penh government in September 2016 to build a port along the coast of the Gulf of Thailand, a few hundred kilometres from the disputed islands in the South China Sea. It was reported that the new port would be deep enough to handle ships,

---

[25] See Steve Mollman, "Political Scientist Richard Javad Heydarian on Rodrigo Duterte, US-Bashing, and the South China Sea", 17 Oct. 2016, https://qz.com/807203/political-scientist-richard-javad-heydarian-on-rodrigo-duterte-us-bashing-and-the-south-china-sea/, accessed 11 Aug. 2017.

[26] "China Hails 'Golden Period' in Ties with Philippines", *Today*, 30 June 2017.

[27] See, for example, "Duterte and End of Asean Neutrality?" *Straits Times*, 12 Jan. 2017; "Philippines Pledges to Uphold Asean's Values as New Chair", *Straits Times*, 16 Jan. 2017.

[28] "Filipinos Favour US over China, but Gap Narrowing", *Straits Times*, 22 Sept. 2017. The survey revealed that four out of five Filipinos still favoured the US, but the percentage was below the Obama period of 92 per cent surveyed in 2015.

both cruise and naval, up to 10,000 tonnes in weight. To the Chinese, Cambodia is an important transportation hub in Southeast Asia. As Chinese Ambassador to Cambodia Xiong Bo noted, "Cambodia holds a key position on the ancient maritime Silk Road connecting the East and the West."[29] This is just one example of the many infrastructure projects built with Chinese money. Beijing also sold military equipment to Cambodia, such as shoulder-fired anti-aircraft missiles and helicopters, and provided military training. As a *Financial Times* investigative report noted, big investment deals had cemented Beijing's relations with Phnom Penh, which had also yielded political dividends for China.[30] Sino-Cambodian relations have indeed come a long way from the Cold War years. In 1988 Hun Sen described China as "everything that is evil in Cambodia",[31] but in 2017 China was perceived to be Cambodia's most reliable friend. Chinese President Xi, who visited Cambodia in October 2016, for the first time since becoming president, described both countries as "good neighbours, real friends who are loyal to each other".[32] Compared to China's generosity, the United States continued to pursue a 45-year loan worth US$500 million (obtained during Sihanouk's tenure) and blocked the International Monetary Fund from lending to Phnom Penh until the debt was repaid. There were fears that the US State Department budget cut, if approved by the Trump administration, would result in American development assistance to Cambodia being reduced to zero.[33] As it happened, assistance was reduced, but not to zero. In January 2017 Phnom Penh cancelled an annual joint US military exercise ostensibly because it was "too busy with domestic commitments", and in April it scrapped a nine-year-old

[29] "Xi Praises Cambodia for Being a Good Neighbour", *Straits Times*, 14 Oct. 2016.
[30] "Cambodia and China to Hold Naval Drills", *Straits Times*, 18 Feb. 2016; "Beijing Draws Cambodia Closer in Diplomatic Embrace", *Today*, 2 Sept. 2016; "FT Investigation: How China Bought Its Way into Cambodia", *Financial Times*, 8 Sept. 2016; "The 'Chinazation' of Cambodia", *Nikkei Asian Review*, 16 Mar. 2017.
[31] "China, Cambodia Cosy up Ahead of Xi's Visit to Phnom Penh", *Today*, 7 Oct. 2016.
[32] "Xi Praises Cambodia for Being a Good Neighbour".
[33] "Breaking News: US Development Assistance to Be Slashed to Zero, Document", *Phnom Penh Post*, 25 Apr. 2017, http://www.phnompenhpost.com/national/breaking-news-us-development-assistance-may-be-slashed-zero-document, accessed 5 Sept. 2017.

US military aid programme.[34] In August 2017 the Hun Sen government closed down the National Democratic Institute office in Cambodia and expelled its foreign staff from the country. The institute, which is supposedly "nonpartisan in its work to promote democracy and strengthen democratic institutions" worldwide and funded by the National Endowment for Democracy, USAid and the US State Department, was accused of attempting to instigate a "color revolution" against the Hun Sen government.[35] Overall, the state of Cambodia-US relations is the inverse of the state of Sino-Cambodian relations.

Beijing is buying its way not just into Cambodia but also into Laos and Myanmar. On 25 December 2016 work started on the controversial China-Laos high-speed railway, which when completed would link Kunming to Vientiane. The Chinese envisioned this to be part of a larger transportation system that would link Yunnan province to key markets in Southeast Asia. This project falls under the OBOR or Belt and Road Initiative (BRI). Given that the proposed railway lines in Vietnam and Myanmar had been shelved, the Kunming-Vientiane railway line was even more important to the Chinese. How beneficial this railway project would be to Laos is not so clear.[36]

Obama was the first-ever sitting US president to visit landlocked Laos, which he did in September 2016. There were reports of that country attempting to tilt away from China towards the United States. However, this is unlikely to become a reality given the amount of Chinese investment in Laos. In contrast, Laos is "not a strong investment draw" for the United States. Beijing views Laos as "a key gateway to Southeast Asia".[37] As Edgar Pang noted, Cambodia and Laos are perceived to be the "most trusted allies" of China in Southeast Asia. However, unlike Cambodia, Laos tries "to keep some semblance of balance" and even-handedness when dealing with China.[38]

[34] "Cambodia Scraps Joint US Military Exercise", *Financial Times*, 18 Jan. 2017; "Cambodia Scraps US Military Aid Deal in Latest Snub to Washington", *Financial Times*, 5 Apr. 2017.

[35] "US and Cambodia Fire Diplomatic Shots After Closure of NGO", *Southeast Asia Globe*, 24 Aug. 2017; "US Denies Conspiracy to Topple Cambodian Government", *Phnom Penh Post*, 30 Aug. 2017.

[36] See "China Starts Controversial Lao Rail Project", *Asia Sentinel*, 7 Mar. 2017.

[37] "Laos Signals a Tilt away from China as Obama Visits", *Today*, 29 Aug. 2016.

[38] Edgar Pang, "'*Same-Same but Different*': Laos and Cambodia's Political Embrace of China", *ISEAS Perspective* 66, 5 Sept. 2017.

As for Myanmar, Yangon is very dependent on Chinese assistance to manage, if not resolve, its ethnic insurgency problems.[39] Although Beijing stressed that it would "consistently persevere in not interfering in other countries' internal affairs and respect the entirety of Myanmar's sovereign rights and territory", Sino-Myanmar relations have often been strained over Chinese support of the ethnic rebels located at the Sino-Myanmar border. Many observers share the view that Beijing uses ethnically Chinese insurgent groups "as a means of leverage over Myanmar".[40] In April 2017, after almost a decade of talks, both countries reached an agreement on the 770km pipeline that would serve as an alternative route to send oil from the Middle East to China, bypassing the Strait of Malacca. As Kavi Chongkittavorn noted, "with both the oil and gas pipelines now in operation, Myanmar has suddenly become a connectivity route for China's Belt and Road Initiative".[41] Beijing sees Myanmar as a land bridge to the Indian Ocean.[42] China is also Myanmar's largest trading partner, accounting for almost 40 per cent of total trade in 2016. The Chinese are also building a special economic zone, power plant and deep-sea port on Myanmar's west coast.[43] On the other hand, the optimism during the time of rapprochement in Myanmar-US relations in 2011, which the Chinese then perceived as a "strategic setback", did not seem to have borne much significant fruit. Myanmar did not, or could not, turn away from China towards the West as many had then hoped or anticipated.[44] Although President Obama visited Myanmar twice, in 2012 and 2014, Washington did little to build on the new relationship whereas Beijing was "energetically bringing more nations into its orbit, wooing American friends and allies with military

[39] "China Captures Myanmar's Peace Process", *Asia Times*, 3 June 2017. See also Enze Han, "Borderland Ethnic Politics and Changing Sino-Myanmar Relations", in *War & Peace in the Borderlands of Myanmar: The Kachin Ceasefire, 1994–2011*, ed. Mandy Sadan (Amsterdam: NIAS Press, 2016), chapter 6.

[40] "Myanmar Praises China for Action on Rebels", *Straits Times*, 23 Mar. 2017.

[41] "Policy Shifts in Myanmar's Ties with Major Powers", *Straits Times*, 22 Apr. 2017.

[42] "China Gains Upper Hand in Myanmar", *Bangkok Post*, 27 May 2017, https://www.bangkokpost.com/news/world/1257494/china-regains-upper-hand-in-myanmar, accessed 12 Apr. 2019.

[43] "China's Investments Changing Its Neighbours", *Straits Times*, 8 Dec. 2016.

[44] The Chinese described the US-Myanmar rapprochement with a Chinese proverb: "The cooked duck flew out of the window" (the "cooked duck" was Myanmar).

hardware, infrastructure deals and diplomatic attention".[45] Analysts do not think the Trump administration will do any better than its predecessor. China's "charm offensive" has helped China regain its foothold in Myanmar.[46]

Sino-Thai relations were discussed in chapter 7. Like the Philippines, Thailand has been diversifying its relations in the wake of the May 2014 coup and the consequent cooling of US-Thai relations—but, unlike the Philippines, not in a dramatic way. Besides China, Bangkok also reached out to Russia, capitalizing on Moscow's ambition to develop its position as an Asian power. In early 2016 the head of Russia's Security Council, Nikolai Patrushev, visited Bangkok, and shortly after two Thai deputy prime ministers visited Moscow.[47] But it is the development of Sino-Thai relations that is most significant at this stage. In April 2017 it was reported that Thailand had agreed to buy tanks as well as a submarine from China, replacing its US-made M41 with Chinese VT-4 tanks.[48] In June Thai Prime Minister Prayuth Chan-o-cha rammed through the Sino-Thai high-speed train project, which had stalled since the signing of the memorandum of understanding on rail cooperation in 2014. The rail project is part of China's long-term plan to link Kunming by rail to Laos, Thailand and eventually Singapore. Political analysts viewed Prayuth's act as a strong and further example of Bangkok's definite tilt towards China.[49] That was before Prayuth's visit to the United States in October 2017, when he met President Donald Trump. The visit marked a "normalization of Thai-US relations after the coup of 2014. Above all, US endorsement helps boost the regime's international legitimacy."[50]

---

[45] "As U.S. Attention Wanes in Southeast Asia, China Woos Myanmar", *New York Times*, 19 July 2017.

[46] Aung Zaw, "China's Charm Offensive Regains Its Foothold in Myanmar", *The Irrawaddy*, 9 Aug. 2017; Amara Thiha, "How China Is Courting Myanmar", *The Diplomat*, 12 Aug. 2017.

[47] "From Russia to Thailand, with Love", *Straits Times*, 7 Apr. 2016.

[48] "Thailand and Cambodia Strengthen Ties with China", *Straits Times*, 5 Apr. 2017.

[49] See "Prayuth Will Invoke 'Absolute Powers' to Push Through Railway Deal with Beijing", *Today*, 14 June 2017; "Prayut Fast-Tracks Sino-Thai Rail Project", *Straits Times*, 17 June 2017.

[50] Pongphisoot Busbarat, "Shopping Diplomacy: The Thai Prime Minister's Visit to the United States and Its Implications for Thai-US Relations", *ISEAS Perspective* 78, 20 Oct. 2017.

Sino-Malaysian relations have also improved considerably. There was such a significant influx of Chinese investment into Malaysia that the Najib government was accused, rightly or wrongly, of allowing China to "come here with tonnes of cash to buy up Bandar Malaysia and make us work for them". One prominent critic is former Prime Minister Mahathir Mohamad.[51] Malaysia, like the Philippines, has benefited considerably from tilting towards China. President Duterte managed to obtain US$24 billion in investment and soft loans during his visit to China in October 2016. Malaysian Prime Minister Najib Razak secured RM144 billion worth of investment and soft loans from Beijing during his November 2016 visit to China.[52] Both Manila and Kuala Lumpur also successfully secured Chinese funding for railway projects in their respective countries. Sino-Malaysian relations have moved beyond trade and investment. In April 2017 Malaysian Defence Minister Hishammuddin Hussein announced that a high-level defence committee would be set up between Malaysia and China to boost security cooperation. Kuala Lumpur also committed to buy four littoral ships from China.[53] In late August 2017 President Xi described relations between China and Malaysia as the "best ever" in history, repeating Najib's remark made in November 2015.[54] Not everyone agrees that Kuala Lumpur has fallen into the Chinese camp. In a 2017 essay Elina Noor and T.N. Qistina attempted to show that Malaysia had "sought to expand and deepen ties with China and the United States simultaneously, consistent with its longstanding policy of maintaining an equidistance between the great powers".[55] In September 2017 Prime

[51] "Mahathir Takes Aim at China Investments in Key Party Speech", *Sunday Times*, 15 Jan. 2017; "Beijing Rebuts Critics Who Say It Is Stealing Locals' Rice Bowls", *Sunday Times*, 15 Jan. 2017; "Beijing, KL to Meet over Port Projects and Bandar Malaysia", *Straits Times*, 31 Mar. 2017. See also "Former Malaysian PM Mahathir Mohamad on the Rise of China", *Financial Times*, 26 May 2017.

[52] "Manila Seeks Billions in Loans from China", *Straits Times*, 28 Jan. 2017.

[53] For details, see Prashanth Parameswaran, "What's Behind the New China-Malaysia Defense Committee?" *The Diplomat*, 25 Apr. 2017.

[54] "Healthy China-Malaysia Ties Could Hurt Ethnic Chinese", *Today*, 28 Aug. 2017; "Najib: China-Malaysia Bilateral Ties at Its Best Now", *The Star Online*, http://www.thestar.com.my/news/nation/2015/11/17/malaysia-china-bilateral-ties-at-its-best/, accessed 6 Sept. 2017.

[55] See Elina Noor and T.N. Qistina, "Great Power Rivalries, Domestic Politics and Malaysian Foreign Policy", *Asian Security*, Sept. 2017, http://www.tandfonline.com/doi/abs/10.1080/14799855.2017.1354568?tab=permissions&scroll=top, accessed 14 Sept. 2017.

Minister Najib visited Washington, DC, where he met President Trump. However, analysts were of the view that Najib was using the visit to shore up his own reputation amidst the 1MDB controversy, which has been an albatross hanging around his neck. As one Malaysian politician noted, "on the one hand, there is 'FDI' from China into Malaysia and now Malaysia makes 'investments' into the US economy" (which was what Najib committed to do).[56]

Among all the Southeast Asian countries, Indonesia and Singapore have not succumbed to Beijing's cash diplomacy. Indonesia has so far been able to "compartmentalize" its claim over the Exclusive Economic Zone around the Natuna Islands and its economic relations with China.[57] Indonesian Foreign Minister Retno Marsudi said, "we have a good relationship with China. We will strive to maintain our good relations along with international laws."[58] On 25 August 2017 China sent an official note to the Indonesian embassy in Beijing demanding that Jakarta rescind its 14 July 2017 move to rename the disputed southwest part of the South China Sea as the North Natuna Sea. The change in an "internationally accepted name", the Chinese insisted, would result in a "complication and expansion of the dispute, and affects peace and stability". The note added that the bilateral relationship was developing in a "healthy and stable way", the South China Sea dispute was being properly managed, and any unilateral name change was not "conducive to maintaining this excellent situation".[59] In the case of Singapore, relations went through a low period because of China's perception that Singapore was focusing unduly on the arbitral tribunal result even though the Philippines had put it aside. However, from August 2017 the relationship appeared to have improved. Prime Minister Lee Hsien

---

[56] "Leong Malaysia", https://www.facebook.com/liewchintong.my/posts/1015484222 1445911, accessed 14 Sept. 2017.

[57] "Indonesia Balances Maritime Sovereignty, Economic Ties to China", 25 Nov. 2016, https://www.voanews.com/a/indonesia-china-south-china-sea/3611198.html, accessed 6 Sept. 2016.

[58] "Indonesia's Complicated Relations with China", *Asia Sentinel*, 5 Aug. 2016.

[59] "China Demands Indonesia Rescind Decision to Rename Part of South China Sea", 2 Sept. 2017, http://www.channelnewsasia.com/news/asiapacific/china-demands-indonesia-rescind-decision-to-rename-part-of-south-9179992, accessed 6 Sept. 2017.

Loong paid, by all accounts, a successful visit to China in September 2017 at the invitation of Chinese Premier Li Keqiang, where he met four of the top Chinese leaders, including President Xi.[60] That said, it is worth noting that Singapore-US relations are close and deep—indeed, one could argue, more so than US relations with the Philippines and Thailand. As Campbell wrote, "Singapore is perhaps the most defining example of a country that has stretched the definition of *partner* by providing uncommon capacity and support to the United States. Singapore is a uniquely strong partner that offers the United States strategic advice and military access."[61] In August 2016 President Obama described the US-Singapore relationship as a "solid-rock" partnership and said that Singapore was "an 'anchor' for US presence in the region".[62] More recently, in May 2017, on announcing the appointment of a new US ambassador to Singapore, the White House described Singapore as "one of America's great allies".[63] Singapore's Prime Minister Lee Hsien Loong noted how far ties had come in the decades since founding Prime Minister Lee Kuan Yew first visited the United States in 1967. In August 2016 he said, "Singapore's own ties with the United States have remained steadfast through nine US presidents—five Republican and four Democratic—and three Singapore prime ministers ... We will maintain these bipartisan links with whichever party wins the elections in November."[64] Although it is still too early to ascertain the Trump administration's Asia policy (it is somewhat wobbly at this point), going by President Trump's remark about Singapore, the relationship will remain steady and sturdy. In June 2017, leaders of the bipartisan

---

[60] "China Lauds Singapore's 'Positive', 'Constructive' Role as Asean Coordinator", *Straits Times*, 6 Aug. 2017; "China Places Great Importance on Ties with S'pore: Premier Li", *Straits Times*, 20 Sept. 2017.

[61] Campbell, *The Pivot*, pp. 220–1.

[62] "Singapore a Solid-Rock Partner, Says US President Obama", *Straits Times*, 3 Aug. 2016.

[63] "Trump Nominates KT McFarland as US Ambassador to Singapore", 20 May 2017, http://www.channelnewsasia.com/news/singapore/trump-nominates-kt-mcfarland-as-us-ambassador-to-singapore-8867110, accessed 6 Sept. 2017.

[64] "Singapore a Solid-Rock Partner".

Congressional Singapore Caucus stressed the importance of maintaining the close relationship between the United States and Singapore.[65]

Sino-Vietnamese relations have been discussed in previous chapters. Suffice it to say here that despite the South China Sea dispute and "despite courting the United States, Vietnam won't break up with China", as Tuong Vu argued. While this author would not agree with Tuong Vu that the ideological connection glues Vietnam and China together, geographical proximity would certainly require Vietnam to manage adroitly its relations with its large neighbour.[66] As Thayer explained, although there had been calls for Vietnam to come out from China's shadow, that was impossible because the two countries shared a common border and because Vietnam had a huge trade deficit with China, in excess of US$32 billion.[67]

Enter President Donald Trump

The third major development in the international politics of Southeast Asia was the electoral victory of Donald Trump (over Hillary Clinton) on 8 November 2016 to become the 45th president of the United States. Much has been said and written about the Trump presidency. What is most pertinent for us is its impact on US-Southeast Asia relations and the international politics of the region. A 275-page report commissioned by the US Congress, prepared by the Center for Strategic Studies and published in January 2016, noted that the United States needed to expand its military presence in Asia-Pacific "to balance the

---

[65] "Singapore Key to US-Asia Relations: Congress Leaders", *Straits Times*, 8 June 2017. For an exposition of the geopolitics of the region and Singapore's relations with the United States and China, see speech by K. Shanmugam, minister for home affairs and minister of law, Asia Economic Forum on "The One-Belt One-Road Initiative: Impact and Implications", 28 Aug. 2017, https://www.mha.gov.sg/newsroom/speeches/Pages/Asia-Economic-Forum-on-The-One-Belt-One-Road-Initiative-Impact-and-Implications.aspx, accessed 6 Sept. 2017.

[66] Tuong Vu, "Vietnam and China: Balancing Geography and History", *YaleGlobal Online*, 24 Aug. 2017, http://yaleglobal.yale.edu/content/vietnam-and-china-balancing-geography-and-history, accessed 6 Sept. 2017. See also Do Thanh Hai, "Vietnam: Riding the Chinese Tide", *Pacific Review* 31, 2 (2018), http://www.tandfonline.com/doi/full/10.1080/09512748.2017.1377282, accessed 12 Apr. 2019.

[67] Carlyle A. Thayer, "Background Briefing: ASEAN at 50: Still a Work in Progress", *Thayer Consultancy Background Brief*, 17 Aug. 2017.

shift in military power" in the region. It further noted that while Washington had taken steps "to reinforce its Asia rebalance", that was insufficient to protect US interests. The report criticized the Obama administration for its failure "to articulate a clear and coherent strategy". In sum, the report painted a bleak picture of the United States' position in the region.[68] If the situation in early 2016 was bleak, it became worse by early 2017. It is common knowledge that the Trump victory came as a shock to Southeast Asia. In the words of Ian Storey and Mustafa Izzuddin, "many, perhaps most, had expected Democratic candidate Hillary Clinton to emerge as the victor, and thus, by and large, see a continuation of the policies implemented by President Barack Obama, including his signature 'pivot' to Asia, and Southeast Asia in particular".[69] On his first working day in the Oval Office, President Trump killed the Trans-Pacific Partnership (TPP), "the signature economic pillar"[70] of the pivot, as he had promised to do on 21 November 2016 during the election campaign. While this was not devastating in the sense that it would not roll back the global free trade momentum, in the words of the six United States ambassadors who took the unusual step to send an open letter to the US Congress to support the TPP:

> [T]he blow to our strategic position is even more worrisome. This is not speculation. To turn our back on our allies and friends at this critical juncture, when the tectonic plates of regional power are shifting faster than ever, would undermine our credibility not only as a reliable trade partner, but as a leader on both sides of the Pacific. It would also create a potentially destabilizing void that might even lead to conflict, an outcome which would hurt everyone in the region, including China.[71]

In the first 100 days of the new administration the White House showed little interest in Southeast Asia, focusing much of its attention

[68] "Military Power in Asia-Pacific 'Shifting Against US'", *Straits Times*, 21 Jan. 2016.

[69] "Roundtable: The Trump Presidency and Southeast Asia", *Contemporary Southeast Asia* 39, 1 (Apr. 2017): 1.

[70] Ankit Panda, "Straight from the US State Department: The 'Pivot' to Asia Is Over", *The Diplomat*, 14 Mar. 2017.

[71] "Final Plea for the TPP", *Today*, 19 Jan. 2017. The TPP was eventually revised and signed without the United States in March 2018 and is now known as the Comprehensive and Progressive Agreement for Trans-Pacific Partnership. The region still harbours hope that Washington will join in the future.

on Northeast Asia. Evan Medeiros, Obama's top adviser on Asia, anticipated that US-ASEAN ties were heading into a "strategic drift" and advised the Southeast Asian states to "have patience, not overreact and keep engaging with the Trump administration".[72] Jonathan Stromseth wrote in May 2017 that the Trump administration "seemed to have little time" for the ten ASEAN countries "which figured prominently in the 'rebalance' policy of President Obama".[73] Washington's focus on the South China Sea also had more to do with US-China rivalry than Southeast Asia per se. In January 2017, nominee for secretary of state Rex Tillerson during his confirmation hearing said that the United States would "have to send China a clear signal that first, the island-building stops", and second, China's "access to those islands is also not going to be allowed", raising concerns that the region would enter a period of volatility.[74] US Secretary of Defence James Mattis subsequently clarified that diplomacy should be a priority in the South China Sea dispute and that "major US military action was not being considered to contend with China's assertive behavior there".[75] A very gradual change apparently began with Vice President Mike Pence's visit to Indonesia in April, followed by a number of phone calls to Southeast Asian leaders by the president. In Jakarta, Pence issued a statement that President Trump would visit Southeast Asia to attend both the US-ASEAN Summit and EAS (in the Philippines) and APEC Summit (in Vietnam) in November 2017.[76] However, the Trump administration's

[72] "US-Asean Ties Headed for Strategic Drift, Says Obama's Asia Adviser", *Straits Times*, 19 Jan. 2017.

[73] "Trump Reassures ASEAN, Previews a Broader Asia Policy", https://www.brookings.edu/blog/order-from-chaos/2017/05/12/trump-reassures-asean-previews-a-broader-asia-policy/, accessed 29 Aug. 2017.

[74] Richard Heydarian argued that if the Trump administration followed through on what Tillerson said, Manila could "outsource the costs of constraining Beijing's maritime assertiveness to Washington". See "Asean Braces for Trump", *Straits Times*, 27 Jan. 2017.

[75] "Beijing Welcomes US Call for Diplomacy on South China Sea Issue", *Straits Times*, 7 Feb. 2017.

[76] "Trump to Visit SE Asia, Attend US-Asean Summit in November", *Today*, 21 Apr. 2017. See also Thitian Pongsudhirak, "Trump's Pragmatic Pivot back to Asia", *Straits Times*, 6 June 2017; "Tillerson Visits Thailand with Focus on Ties and Pyongyang", *Straits Times*, 9 Aug. 2017; "US to Enlist Malaysia's Help to Rein in N. Korea", *Straits Times*, 9 Aug. 2017.

interest in Southeast Asia had mostly to do with developments in the Korean Peninsula, which was reminiscent of the Bush administration's renewed interest in Southeast Asia in the wake of the terrorist attacks on 11 September 2001.[77] Washington wanted the support of the ASEAN countries in dealing with Pyongyang, which had persisted in its missile tests, beginning with the firing of four ballistic missiles into the Sea of Japan on 6 March 2017.

Two polls conducted in March–April 2017, one by the Asian Research Network[78] and the other by the ISEAS-Yusof Ishak Institute (Singapore),[79] revealed the following: There was a general perception that American influence in the region was diminishing vis-à-vis China. China was seen to be the most influential player in Southeast Asia, but there was little trust that Beijing would be a good leader in maintaining peace and stability in the region. The United States, on the other hand, was no longer seen as a dependable ally and could not be relied on to uphold free trade, human rights and international law in the region. Everyone, however, viewed trade with the United States as "overwhelmingly positive" and wanted the United States to remain in the region to balance China. Hugh White was not wide of the mark when he wrote that the Trump administration's "narrowly defined 'America First' approach towards Asia has effectively ceded US leadership in the region to a rising China".[80]

On Terrorism, Southern Philippines and the Rohingya Crisis

Two other issues that need to be discussed before the end of this narrative are (a) the terrorist threat in Southeast Asia, and (b) the Rohingya crisis in Myanmar, which have consequences that could affect the cohesion of ASEAN.

---

[77] "US Wants Asean to Review Relations with N. Korea", *Straits Times*, 6 May 2017.

[78] "The Asian Research Network: Survey on America's Role in the Indo-Pacific 2017", https://www.ussc.edu.au/analysis/the-asian-research-network-survey-on-americas-role-in-the-indo-pacific, accessed 6 Sept. 2017.

[79] "How Do Southeast Asians View the Trump Administration?" https://www.iseas.edu.sg/images/centres/asc/pdf/ASCSurvey40517.pdf, accessed 6 Sept. 2017.

[80] Hugh White, "Dawn of the Post-American Order in Asia", *Straits Times*, 30 Dec. 2017.

Chapter 3 discussed how the issue of terrorism came about and how ASEAN and its constituent parts were able to manage, if not resolve, the threat. Then, the threat was from Al Qaeda. Writing in 2008, Daljit Singh noted that Southeast Asia had had "important successes in the fight against terrorism" and while "the threat has by no means been eliminated, it has been reduced compared to its peak in 2001–02".[81] From 2014, the threat from Al Qaeda was replaced by that from the Islamic State in Iraq and Syria (ISIS), which grew out of Al Qaeda and became a force of its own in early 2014. ISIS, disowned by Al Qaeda, became known to be "more brutal and more effective at controlling territory it has seized" and "more cold-blooded than Al Qaeda".[82] Some revisionist scholars, such as Stephen Walt, viewed ISIS as "a revolutionary state-building organization" as opposed to the conventional view that "its evil ensures its eventual destruction".[83]

In September 2014, ASEAN foreign ministers issued their first joint statement (although individual Southeast Asian states had condemned ISIS and its actions before) expressing concerns about the situation in Syria and Iraq, which had wrought ISIS. The ISIS threat was moving closer to Southeast Asia. The Abu Sayyaf group in the Philippines had pledged allegiance to ISIS, and a number of Malaysians were reported to be heading to Syria to fight alongside ISIS. Young Indonesians were reported to have been radicalized and recruited by ISIS. In the following years, more Muslims from various Southeast Asian countries would be arrested for supporting the organization.[84] In March 2015 ASEAN defence ministers signed a joint declaration to strengthen regional security, especially against threats posed by ISIS.[85] In November 2015 it was reported that wanted Malaysian militants hiding in the southern Philippines were planning to form an "official" faction of ISIS in Southeast Asia by bringing together terrorist groups in Malaysia, the

[81] "Asean Strategy Works in Keeping Terrorism at Bay", *Straits Times*, 4 Aug. 2008.

[82] "ISIS: Everything You Need to Know About the Rise of the Militant Group", 25 Sept. 2014, http://edition.cnn.com/interactive/2014/09/world/isis-explained/, accessed 13 Sept. 2017; "Islamic State Transforming into Functioning State with Terror as Tool", *Today*, 23 July 2015.

[83] "Islamic State Transforming into Functioning State with Terror as Tool".

[84] "Asean Issues First Joint Statement on ISIS Crisis", *Sunday Times*, 28 Sept. 2014; "Malaysian ISIS Suspects Are 'Fresh Recruits'", *Sunday Times*, 28 Sept. 2014.

[85] "ASEAN Ministers Sign Joint Declaration to Fight Security Threats", *Today*, 17 Mar. 2015.

Philippines and Indonesia, including Jemaah Islamiyah and Abu Sayyaf.[86] The objective was to create a caliphate in Southeast Asia. The ISIS threat appeared imminent when a series of deadly suicide bombings occurred in Jakarta on 14 January 2016, which ISIS claimed responsibility for. Analysts were divided as to whether this episode was evidence that a full-blown ISIS campaign in Southeast Asia had started. However, they agreed on two points. One, Southeast Asia was "fertile ground" for ISIS to operate given its enormous Muslim population, which made it a rich recruiting ground for disaffected Muslims. Mindanao (southern Philippines), where there has been a long-running Islamic insurgency, was flagged as a particularly soft spot that the ISIS leadership was targeting. There had also been an insurgency in southern Thailand since 2004, but so far the Thai-Muslim separatists had not shown an interest in linking up with ISIS. However, that did not mean it would never happen. Indeed, analysts warned that ISIS could exploit the present low-grade insurgency in southern Thailand.[87]

In 2016–17 the Jakarta bombings, a grenade attack outside Kuala Lumpur and an unsuccessful plot to launch a rocket attack on Marina Bay in Singapore by a Batam-based ISIS cell all brought terrorism back to the headlines.[88] The terrorism threat in Southeast Asia appeared to get more serious as ISIS lost ground in its fight in Syria and Iraq. Towards the end of 2016, ISIS was fighting to hold onto its last stronghold in Iraq, the city of Mosul.[89] In January 2017 it was reported that there was a rise in the number of Malaysians arrested for trying to join

[86] "Malaysian Militants Plan to Start ISIS Faction in S-E Asia", *Straits Times*, 15 Nov. 2015.

[87] "Conflict in Thai South Could Be Exploited by ISIS, Warn Analysts", *Straits Times*, 10 June 2017.

[88] "Jakarta Attacks: Is ISIS' Presence in South-east Asia Overstated?" *Straits Times*, 16 Jan. 2016; "Jakarta Attacks Could Mark Start of ISIS Campaign in S-E Asia", *Straits Times*, 20 Jan. 2016; Joseph Chinyong Liow, "ISIS Reaches Indonesia: The Terrorist Group's Prospects in Southeast Asia", *Foreign Affairs*, 8 Feb. 2016; "'JI, Not ISIS, Is Bigger Threat' to South-east Asia", *Straits Times*, 29 Apr. 2016; "ISIS 'May Set up Caliphate in S-E Asia'", *Straits Times*, 30 Apr. 2016; "S-E Asia Could Be Next ISIS Battleground, Say Experts", *Straits Times*, 26 Oct. 2016; "ISIS Plan for Mindanao Poses Threat to Indonesia", *Straits Times*, 8 Dec. 2016; "Manila Finds Strong Links Between ISIS and Rebels in South", *Straits Times*, 11 Feb. 2017.

[89] "ISIS Losing Ground, but Extending Reach", *Sunday Times*, 20 Nov. 2016; "ISIS Terror Threat Greater Now, Says Shanmugam", *Straits Times*, 3 Dec. 2016.

ISIS.[90] In September 2017 ISIS issued a recruitment video featuring a Singaporean fighter (who left Singapore in 2014 for the Middle East, where he—one of three Singaporeans so far—was supposedly radicalized). Terrorism experts were of the view that the video showed that ISIS was focusing on Southeast Asia.[91] Meanwhile, analysts noted that Jemaah Islamiyah, which was prominent in the early 2000s and was responsible for the 2002 Bali bombings, was "regaining strength" in Indonesia, and while it was not an immediate threat it "could spawn a new generation of extremists".[92]

In May 2017 fighting flared up in Marawi, a mainly Muslim city in the southern Philippines, after security forces raided an apartment to arrest Isnilon Hapilon, who analysts believed to be the top ISIS representative in Southeast Asia. This led President Duterte to declare martial law across Mindanao. Abu Sayyaf and a new group known as Maute, both allied to ISIS, were fighting together in Marawi. It was reported in June that Indonesian militants were fighting alongside Maute combatants.[93] There was a fear that if the Islamic militants were not contained, the terrorist threat might spread to Singapore, Malaysia and Indonesia. At the same time, if defeated, the militants could escape to the neighbouring states.[94]

Finally, there is the Rohingya crisis in Myanmar. Like the insurgencies in southern Thailand and southern Philippines, the Rohingya crisis is a domestic issue with a long history that has regional, if not international, ramifications. Space does not allow us to delve into the origins and history of the Rohingya issue here, except to note that the Myanmar government does not recognize the Rohingya as one of its 135 ethnic groups and there has been a long-standing animosity between

---

[90] "Rise in Number of Malaysians Arrested for Trying to Join ISIS", *Straits Times*, 2 Jan. 2017.

[91] "Latest Video a Sign of ISIS' Focus on South-east Asia: Experts", *Straits Times*, 25 Sept. 2017.

[92] "JI 'Regaining Strength' in Indonesia", *Today*, 28 Apr. 2017.

[93] "Indonesian Militants' Presence in Marawi City Sparks Alarm", *Straits Times*, 12 June 2017.

[94] "Defeat of Rebels in Marawi Could Spell More Trouble for S-E Asia, Say Analysts", *Today*, 30 May 2017. In August 2018 President Duterte signed a law (that enforced the 2014 peace deal with the Moro Islamic Liberation Front) granting greater autonomy to Muslims in the southern Philippines. The autonomous region is known as Bangsamoro.

Buddhists and Rohingya Muslims. For our purposes, a convenient place to begin would be Myanmar's transition to relative democracy from 2011. One unintended consequence was the rise of extremist Buddhist groups, which led to the revival of sectarian violence between the Buddhists and Rohingya Muslims in Rakhine State in June 2012. Three Muslims, two of whom were allegedly Rohingya, raped a Rakhine woman, which led to revenge attacks. The Myanmar government took the side of the ethnic Arakan Buddhists.[95] The conflict simmered and flared up again on 9 October 2016, when a few hundred men crossed from Bangladesh into Rakhine State and attacked three border guard posts, killed nine police officers and stole thousands of bullets. The Myanmar government came down heavily on the Rohingya, as it had always done since 1962. Kuala Lumpur went as far as to accuse the Myanmar army of "genocide".[96] Apart from human rights concerns—there were reports in late 2016 of hundreds of thousands of Rohingya being displaced and crossing over into Bangladesh; complete villages being razed to the ground; rape, torture and murder by the Myanmar military—there was the worry that ISIS could exploit the Rohingya crisis if the issue was not resolved.[97] In its December 2016 report, the International Crisis Group warned that continued use of disproportionate force without any effort at reconciliation could create "conditions to further radicalize sections of the Rohingya population that transnational jihadists could exploit for their own agenda".[98] The situation has only worsened. In September 2017 UN Secretary-General Antonio Guterres, in a letter to the Security Council, warned of the "risk of ethnic cleansing in Myanmar".[99] UN High Commissioner for Human Rights Zeid Ra'ad al-Hussein, in fact, described the actions of the Myanmar military as "a textbook example of ethnic cleansing".[100]

---

[95] "The Government Could Have Stopped This", 31 July 2012, https://www.hrw.org/report/2012/07/31/government-could-have-stopped/sectarian-violence-and-ensuing-abuses-burmas-arakan, accessed 15 Sept. 2017.

[96] "UN Calls on Suu Kyi to Visit Crisis-Hit Rakhine", *Straits Times*, 10 Dec. 2016.

[97] "ISIS Could Exploit Rohingya Crisis: KL", *Straits Times*, 9 Dec. 2016; "Malaysia Warns of ISIS Threat to Myanmar", *Straits Times*, 5 Jan. 2017.

[98] Cited in Jera Lego, "Why Asean Can't Ignore the Rohingya Crisis", *The Diplomat*, 17 May 2017.

[99] "Myanmar Crisis Could 'Unsettle Region'", *Straits Times*, 7 Sept. 2017.

[100] "UN Official Slams 'Textbook Ethnic Cleansing' in Myanmar", *Straits Times*, 12 Sept. 2017.

ASEAN has so far not been able to play an effective role in addressing the crisis. As Hoang Thi Ha noted, "For years, Asean's response to the Rohingya problem has been mute and passive, constrained by its non-intervention principle ... It is increasingly untenable for Asean to insulate itself from this thorny matter behind the shield of non-interference", particularly "as the region is getting more connected and integrated".[101]

It was against the above setting that ASEAN celebrated the 50th year of its founding in 2017. It is also where we end this book. Not surprisingly, celebrations were muted given the immense and difficult challenges faced by the organization, internal and external. The pursuit of a post-Cold War order centred on ASEAN remains the goal. As this book has shown and others have pointed out, "it has to be earned rather than simply assumed or proclaimed ... there can be no ASEAN centrality without ASEAN unity and ASEAN neutrality".[102] Can ASEAN stay united? Kishore Mahbubani, in his commemorative book marking ASEAN's 50th year,[103] wrote that the things holding the organization together were fear, luck and golf. Of the three, fear and luck remain pertinent. The fear of China, for one, will keep ASEAN intact. As George Yeo eloquently put it:

> We [ASEAN] are being driven together not so much by a natural affection for one another as by the huge challenges which confront us collectively. Either we accept a common destiny, or we will be cast aside with individual Asean countries having to strike separate deals with different major powers. A divided Asean will see all of them jostling for power and influence in the region.[104]

As for ASEAN neutrality, much depends on the actions of external powers (which are outside the control of the ASEAN countries), particularly the United States, and this is where perhaps luck will play a part.

---

[101] "What Can Asean Do About the Rohingya Crisis?" *Today*, 22 Dec. 2016. See also Lego, "Why Asean Can't Ignore the Rohingya Crisis".

[102] Acharya, "Myth of ASEAN Centrality?": 279; "ASEAN's Biggest Challenge Is to Stay United: Tommy Koh", 8 Aug. 2017, http://www.channelnewsasia.com/news/singapore/asean-s-biggest-challenge-is-to-stay-united-tommy-koh-9105084, accessed 22 Sept. 2017.

[103] Kishore Mahbubani and Jeffery Sng, *The ASEAN Miracle: A Catalyst for Peace* (Singapore: NUS Press, 2017).

[104] George Yeo, "Repositioning Asean for a New World", *Straits Times*, 8 Sept. 2005.

Conclusion

This book focuses on the international politics of Southeast Asia from 1990 to 2017 from the perspectives of the Southeast Asian states. It weaves together multiple issues as they emerge and develop into what I hope in the end is a coherent and readable narrative. As stated in the Introduction, the objective of the book is to describe the international politics of Southeast Asia from the early post-Cold War years—the goals and aspirations of the regional states, and the extent to which those goals were achieved over a span of almost 30 years. During those years there were many developments within each Southeast Asian country, such as changes of government, ethnic strife, and natural and man-made disasters. Important as these were within the context of each country's history, this book refers to them only when they affect regional or international politics in significant ways.

The book has eight chapters starting with an account of what Southeast Asia was like in 1990, when the Cold War officially ended. Following that, the chapters move through vicissitudes, twists and turns over the last almost 30 years. Everyone may like to believe that life moves forward towards an end goal, but in reality, just as the French philosopher and historian Paul Ricoeur noted, "There is no story if our attention is not moved along by a thousand contingencies."[1] Along the course, "a thousand contingencies" can delay, change and even derail the final expectation, for example, the emergence of Donald Trump (chapter 8), whom Henry Kissinger memorably describes as "one of those figures in history who appears from time to time to mark the end of an era and to force it to give up its old pretences". Kissinger opined,

[1] Paul Ricoeur, "Narrative Time", *Critical Enquiry* 7, 1 (Autumn 1980): 174.

"it doesn't necessarily mean that he knows this, or that he is considering any great alternative. It could just be an accident."[2]

The substantial narrative ends in 2017. In *The Sense of an Ending*, Frank Kermode argues that we use narratives to make sense of our world, and endings are necessary to narratives because they make sense of what has gone before.[3] The year 2017 is an appropriate place to end as it marked the 50th anniversary of the formation of ASEAN, which started as a subregional organization during the Cold War before it became a full-fledged regional organization in 1999, almost a decade after the Cold War ended. Anniversaries are generally an appropriate time for looking back and looking forward. Reflecting on the past three decades covered in this book, the Southeast Asian states together have been attempting to do two things simultaneously: (a) develop a strong and cohesive region, and (b) construct a new regional order to replace the Cold War structures. The two are related.

The first is in the hands of the ASEAN states. In the words of former Indonesian Foreign Minister Natalegawa, writing about the evolution of ASEAN from 1967 to the present, "Countries or issues are not predetermined to be permanently mired in vicious dynamics; nor however are they perpetually ensconced in a virtuous setting. The dynamics are the direct outcomes of policy decisions and policy choices."[4] The ASEAN states have, however, been slow in achieving the first objective. One can argue that developments outside their control slowed the process, for example, the formation of ASEAN-10 coincided with the Asian Financial Crisis (chapter 2); and just at the cusp of its recovery, September 11 occurred (chapter 3). However, it is also true that had it not been for the financial crisis, ASEAN would probably not have speeded up its economic integration. Another example, as pointed out by George Yeo, former foreign minister of Singapore, is how Kevin Rudd's proposal for a new Asia Pacific Community catalyzed the

---

[2] "Henry Kissinger, 'We Are in a Very, Very Grave Period'", 20 July 2018, https://www.ft.com/content/926a66b0-8b49-11e8-bf9e-8771d5404543, accessed 17 Aug. 2018.

[3] Frank Kermode quoted in John Ellis, *Documentary: Witness and Self-revelation* (London: Routledge, 2011), p. 69.

[4] Natalegawa, *Does ASEAN Matter?* p. 3.

ASEAN decision on whether to include the United States and Russia in the EAS (chapter 4). Looking back to before 1990, there were two other occasions when ASEAN was jolted into action. In the wake of the fall of Saigon in 1975, ASEAN finally convened the first head of state summit ten years after its formation. It is common knowledge that the Vietnamese invasion and subsequent occupation of Kampuchea was a key factor in the growth of ASEAN's unity and credibility in the 1980s.[5] In sum, it would appear that ASEAN only reacts quickly and effectively when it is confronted with an existential threat—of disintegrating or being sidelined. ASEAN's greatest fear is to be sidelined. It therefore needs to be more proactive. In the last 30 years, ASEAN was most proactive in the early 1990s.

The second objective is much harder for ASEAN to control because it involves external powers, most, if not all of them, larger than the sum total of ASEAN. It requires their buy-in. It is indeed a rather prolonged order transition. Since the end of the Cold War, ASEAN has spearheaded the formation of multiple and overlapping scaffoldings or platforms (described throughout the book) to replace the Cold War structures. Why is there the need for so many, one may ask. This is because the region is still exploring and experimenting in the search for a new post-Cold War order, for example with the ASEAN Regional Forum (ARF), the first regional security platform, which marked its 25th anniversary in 2018. After a quarter century, it is stuck at the second stage of its development, unable to move beyond the Preventive Diplomacy stage to that of Conflict Resolution, the ultimate goal of the ARF (chapter 4). Consequently, the US, Japan, Australia and India have come up with their own initiatives, such as the quadrilateral security cooperation under the Free and Open Indo-Pacific (FOIP) concept, "as a potential parallel track to the ARF".[6] This threatens to sideline the Southeast Asian states, which ASEAN is sensitive about. The swift dismissal of the Rudd and White proposals (chapter 6)

---

[5] See Ang, *Southeast Asia's Cold War*.

[6] Termsak Chalermpalanupap, "The ASEAN Regional Forum: Genesis, Development, and Challenges", *ASEAN Matters for All of Us*, Issue 3 (6 Aug.) (Singapore: Institute of Southeast Asian Studies, 2018); Lucio Blanco Pilo III, "Making a 'Free Open Indo-Pacific' Appealing to Southeast Asia", https://amti.csis.org/making-foip-appealing-southeast-asia/, accessed 17 Aug. 2018.

showed how sensitive ASEAN is over the slightest whiff of being relegated to secondary importance. Meanwhile, ASEAN has initiated the ADMM-Plus, which addresses "the same non-traditional security challenges as the ARF"[7] (chapter 4). ASEAN will, therefore, as Termsak Chalermpalanupap rightly pointed out, need to re-examine its modus operandi if it wants to create an order that is ASEAN-led or ASEAN-centred. According to Natalegawa, "in the immediate future, ASEAN needs to contend with an apparent 'lag' or 'gap' between reliance on the so-called 'ASEAN way' and a more formal rule-based ASEAN".[8] If Natalegawa is right, the gap between the two is unlikely to close soon. The question is whether the two need to be mutually exclusive.

Looking forward, having listened to and conversed with many scholars and regional analysts, my key takeaway is the word "uncertainty". There are a number of balls—perhaps too many—in the air, and no one is certain where and how they will land: How will the FOIP idea evolve? Will there be a bounded or more inclusive order in the region?[9] Whether there will be a code of conduct for the South China Sea in the near future remains uncertain. Many would agree with Natalegawa that how well ASEAN negotiates the code of conduct with China will be "the litmus test for ASEAN".[10] Will East Timor eventually become the 11th member of ASEAN?[11] Another unknown is the important question of political leadership in ASEAN.[12] Yet another uncertainty is the effect of Trump's "America First" policy on the region. Perhaps the biggest ball in the air is the growing Sino-US rivalry. It is clear that China is determined to be the dominant power in the region, while

[7] Termsak Chalermpalanupap, "ASEAN Regional Forum".

[8] Natalegawa, *Does ASEAN Matter?* p. 3.

[9] See John J. Mearsheimer, "The Rise and Fall of the Liberal International Order", paper presented at Notre Dame International Security Center, 11 Sept. 2018, for a useful discussion of "order", https://ndisc.nd.edu/assets/288231/rise_and_fall_of_the_liberal_international_order.september_11_2018.pdf, accessed 8 Jan. 2019.

[10] Natalegawa, *Does ASEAN Matter?* pp. 115, 139. On 3 August 2018, ASEAN and China announced an agreement on a Single Draft South China Sea Code of Conduct Negotiating Text, finally opening the way for the start of negotiations on the elusive code of conduct.

[11] For a discussion by an insider, see Natalegawa, *Does ASEAN Matter?* pp. 61–6.

[12] See chapter 4.

the United States is unwilling to concede its predominant status.[13] Will ASEAN be able to continue its balancing act between these two powers? Going by the view of Singapore's most internationally known diplomat, Tommy Koh, who generally exudes optimism and has been described as a "pragmatic idealist", it would be extremely challenging.[14] Koh hoped that "wisdom will prevail in the Asean family", echoing Natalegawa, who wrote of "the responsibility of ASEAN's current decision-makers not to fail ASEAN's future generations".[15]

In *Destined for War? Can America and China Escape Thucydides's Trap?* Allison argues that the United States and China are headed towards a war neither wants (although, in his view, war is not inevitable).[16] The book has generated much discussion, not unlike Kennedy's *The Rise and Fall of the Great Powers* and scholars who wrote about the "China Threat" thesis in the early 1990s. Jean-Pierre Lehmann describes the period we now live in as not "post-Cold War" but "pre-war" (although, like Allison, he argues that war in Asia is not a foregone conclusion). Recalling the debate over the origins of World War I, Lehman notes that "there are always choices" but "the problem was that many wrong choices were made then and are made now".[17] Here I am reminded of E.H. Carr's *The Twenty Years' Crisis, 1919–1939*, which, as I mentioned in the Introduction, inspired me to write this book. Carr wrote that although "war was already casting its shadow in the world", all was not yet lost, as there was hope to avert it. Carr's book reached the page proofs stage when World War II broke out in Europe. We should be

---

[13] Sino-US relations have deteriorated significantly from 2018. This is especially manifested in the ongoing spat over trade issues.

[14] "An Independent, United and Neutral Asean is Key for Singapore and the Region: Tommy Koh", *Straits Times*, 16 Aug. 2018, https://www.straitstimes.com/singapore/an-independent-united-and-neutral-asean-is-key-for-singapore-and-the-region-tommy-koh, accessed 20 Aug. 2018.

[15] Natalegawa, *Does ASEAN Matter?* p. 131.

[16] Allison, *Destined for War?*

[17] Jean-Pierre Lehmann, "Learn from History to Scatter Asia's Gathering Clouds of War", *Straits Times*, 11 Oct. 2016. Lehman used World War I as his analogy. See also Thitinan Pongsudhirak, "Will Asia-Pacific Tensions Lead to Conflict?" *Today*, 1 Sept. 2016. Thitinan argued that "short of new rules and institutions that can govern the Asia-Pacific, the regional states will likely be heading towards dangerous outcomes that used to be unthinkable not too long ago".

prepared to ponder the improbable. To borrow the title of a song by Primal Fear, "Don't Say You've Never Been Warned".[18] Some analysts have pointed out that we are moving into a "New Cold War" period (or some version of it), describing US Vice President Mike Pence's 4 October 2018 speech on the Trump administration's policy towards China as another edition of Winston Churchill's 1946 Iron Curtain speech.[19] Kenneth Waltz reminds us that "the origins of hot wars lie in cold wars, and the origins of cold wars are found in the anarchic ordering of the international arena".[20] There is also a view that with "modern and future wars, there is no war or peace—only *war and peace*", and perhaps we are already living in this new environment.[21]

Southeast Asia appears to be once again, to borrow the words of S. Rajaratnam (Singapore's first foreign minister) writing on a different period:

> … standing uncertainly at the cross-roads scrutinising signboards that point not in one but many directions … We know that they are all pointing in definite directions. But only one of them is pointing in

[18] See https://genius.com/Primal-fear-dont-say-youve-never-been-warned-lyrics, accessed 7 Nov. 2018.

[19] "Pence's China Speech as Portent of 'New Cold War'", *New York Times*, 5 Oct. 2018; Walter Russell Mead, "Mike Pence Announces Cold War II", *Wall Street Journal*, 8 Oct. 2018; Mie Oba, "The Unpredictable, Conflicting Structure of the New Cold War", *The Diplomat*, 29 Dec. 2018. Not all agree. See, for example, Odd Arne Westad, "Has a New Cold War Really Begun? Why the Term Shouldn't Apply to Today's Great-Power Tensions", https://www.foreignaffairs.com/articles/china/2018-03-27/has-new-cold-war-really-begun, accessed 3 Jan. 2019; Harish C. Mehta, "Is There a 'New Cold War' in Asia Between China and the United States?" *Calcutta Journal of International Affairs* 3, 1 (Jan. 2019), https://www.globaljournalceners.org/article.php?e=52, accessed 4 Jan. 2019; "Joseph Nye: China, US Not in 'Cold War', but Cooperative Rivalry", http://www.china.org.cn/world/2019-01/11/content_74364478.htm, accessed 18 Jan. 2019.

[20] Kenneth N. Waltz, "The Origins of War in Neorealist Theory", *Journal of Interdisciplinary History* 18, 4 (Spring 1988): 620. See also Richard Haass, "How a World Ends, and What Comes in Its Wake", *Foreign Affairs*, Jan./Feb. 2019, https://www.foreignaffairs.com/articles/2018-12-11/how-world-order-ends, accessed 17 Dec. 2018.

[21] R. Jordan Prescott, "Goodbye Conventional War. It's Been Fun", https://mwi.usma.edu/goodbye-conventional-war-fun/, accessed 22 Mar. 2019.

> the right direction and we shall never know which one until we get there—or what is more likely, we do not get there.[22]

It is my hope that the reader will have gained a better understanding of the international politics of Southeast Asia in the nearly 30 years after the Cold War ended, how events unfolded, and how we arrived at where we are today. As David C. McCullough wrote, "History is a guide to navigation in perilous times",[23] and indeed, we live in perilous times.[24]

---

[22] "Opening Address by Mr S. Rajaratnam, Minister for Foreign Affairs of the Republic of Singapore", in *New Directions in the International Relations of Southeast Asia: The Great Powers and Southeast Asia*, ed. Lau Teik Soon (Singapore: Institute of Southeast Asian Studies, 1973).

[23] The quote is from https://www.goodreads.com/quotes/113207-history-is-a-guide-to-navigation-in-perilous-times-history, accessed 21 Sept. 2017.

[24] According to Henry Kissinger, we are living in an extremely grave period. "Henry Kissinger: 'We Are in a Very, Very Grave Period'".

Glossary

ADIZ	Air Defence Identification Zone
ADMM	ASEAN Defence Ministers Meeting
ADMM-Plus	ASEAN Defence Ministers Meeting-Plus
AEC	ASEAN Economic Community
AFTA	ASEAN Free Trade Area
APEC	Asia-Pacific Economic Cooperation
APT	ASEAN Plus Three
ARF	ASEAN Regional Forum
ASC	ASEAN Security Community
ASCC	ASEAN Socio-Cultural Community
ASEM	Asia-Europe Meeting
BRI	Belt and Road Initiative
CAFTA	Central America Free Trade Agreement
CBM	Confidence Building Measures
COC	Code of Conduct
CPP	Cambodian People's Party
CPTPP	Comprehensive and Progressive Agreement for Trans-Pacific Partnership
CSIS	Centre for Strategic and International Studies
DOC	Declaration on the Conduct of Parties in the South China Sea
DOD	Department of Defense
EAEC	East Asian Economic Caucus
EAEG	East Asian Economic Group
EAI	Enterprise for ASEAN Initiative
EAS	East Asia Summit
EASR	East Asian Strategy Reports
EASI	East Asia Strategic Initiative
FOIP	Free and Open Indo-Pacific

FTA	Free Trade Agreement
FTAAP	Free Trade Area of the Asia-Pacific
FUNCINPEC	National United Front for an Independent, Neutral, Peaceful and Cooperative Cambodia
ICG	International Crisis Group
IDSS	Institute of Defence and Strategic Studies
IISS	International Institute for Strategic Studies
ISIS	Islamic State in Iraq and Syria
JMSU	Joint Maritime Seismic Undertaking
NLD	National League for Democracy
NSC	National Security Council
NTS	Non-traditional Security
OBOR	One Belt One Road
PD	Preventive Diplomacy
PLAN	People's Liberation Army Navy
RCEP	Regional Comprehensive Economic Partnership
RSIS	S. Rajaratnam School of International Studies
SLORC	State Law and Order Restoration Council
TPP	Trans-Pacific Partnership
UNCLOS	United Nations Convention on the Law of the Sea
WTO	World Trade Organization
ZOPFAN	Zone of Peace, Freedom and Neutrality

Selected Bibliography

Articles

"A Landmark Decision in the South China Sea: The Scope and Implications of the Arbitral Tribunal's Award". *Contemporary Southeast* Asia 38, 3 (Dec. 2016).

"ARF Senior Officials Agree on Membership Criteria". *Straits Times*, 11 May 1996.

"ASEAN Charter: The Model Decision". *Straits Times*, 9 Sept. 2005.

"ASEAN Defense Ministers' Meeting (ADMM) and ADMM Plus: A Japanese Perspective". *NIDS Journal of Defense and Security* 14 (Dec. 2013).

"ASEAN Faces Difficulty in Beijing Negotiations: Divisions Within Group Block Consensus on Code for South China Sea". *Wall Street Journal Asia*, 1 Aug. 2002.

"Asian Financial Crisis and China". *Hong Kong Ta Kung Pao*, 2 Nov. 1998, FBIS-CHI-98-310.

"Call to Set up Regional Security Forum". *Straits Times*, 19 Jan. 1992.

"Cambodia-Thailand Sovereignty Disputes: Implications for Cambodia's Strategic Environment and Defence Organisation". *Strategic Analysis* 41, 2 (2017).

"Can S-E Asia Ride the Next FDI Wave?" *Straits Times*, 9 June 2007.

"CSCAP Retreat: Reviewing of Regional Security Order and Architecture". *Think Tank* 40 (Apr. 2017), S. Rajaratnam School of International Studies.

"Deputy Foreign Minister Vu Khoan's Exclusive Interview". *Vietnam Southeast Asia Today*, Special Issue, 25 July 1995.

"G. Barraclough, 76, Historian". *New York Times*, 10 Jan. 1985, http://www.nytimes.com/1985/01/10/world/g-barraclough-76-historian.html, accessed 30 Mar. 2016.

"Inevitable That Asean Membership Will Grow: KL Minister". *Straits Times*, 17 Jan. 1992.

"Korea and Kashmir Clashes 'Too Big' for ARF". *Straits Times*, 20 June 1999.

"Pavlovian Conditioning and 'Correct Thinking' on the South China Sea". *Straits Times*, 1 Apr. 2016.

"Reaction to SRV Offer to Host ASEAN Summit". *The Nation*, 30 Nov. 1995, *FBIS-EAS*-95-231.

"Reassessing Multilateralism: A New Agenda for the ASEAN Regional Forum: A Report of the IDSS Project on the Future of the ASEAN Regional Forum". Singapore: Institute of Defence and Strategic Studies, June 2002.

"Regional Perspective: Making the ARF Relevant Post-September 11". *The Nation*, 8 July 2002.

"Roundtable: The ADMM-Plus and the Future of Defense Diplomacy". *Asia Policy* 22 (July 2016).

"Settle Spratlys Dispute Amicably: ASEAN Ministers". *Straits Times*, 22 July 1992.

"S'pore to Push for More Talks Among Members with Dialogue Partners". *Straits Times*, 27 July 1992.

"Spratlys Declaration 'Gives Asean New Role in Dispute'". *Straits Times*, 31 July 1992.

"What Makes the 4th Asean Summit Historic". *Straits Times*, 23 Jan. 1992.

Abuza, Zachary. "Tentacles of Terror: Al Qaeda's Southeast Asian Network". *Contemporary Southeast Asia* 24, 3 (2002): 427–65.

Acharya, Amitav. "The Myth of ASEAN Centrality?" *Contemporary Southeast Asia: A Journal of International & Strategic Affairs* 39, 2 (2017): 273–9.

Ad'ha Aljunied Syed Mohammed. "Countering Terrorism in Maritime Southeast Asia: Soft and Hard Power Approaches". *Journal of Asian & African Studies* 47, 6 (2012): 652–65.

Ahmad, Zakaria Haji and Baladas Ghoshal. "The Political Future of ASEAN After the Asian Crisis". *International Affairs* 75, 4 (1999): 759–78.

Amer Ramses. "The South China Sea: Achievements and Challenges to Dispute Management". *Asian Survey* 55, 3 (2015): 618–39.

Ang Cheng Guan. "The South China Sea Dispute Revisited". *Australian Journal of International Affairs* 54, 2 (July 2000).

Ba, Alice D. "Southeast Asia in an Age of Strategic Uncertainty: Legal Rulings, Domestic Impulses, and the Ongoing Pursuit of Autonomy". *Southeast Asian Affairs* (2017): 3–17.

Barro, Robert J. "The East Asian Tigers Have Plenty to Roar About". *BusinessWeek*, 27 Apr. 1998, p. 24.

Bellamy, A. and C. Drummond. "The Responsibility to Protect in Southeast Asia: Between Non-interference and Sovereignty as Responsibility". *Pacific Review* 24, 2 (2011): 179–200.

Blumenson, Martin. "Can Official History Be Honest History?" *Military Affairs* 26, 4 (Winter 1962–63): 158.

Bull, Hedley and Adam Watson, eds. *Expansion of International Society*. Oxford: Oxford University Press, 1984.

Castro, Renato Cruz De. "China, the Philippines, and US Influence in Asia". *Asian Outlook* 2 (July 2017).

Catterall, Peter. "What (if Anything) Is Distinctive About Contemporary History?" *Journal of Contemporary History* 32, 4 (1997).

Cheeseman, Graeme. "Asian-Pacific Security Discourse in the Wake of the Asian Economic Crisis". *Pacific Review* 12, 3 (1999): 333–56.

Chong, Ian. "Deconstructing Order in Southeast Asia in the Age of Trump". *Contemporary Southeast Asia: A Journal of International & Strategic Affairs* 39, 1 (2017): 29–35.

Ciorciari, John D. "ASEAN and the Great Powers". *Contemporary Southeast Asia: A Journal of International & Strategic Affairs* 39, 2 (2017): 252–8.

Davenport, T. "Legal Implications of the South China Sea Award for Maritime Southeast Asia". *Australia Year Book of International Law* 34 (2016): 65–86.

Davies, Mathew. "An Agreement to Disagree: The ASEAN Human Rights Declaration and the Absence of Regional Identity in Southeast Asia". *Journal of Current Southeast Asian Affairs* 33, 3 (2014): 107–29.

Denoon, David B.H. and Evelyn Colbert. "Challenges for the Association of Southeast Asian Nations (ASEAN)". *Pacific Affairs* 71, 4 (Winter 1998–99): 505.

Desker, Barry. "Is the ARF Obsolete? Three Moves to Avoid Irrelevance". *IDSS Commentaries*, 20 July 2006.

Dibb, Paul. "The End of the Asian Miracle? Will the Current Economic Crisis Lead to Political and Social Instability?" *SDSC Newsletter*, Summer 1998, p. 1.

———. "The Prospects for Southeast Asia's Security". ANU, SDSC Working Paper no. 347, June 2000.

Dibb, P., D. Hale and P. Prince. "The Strategic Implications of Asia's Economic Crisis". *Survival* 40, 2 (Summer 1998): 5–26.

Dillon, Dana R. "Countering Beijing in the South China Sea". *Policy Review* 167 (2011): 51–67.

Emmers, Ralf. "Regional Hegemonies and the Exercise of Power in Southeast Asia: A Study of Indonesia and Vietnam". *Asian Survey* 45, 4 (2005): 645–65.

———. "ASEAN Regional Forum: Time to Move Towards Preventive Diplomacy". *IDSS/RSIS Commentaries*, 25 Oct. 2007.

———. "Indonesia's Role in ASEAN: A Case of Incomplete and Sectorial Leadership". *Pacific Review* 27, 4 (2014): 543–62.

Emmers, Ralf and See Seng Tan. "The ASEAN Regional Forum and Preventive Diplomacy: Built to Fail?" *Asian Security* 7, 11 (1 Nov. 2011): 44–60.

Emmerson, Donald K. "Mapping ASEAN's Futures". *Contemporary Southeast Asia: A Journal of International & Strategic Affairs* 39, 2 (2017): 280–7.

Evans, Richard J. "The Journal of Contemporary History and Its Editors". *Journal of Contemporary History* 50, 4 (2015): 710–37.

Febrica, Senia. "Securitizing Terrorism in Southeast Asia: Accounting for the Varying Responses of Singapore and Indonesia". *Asian Survey* 50, 3 (2010): 569–90.

Finnbogason, Daniel and Isak Svensson. "The Missing Jihad: Why Have There Been No Jihadist Civil Wars in Southeast Asia?" *Pacific Review* 31, 1 (2018): 96–115.

Foot, Rosemary. "China in the ASEAN Regional Forum: Organisational Processes and Domestic Modes of Thought". *Asian Survey* 38, 5 (May 1998): 425–40.

Graham, Euan. "Southeast Asia in the US Rebalance: Perceptions from a Divided Region". *Contemporary Southeast Asia* 35, 3 (2013): 305–32.

Hamilton-Hart, Natasha. "Deal-makers and Spoilers: Trump and Regime Security in Southeast Asia". *Contemporary Southeast Asia: A Journal of International & Strategic Affairs* 39, 1 (2017): 42–9.

Hara, Kimie. "Rethinking the 'Cold War' in the Asia-Pacific". *Pacific Review* 12, 4 (1999): 515–36.

Hart, Bradley W. "The Journal of Contemporary History: Fifty Years of Change and Continuity". *Journal of Contemporary History* 50, 4 (2015): 738–49.

Hartnett, Stephen K. and Bryan Reckard. "Sovereign Tropes: A Rhetorical Critique of Contested Claims in the South China Sea". *Rhetoric & Public Affairs* 20, 2 (2017): 291–337.

Haslam, Jonathan. "The Cold War as History". *Annual Review of Political Science* 6 (2003): 77–98.

Hassan, Mohamed Jawher. *A Pacific Peace: Issues and Responses: Papers Presented at the 11th Asia-Pacific Roundtable, 5–8 June 1997, Kuala Lumpur*. Kuala Lumpur: Institut Kajian Strategi Dan Antarabangsa, 1998.

Hongzhou Zhang and Sam Bateman. "Fishing Militia, the Securitization of Fishery and the South China Sea Dispute". *Contemporary Southeast Asia: A Journal of International & Strategic Affairs* 39, 2 (2017): 288–314.

Johnes, Martin. "On Writing Contemporary History". *North American Journal of Welsh Studies* 6, 1 (Winter 2011).

———. "Category: Contemporary History", 12 Sept. 2017, https://martinjohnes.wordpress.com/category/contemporary-history/, accessed 28 Mar. 2019.

Jones, Catherine. "Great Powers, ASEAN, and Security: Reason for Optimism?" *Pacific Review* 28, 2 (2015): 259–80.

Jonsson, Kristina. "Unity-in-Diversity? Regional Identity-Building in Southeast Asia". *Journal of Current Southeast Asian Affairs* 29, 2 (2010): 41–72.

Kandiah, Michael D. "Contemporary History". Making History, http://www.history.ac.uk/makinghistory/resources/articles/contemporary_history.html, accessed 28 Mar. 2016.

Kassim, Yang Razali. "ASEAN at 40: The End of a Two-Speed Grouping?" *RSIS Commentaries*, 6 Sept. 2007.

Kausikan, Bilahari. "Dealing with an Ambiguous World Lecture IV: The Myth of Universality: The Geopolitics of Human Rights". Fourth IPS-Nathan Lecture, Institute of Policy Studies, Singapore, 26 Apr. 2016.

Khong Yuen Foong. "Making Bricks Without Straw in the Asia Pacific?" *Pacific Review* 10, 2 (1997): 289–300.

———. "The Elusiveness of Regional Order: Leifer, the English School and Southeast Asia". *Pacific Review* 18, 1 (2005).

Kim Hyung Jong and Lee Poh Pin. "The Changing Role of Dialogue in the International Relations of Southeast Asia". *Asian Survey* 51, 5 (2011): 953–70.

Klintworth, Gary. "Greater China and Regional Security". *Australian Journal of International Affairs* 48, 2 (Nov. 1994).

Koh, Tommy. "ASEAN Charts a New Regional Order". *Wall Street Journal Asia*, 21 Aug. 1992.

Kraft, Herman Joseph S. "Great Power Dynamics and the Waning of ASEAN Centrality in Regional Security". *Asian Politics & Policy* 9, 4 (2017): 597–612.

Krauthammer, Charles. "The Unipolar Moment". *Foreign Affairs: America and the World* (1990–91).

———. "The Unipolar Moment Revisited". *National Interest* (Winter 2002/03): 5–17.

Leifer, Michael. "ASEAN: Now for the Next 25 Years". *International Herald Tribune*, 12 Aug. 1992.

Llewelyn, James. "Preventive Diplomacy and the Role of Civil Maritime Security Cooperation in Southeast Asia". *Strategic Analysis* 41, 1 (2017): 49–60.

Loretta Malintoppi. "Trends and Perspectives of Settlement of Law of the Sea Disputes in Southeast Asia". *ASIL Annual Meetings Proceedings*, 107 (2013): 56–60.

Mansfield, Edward D. and Etel Solingen. "Regionalism". *Annual Review of Political Science* 13 (2010): 145–63.

Martinez, Andres. "The 1990s: Exuberant Interlude Between Cold War and Sept. 11". *Sunday Times*, 8 May 2016.

Marwick, Arthur. "A New Look, A New Departure: A Personal Comment on Our Changed Appearance". *Journal of Contemporary History* 32, 1 (Jan. 1997): 5–8.

Mazlish, Bruce. "Revisiting Barraclough's Contemporary History". *Historically Speaking* 8, 6 (July/Aug. 2007).

Mearsheimer, John J. "The Rise and Fall of the Liberal International Order". Paper presented at Notre Dame International Security Center, 11 Sept. 2018, https://ndisc.nd.edu/assets/288231/rise_and_fall_of_the_liberal_international_order.september_11_2018.pdf, accessed 8 Jan. 2019.

Midford, Paul. "Japan's Leadership Role in East Asian Security Multilateralism: The Nakayama Proposal and the Logic of Reassurance". *Pacific Review* 13, 3 (2000): 367–97.

Mohan, C. Raja. "An Uncertain Trumpet? India's Role in Southeast Asian Security". *India Review* 12, 3 (2013): 134–50.

Mueller, John. "What Was the Cold War About? Evidence from Its Ending". *Political Science Quarterly* 119, 4 (2004–05): 609–31.

Natalegawa, M. and R.M. Marty. "The Expansion of ASEAN and the Changing Dynamics of Southeast Asia". *Contemporary Southeast Asia: A Journal of International & Strategic Affairs* 39, 2 (2017): 232–8.

Ninkovich, Frank. "Trumpism, History, and the Future of U.S. Foreign Relations". H-Diplo|ISSF Policy Series, 18 Apr. 2017, https://issforum.org/roundtables/policy/1-5ad-ninkovich, accessed 18 Sept. 2017.

Nguyen Vu Tung, "Vietnam's Membership of ASEAN: A Constructivist Interpretation". *Contemporary Southeast Asia* 29, 3 (2007): 483–505.

Nurhidayah, L., S. Alam and Z. Lipman. "The Influence of International Law upon ASEAN Approaches in Addressing Transboundary Haze Pollution in Southeast Asia". *Contemporary Southeast Asia: A Journal of International and Strategic Affairs* 37, 2 (2015): 183–210.

Oba Mie. "ASEAN and the Creation of a Regional Community". *Asia-Pacific Review* 21, 1 (2014): 63–78.

Oishi Mikio. "Is a New ASEAN Way of Conflict Management Emerging?" In *Contemporary Conflicts in Southeast Asia: Towards a New ASEAN Way of Conflict Management*, ed. Mikio Oishi, pp. 181–96. Singapore: Springer, 2016.

Ooi Giok Ling and Ramkishen S. Rajan. *Singapore: The Year in Review 1998*. Singapore: Times Academic, 1999.

Pepinsky, Thomas B. "Disciplining Southeast Asian Studies". *Sojourn: Journal of Social Issues in Southeast Asia* 30, 1 (2015): 215–26.

Pietsch, Juliet. "Authoritarian Durability: Public Opinion Towards Democracy in Southeast Asia". *Journal of Elections, Public Opinions & Parties* 25, 1 (2015): 31–46.

Pitakdumrongkit, Kaewkamol. "Coordinating the South China Sea Issue: Thailand's Roles in the Code of Conduct Development". *International Relations of the Asia-Pacific* 15, 3 (2015): 403–31.

Powell, Bill. "Here's to a Rapid Recovery". *Newsweek*, 2 Feb. 1998.

Ramakrishna, Kumar. "Terrorism in Southeast Asia: The Ideological and Political Dimensions". *Southeast Asian Affairs 2004*. Singapore: Institute of Southeast Asian Studies, 2004.

———. "The Growth of ISIS Extremism in Southeast Asia: Its Ideological and Cognitive Features—and Possible Policy Responses". *New England Journal of Public Policy* 29, 1 (2017): 1–22.

Raymond, Gregory Vincent. "Naval Modernization in Southeast Asia: Under the Shadow of Army Dominance?" *Contemporary Southeast Asia: A Journal of International & Strategic Affairs* 39, 1 (2017): 149–77.

Roberts, Christopher. "Region and Identity: The Many Faces of Southeast Asia". *Asian Politics & Policy* 3, 3 (2011): 365–82.

Rolfe, Jim. "Security in Southeast Asia: It's Not About the War on Terrorism". *Asia Pacific Security Studies* 1, 3 (June 2002).

Roy, Denny. "'The China Threat' Issue". *Asian Survey* 36, 8 (Aug. 1996).

Ruland, J. "Southeast Asian Regionalism and Global Governance: 'Multilateral Utility' or 'Hedging Utility'?" *Contemporary Southeast Asia* 33, 1 (2011): 83–112.

Schlesinger, Arthur Jr. "On the Writing of Contemporary History". *The Atlantic*, 22 Dec. 2017, http://www.theatlantic.com/magazine/archive/1967/03/on-the-writing-of-contemporary-history/305731/, accessed 18 Mar. 2019.

Scott, David. "Conflict Irresolution in the South China Sea". *Asian Survey* 52, 6 (2012): 1019–42.

Scott, Shirley V. "What Lessons Does the Antarctic Treaty System Offer for the Future of Peaceful Relations in the South China Sea?" *Marine Policy* 87 (2018): 295–300.

Severino, Rodolfo C. "ASEAN in Need of Stronger Cohesion". *Straits Times*, 9 Dec. 2006.

Silove, Nina. "The Pivot Before the Pivot: U.S. Strategy to Preserve the Power Balance in Asia". *International Security* 40, 4 (2016): 45–88.

Simon, Sheldon W. "The Economic Crisis and ASEAN States' Security". Strategic Studies Institute, US Army War College, 23 Oct. 1998.

Smith, Paul J. "Terrorism in Southeast Asia: A Strategic Assessment". *Regional Outlook* (2010): 12–6.

Sodhy, Pamela. "US-Malaysian Relations During the Bush Administration: The Political, Economic, and Security Aspects". *Contemporary Southeast Asia* 25, 3 (2003): 363–86.

Steiner, Zara. "On Writing International History: Chaps, Maps and Much More". *International Affairs* 73, 3 (1997): 531–46.

Storey, Ian James. "Creeping Assertiveness: China, the Philippines and the South China Sea Dispute". *Contemporary Southeast Asia* 21, 1 (1999): 95–118.

Sumanto Al Qurtuby. "Public Islam in Southeast Asia: Late Modernity, Resurgent Religion, and Muslim Politics". *Studia Islamika* 20, 3 (2013): 399–442.

Tan See Seng. "Spectres of Leifer: Insights on Regional Order and Security for Southeast Asia Today". *Contemporary Southeast Asia* 34, 3 (Dec. 2012).

Tan See Seng and Nasu Hitoshi. "ASEAN and the Development of Counter-Terrorism Law and Policy in Southeast Asia". *University of New South Wales Law Journal* 39, 3 (2016): 1219–38.

Tan, Andrew T.H. and Kenneth Boutin. *Non-traditional Security Issues in Southeast Asia*. Singapore: Select, 2001.

Tang Siew Mun. "Is ASEAN Due for a Makeover?" *Contemporary Southeast Asia: A Journal of International & Strategic Affairs* 39, 2 (2017): 239–44.

Thayer, Carlyle. "China and Vietnam: An Uneasy Modus Vivendi?" *Thayer Consultancy*, 6 July 2012.

———. "ASEAN's Code of Conduct in the South China Sea: A Litmus Test for Community-Building". *Asia-Pacific Journal*, 4th ser., 10, 34 (Aug. 2012).

———. "Southeast Asia's Regional Autonomy Under Stress". *Southeast Asian Affairs* (2016): 3–18.

Thomson, David. "The Writing of Contemporary History". *Journal of Contemporary History* 2, 1 (Jan. 1967).

Tofangsaz Hamed. "Confiscation of Terrorist Funds: Can the EU Be a Useful Model for ASEAN?" *UCLA Pacific Basin Law Journal* 34, 2 (2017): 149–213.

Tosh, John. *The Pursuit of History: Aims, Methods and New Directions in the Study of Modern History*. London: Pearson Longman, 2006.

Truong-Minh Vu. "International Leadership as a Process: The Case of China in Southeast Asia". *Revista Brasileira de Política Internacional* 60, 1 (2017): 1–21.

Tung Nguyen Vu. "Vietnam's Membership of ASEAN: A Constructivist Interpretation". *Contemporary Southeast Asia* 29, 3 (2007): 483–505.

Ugarte, Eduardo F. and Mark Macdonald Turner. "What Is the 'Abu Sayyaf'? How Labels Shape Reality". *Pacific Review* 24, 4 (2011): 397–420.

"US-Japan Move on Security 'Positive'. *Straits Times*, 3 June 1996.

"US Needs Consistent Policy Towards Asia". *Straits Times*, 5 June 1996.

Van Schendel, William. "Southeast Asia: Whose Time Is Past?" *Journal of Humanities and Social Sciences of Southeast Asia and Oceania* 168, 4 (2012): 497–503.

Watt, Donald C. "Contemporary History: Problems and Perspectives". *Journal of the Society of Archivists* 3, 10 (1969): 511–25.

Weatherbee, Donald E. "Southeast Asia and ASEAN: Running in Place". *Southeast Asian Affairs* (2012): 3–22.

Weissmann, M. "The South China Sea Conflict and Sino-ASEAN Relations: A Study in Conflict Prevention and Peace Building". *Asian Perspective* 34, 3 (2010): 35–69.

Welch, Anthony. "China-ASEAN Relations in Higher Education: An Analytical Framework". *Frontiers of Education in China* 7, 4 (2012): 465–85.

Wen Zha. "Personalized Foreign Policy Decision-Making and Economic Dependence: A Comparative Study of Thailand and the Philippines' China Policies". *Contemporary Southeast Asia* 37, 2 (2015): 242–68.

Wenjuan Nie. "China's Domestic Strategic Debate and Confusion over the South China Sea Issue". *Pacific Review* 31, 2 (2018): 188–204.

White, Hugh. "Power Shift: Australia's Future Between Washington and China". *Quarterly Essay* 39 (2010): 1–74.

Woodward, Llewellyn. "The Study of Contemporary History". *Journal of Contemporary History* 1, 1 (1966): 1–13.

Yates, Robert. "ASEAN as the 'Regional Conductor': Understanding ASEAN's Role in Asia-Pacific Order". *Pacific Review* 30, 4 (2017): 443–61.

Zhou Fangyin. "Between Assertiveness and Self-Restraint: Understanding China's South China Sea Policy". *International Affairs* 92, 4 (2016): 869–90.

Books

Acharya, Amitav. *The Quest for Identity: International Relations of Southeast Asia.* Singapore: Oxford University Press, 2000.

______. *Constructing a Security Community in Southeast Asia: ASEAN and the Problem of Regional Order*. London: Routledge, 2001.

______. *The Making of Southeast Asia: International Relations of a Region*. Ithaca: Cornell University Press, 2012.

______. *Constructing Global Order: Agency and Change in World Politics.* Cambridge: Cambridge University Press, 2018.

Allison, Graham. *Destined for War: Can America and China Escape Thucydides's Trap?* Boston: Houghton Mifflin Harcourt, 2017.

Almonte, Jose T. *Towards One Southeast Asia.* Quezon City: Institute for Strategic and Development Studies, 2004.

Almonte, Jose T. and Marites Danguilan Vitug. *Endless Journey: A Memoir.* Quezon City: Cleverheads, 2015.

Andaya, Barbara Watson and Leonard Y. Andaya. *A History of Early Modern Southeast Asia, 1400–1830*. Cambridge: Cambridge University Press, 2015.

Ang Cheng Guan. *Lee Kuan Yew's Strategic Thought*. London: Routledge, 2013.

______. *Singapore, ASEAN and the Cambodian Conflict 1978–1991*. Singapore: NUS Press, 2013.

______. *Southeast Asia's Cold War: An Interpretive History*. Honolulu: University of Hawai'i Press, 2018.

Archer, Clive, Alyson J.K. Bailes and Anders Wivel, eds. *Small States and International Security*, chapters 1, 12. London: Routledge, 2014.

Bond, Christopher S. and Lewis M. Simons. *Southeast Asia and the Road to Global Peace with Islam*. Hoboken: John Wiley & Sons, 2009.

Brands, H.W., ed. *The Use of Force After the Cold War*. College Station: Texas A&M University Press, 2000.

Brands, Hal. *Making the Unipolar Moment: U.S. Foreign Policy and the Rise of the Post-Cold War Order*. Ithaca: Cornell University Press, 2016.

Brivati, Brian, Julia Buxton and Anthony Seldon, eds. *The Contemporary History Handbook*. Manchester: Manchester University Press, 1996.

Bundy, W.P. *Foreign Affairs: America and the World*. New York: Pergamon, 1982.

Burton, W.H. and D. Thompson, eds. *Studies in the Nature and Teaching of History*. New York: Humanities Press, 1967.

Caballero-Anthony, Mely, Amitav Acharya and Ralf Emmers, eds. *Non-traditional Security in Asia: Dilemmas in Securitisation*. London: Ashgate, 2006.

Caballero-Anthony, Mely and Alistair D.B. Cook. *Non-traditional Security in Asia: Issues, Challenges and Framework for Action*. Singapore: Institute of Southeast Asian Studies, 2013.

Campbell, Kurt M. *The Pivot: The Future of American Statecraft in Asia*. New York: Twelve, 2016.

Capie, David H. and Paul M. Evans. *The Asia-Pacific Security Lexicon*. Singapore: Institute of Southeast Asian Studies, 2002.

Carr, Bob. *Diary of a Foreign Minister*. Sydney: NewSouth, 2014.

Carr, Edward Hallett. *The Twenty Years' Crisis, 1919–1939: An Introduction to the Study of International Relations*. New York: HarperCollins, 2001.

Case, Williams. *Populist Threats and Democracy's Fate in Southeast Asia: Thailand, the Philippines and Indonesia*. New York: Routledge, 2017.

Chalermpalanupap, Termsak. "The ASEAN Regional Forum: Genesis, Development, and Challenges". *ASEAN Matters for All of Us*, Issue 3 (6 Aug.). Singapore: Institute of Southeast Asian Studies, 2018.

Chong, Alan. "Southeast Asia: Theory Between Modernisation and Tradition?" In *Non-Western International Relations Theory: Perspectives on and Beyond Asia*, ed. Amitav Acharya and Barry Buzan, pp. 117–47. London: Routledge, 2010.

———, ed. *International Security in the Asia-Pacific*. Cham: Palgrave Macmillan, 2018.

Clinton, W. David. *The Realist Tradition and Contemporary International Relations*. Baton Rouge: Louisiana State University Press, 2007.

Clymer, Kenton J. *A Delicate Relationship: The United States and Burma/Myanmar Since 1945*. Ithaca: Cornell University Press, 2015.

Collins, Alan. *The Security Dilemmas of Southeast Asia*. London: Macmillan, 2000.

Connors, Michael K., Remy Davison and Jorn Dosch. *The New Global Politics of the Asia-Pacific: Conflict and Cooperation in the Asian Century*. London: Routledge, 2018.

Cossa, Ralph A. "Security Implications of Conflict in the South China Sea: Exploring Potential Triggers of Conflict". Honolulu: Pacific Forum CSIS Special Report, 1996.

Dayley, Robert and Clark D. Neher. *Southeast Asia in the New International Era*. Boulder: Westview, 2013.

De Cunha, Derek, ed. *Southeast Asian Perspectives on Security*. Singapore: Institute of Southeast Asian Studies, 2000.

Denoon, David B.H., ed. *US-China Relations*, Vol. 2: *China, the United States, and the Future of Southeast Asia*. New York: New York University Press, 2017.

Do Thanh Hai. *Vietnam and the South China Sea: Politics, Security and Legality*. London: Routledge, 2017.

Duignan, Peter and Lewis H. Gann. *The Cold War: End and Aftermath*. Stanford: Hoover Institution on War, Revolution, and Peace, 1996.

Ellings, Richard J. and Aaron L. Friedberg, eds. *Strategic Asia: Power and Purpose 2001–02*. Seattle: National Bureau of Asian Research, 2001.

Ellis, John. *Documentary: Witness and Self-revelation*. London: Routledge, 2011.

Elson, R.E. *Suharto: A Political Biography*. Cambridge: Cambridge University Press, 2001.

Fealy, Greg and Carlyle A. Thayer. "Problematising 'Linkages' Between Southeast Asian and International Terrorism". In *Security Politics in the Asia-Pacific: A Regional-Global Nexus?* ed. William T. Tow. Cambridge: Cambridge University Press, 2009.

Finney, Patrick, ed. *International History*. Houndmills: Palgrave Macmillan, 2005.

Fitriani, Evi. *Southeast Asians and the Asia-Europe Meeting: State's Interests and Institution's Longevity*. Singapore: Institute of Southeast Asian Studies, 2014.

Freedman, Amy L. "Malaysia, Thailand, and the ASEAN Middle Power Way". In *Middle Powers and the Rise of China*, ed. Gilley Bruce and Andrew O'Neil, pp. 104–25. Washington, DC: Georgetown University Press, 2014.

Frost, Frank. *Engaging the Neighbours: Australia and ASEAN Since 1974*. Canberra: ANU Press, 2016.

Gaddis, John Lewis. *On Contemporary History: An Inaugural Lecture Delivered Before the University of Oxford on 19 May 1993*. Oxford: Clarendon Press, 1995.

Ganesan, N. and Ramses Amer, eds. *International Relations in Southeast Asia: Between Bilateralism and Multilateralism*. Singapore: Institute of Southeast Asian Studies, 2010.

Ganguly, Sumit, Andrew Scobell and Joseph Chinyong Liow, eds. *The Routledge Handbook of Asian Security Studies*, chapters 15–21. London: Routledge, 2010.

Goh, Evelyn. *The Struggle for Order: Hegemony, Hierarchy, and Transition in Post-Cold War East Asia*. Oxford: Oxford University Press, 2013.

Gunaratna, Rohan and Stefanie Kam, eds. *Handbook of Terrorism in the Asia-Pacific*. Singapore: World Scientific, 2016.

Gramsci, Antonio. *Selections of the Prison Note-books of Antonio Gramsci*, transl. Quentin Hoare and Geoffrey Nowell Smith. London: Lawrence and Wishart, 1971.

Haake, Jurgen. *ASEAN's Diplomatic and Security Culture: Origins, Developments and Prospects*. London: RoutledgeCurzon, 2003.

Hoadley, Stephen and Jurgen Ruland, eds. *Asian Security Reassessed*, chapter 1. Singapore: Institute of Southeast Asian Studies, 2006.

Hobsbawm, Eric. *The Age of Extremes*. New York: Vintage Books, 1996.

Huang, David W.F., ed. *Asia Pacific Countries and the US Rebalancing Strategy*. New York: Palgrave Macmillan, 2016.

Hughes, H. Stuart. *History as Art and as Science: Twin Vistas on the Past*. Chicago: University of Chicago Press, 1964.

Hughes-Warrington, Marnie. *Fifty Key Thinkers on History*. London: Routledge, 2000.

Koh, Tommy, Sharon Seah Li-Lian and Chang Li Lin. *50 Years of ASEAN and Singapore*. Singapore: World Scientific, 2017.

Keating, Paul. *Engagement: Australia Faces the Asia-Pacific*. Sydney: Macmillan, 2000.

Kennedy, Paul. *The Rise and Fall of the Great Powers*. New York: Vintage Books, 1987.

Key Issues in Asia Pacific Security. Senior Policy Seminar 2001, East-West Center, Honolulu, 2001.

Kingsbury, D. *Politics in Contemporary Southeast Asia: Authority, Democracy and Political Change*. New York: Routledge, 2017.

Klintworth, Gary. *Vietnam's Withdrawal from Cambodia: Regional Issues and Realignments*. Canberra: Australian National University, 1990.

Kranrattanasuit, Naparat. *ASEAN and Human Trafficking: Case Studies of Cambodia, Thailand and Vietnam*. Leiden, Boston: Brill Nijhoff, 2014.

Lee, Jones. *ASEAN, Sovereignty and Intervention in Southeast Asia*. London: Palgrave Macmillan, 2012.

Liow, Joseph Chinyong. *Ambivalent Engagement: The United States and Regional Security in Southeast Asia After the Cold War*. Washington, DC: Brookings Institution Press, 2017.

Mahbubani, Kishore and Jeffery Sng. *The ASEAN Miracle: A Catalyst for Peace*. Singapore: NUS Press, 2017.

Maier-Knapp, Naila. *Southeast Asia and the European Union: Non-traditional Security Crises and Cooperation*. New York: Routledge, 2015.

McBeth, John. *The Loner: President Yudhoyono's Decade of Trial and Indecision*. Singapore: Straits Times Press, 2016.

Mukherjee, Anit, ed. *The Merlion and the Ashoka: Singapore-India Strategic Ties*. Singapore: World Scientific, 2016.

Natalegawa, Marty. *Does ASEAN Matter? A View from Within*. Singapore: Institute of Southeast Asian Studies, 2018.

Nguitragool, Paruedee. *Environmental Cooperation in Southeast Asia: ASEAN's Regime for Trans-boundary Haze Pollution*. New York: Routledge, 2011.

Pekkanen, Saadia, John Ravenhill and Rosemary Foot, eds. *Oxford Handbook of the International Relations of Asia*, chapter 5. Oxford: Oxford University Press, 2014.

Quayle, Linda. *Southeast Asia and the English School of International Relations*. London: Palgrave Macmillan, 2013.

Rodan, Garry and Caroline Hudges. *The Politics of Accountability in Southeast Asia: The Dominance of Moral Ideologies*. Oxford: Oxford University Press, 2014.

Rothkopf, David J. *Running the World: The Inside Story of the National Security Council and the Architects of American Power*. New York: Public Affairs, 2005.

Savic, Ivan and Zachary C. Shirkey. *Uncertainty, Threat, and International Security: Implications for Southeast Asia*. New York: Routledge, 2017.

See Seng Tan and Amitav Acharya, eds. *Asia-Pacific Security Cooperation: National Interests and Regional Order*. Armonk: M.E. Sharpe, 2004.

Shambaugh, David. "Prospects for Asian Security After the Cold War". In *After the Cold War: Security and Democracy in Africa and Asia*, ed. William Hale and Eberhard Kienle. London: I.B. Tauris, 1997.

Shao Binhong. *Looking for a Road: China Debates Its and the World's Future*. Leiden: Brill, 2017.

Sharma, B.K. and Nivedita Das Kundu, eds. *China's One Belt One Road: Initiative, Challenges and Prospects*. New Delhi: Vij Books, 2016.

Sidel, John. *The Islamist Threat in Southeast Asia: A Reassessment*. Washington, DC: East-West Center in Washington, 2007.

Siegel, James T. and Audrey R. Kahin, eds. *Southeast Asia over Three Generations*. Ithaca: Southeast Asia Program, Cornell University, 2003.

Simon, Sheldon W., ed. *The Many Faces of Asian Security*. Lanham: Rowman & Littlefield, 2001.

Singh, Bhubhindar and See Seng Tan. *From Boots to Brogues: The Rise of Defence Diplomacy in Southeast Asia*. Singapore: S. Rajaratnam School of International Studies, 2011.

Smith, Jeff M., ed. *Asia's Quest for Balance: China's Rise and Balancing in the Indo-Pacific*. Lanham: Rowman & Littlefield, 2018.

Smith, Ralph B. *An International History of the Vietnam War*, Vol. 1: *Revolution Versus Containment, 1955–61*. London: Macmillan, 1983.

———. *An International History of the Vietnam War*, Vol. 2: *The Struggle for Southeast Asia, 1961–65*. London: Macmillan, 1985.

______. *An International History of the Vietnam War*, Vol. 3: *The Making of a Limited War, 1965–66*. London: Macmillan, 1991.

Smith, R.B. *Changing Visions of East Asia, 1943–93: Transformations and Continuities*. London: Routledge, 2007.

Smith, Terry. *What Is Contemporary Art?* Chicago: University of Chicago Press, 2009.

Sng, Jeffery and Phimpraphai Bisalputra. *A History of the Thai-Chinese*. Singapore: Editions Didier Millet, 2015.

Soesastro, Hadi and Clara Joewono, eds. *The Inclusive Regionalist: A Festschrift Dedicated to Jusuf Wanandi*. Jakarta: Centre for Strategic and International Studies, 2007.

Sparrow, Bartholomew H. *Brent Scowcroft and the Call of National Security: The Strategist*. New York: Public Affairs, 2015.

Stolte, Carolien and Alicia Schrikker, eds. *World History: A Genealogy, Private Conversations with World Historians, 1996–2016*. Leiden: Leiden University Press, 2017.

Tan, Andrew T.H., ed. *Security and Conflict in East Asia*. London: Routledge, 2015.

Tarling, Nicholas. *Imperialism in Southeast Asia*. London: Routledge, 2001.

______. *Nationalism in Southeast Asia*. London: Routledge, 2004.

______. *Regionalism in Southeast Asia: To Foster the Political Will*. London: Routledge, 2006.

______. *Southeast Asia and the Great Powers*. London: Routledge, 2010.

______. *Neutrality in Southeast Asia: Concepts and Contexts*. New York: Routledge, 2017.

Tay, Simon S.C., Jesus P. Estanislao and Hadi Soesastro, eds. *Reinventing ASEAN*. Singapore: Institute of Southeast Asian Studies, 2001.

Thatcher, Margaret. *Statecraft: Strategies for a Changing World*. London: HarperCollins, 2002.

Thayer, Carlyle A. *Multilateral Institutions in Asia: The ASEAN Regional Forum*. Honolulu: Asia-Pacific Center for Security Studies, 2000.

The WikiLeaks Files: The World According to US Empire, introd. Julian Assange. London: Verso, 2015.

Tien Hung-Mao and Tun-jen Cheng, eds. *The Security Environment in the Asia-Pacific*. Armonk: M.E. Sharpe, 2000.

Trachtenberg, Marc. *The Craft of International History: A Guide to Method*. Princeton: Princeton University Press, 2006.

Verico, Kiki. *The Future of the ASEAN Economic Integration*. London: Palgrave Macmillan, 2016.

Viraphol, Sarasin and Werner Pfenning, eds. *ASEAN-UN Cooperation in Preventive Diplomacy*. Bangkok: Ministry of Foreign Affairs, 1995.

Wang Gungwu. *Nation-Building: Five Southeast Asian Histories*. Singapore: Institute of Southeast Asian Studies, 2005.

Weatherbee, Donald E. *International Relations in Southeast Asia: The Struggle for Autonomy*. Lanham: Rowman & Littlefield, 2015.

White, Hugh. *The China Choice: Why America Should Share Power*. Oxford: Oxford University Press, 2012.

Wong, John and Zheng Yongnian. *The Nanxun Legacy and China's Development in the Post-Deng Era*. Singapore: Singapore University Press, 2001.

Woolcott, Richard. *The Hot Seat: Reflections on Diplomacy from Stalin's Death to the Bali Bombings*. Sydney: HarperCollins, 2003.

Wright, Gordon. "Contemporary History in the Contemporary Age". In *The Future of History: Essays in the Vanderbilt University Centennial Symposium*, ed. Charles F. Delzell. Nashville: Vanderbilt University Press, 1977.

Yahuda, Michael. *The China Threat*. Kuala Lumpur: Institute of Strategic and International Studies, 1986.

Yong Deng. *China's Struggle for Status: The Realignment of International Relations*. Cambridge: Cambridge University Press, 2008.

Zheng Yongnian and John Wong, eds. *Goh Keng Swee on China: Selected Essays*. Singapore: World Scientific, 2013.

Index